A VOLUNTARY CRUCIFIXION

ESSENTIAL PROSE SERIES 153

Canada Council for the Arts
Conseil des Arts du Canada

ONTARIO ARTS COUNCIL
CONSEIL DES ARTS DE L'ONTARIO
an Ontario government agency
un organisme du gouvernement de l'Ontario

Canada

Guernica Editions Inc. acknowledges the support of the Canada Council for the Arts and the Ontario Arts Council. The Ontario Arts Council is an agency of the Government of Ontario.

We acknowledge the financial support of the Government of Canada.

A VOLUNTARY CRUCIFIXION

DAVID MacKINNON

GUERNICA
EDITIONS
TORONTO • BUFFALO • LANCASTER (U.K.)
2019

Michael Mirolla, editor
David Moratto, cover design
David Moratto, interior design
Guernica Editions Inc.
1569 Heritage Way, Oakville, (ON), Canada L6M 2Z7
2250 Military Road, Tonawanda, N.Y. 14150-6000 U.S.A.
www.guernicaeditions.com

Distributors:
University of Toronto Press Distribution,
5201 Dufferin Street, Toronto (ON), Canada M3H 5T8
Gazelle Book Services, White Cross Mills
High Town, Lancaster LA1 4XS U.K.

First edition.
Printed in Canada.

Legal Deposit — First Quarter
Library of Congress Catalog Card Number: 2018943221
Library and Archives Canada Cataloguing in Publication
MacKinnon, David, 1953-, author
A voluntary crucifixion / David MacKinnon. -- First edition.

(Essential prose series ; 153)
Essays.
Issued in print and electronic formats.
ISBN 978-1-77183-272-4 (softcover).--ISBN 978-1-77183-273-1 (EPUB).
--ISBN 978-1-77183-274-8 (Kindle)

I. Title. II. Series: Essential prose series ; 153

PS8625.K553V65 2018 C814'.6 C2018-902774-6 C2018-902775-4

麥天麟

No man taketh it from me,
but I lay it down of myself.
—**John 10:18**

If liberty means anything at all,
it means the right to tell people
what they do not want to hear.
—**George Orwell**

DEDICACIO[1]

This tome is dedicated:

Primo, to	**Henry Miller, Chuang-Tzu, Blaise Cendrars, François Villon** and **Curzio Malaparte** who transformed life's calamities into sublime song
Secundo, to	**Rory Wickes**, rodeo man, & **"Red Fred" Naylor**, Ground Zero saviour, who foresaw their doom writ large in the stars
Tertio, to	**Sandra**, the last Anthropologist
Quattro, to	**Jean Giono**, writer and peasant
Quinto, to	**L & C**, who retain the memory of the Ancients

1. *Inscripcio que relata la consagracio d'un temple. Diccionari de la llengua catalan. Segona edicio*

CONTENTS

JE *EST* L'AUTRE

麥天麟

CRIME & PUNISHMENT

AUTO-DA-FE

ACKNOWLEDGEMENTS

The word "acknowledgement" has a particular resonance in the indigenous world. The first person to utter the word to me was Ariki, the Maori hereditary chief with whom I had extensive dealings when I directed a project to bring a group of indigenous leaders to Rome. The effect upon me was immediate, as if I'd passed through a looking glass into a world where a lifetime of preconceptions was annihilated instantaner.

Let me explain. Most people are aware that European explorers conquered the New World and settled lands hitherto owned by indigenous peoples during the Age of Discovery. It is less known that the conquest of indigenous peoples was originally ordered by the Vatican via several papal bulls that have never been revoked, an aberration brought about in part because the notorious Borgia family of Spain had succeeded in hijacking the Papacy.

In order to address the ongoing suffering of the indigenous, some argue for a Truth and Reconciliation Commission. Those with longer memories insist that only a complete restoration of everything stolen since the Age of Discovery by the European settlers and their Church will suffice. Ariki, however, put it more succinctly: "We need an acknowledgement."

Ariki was referring to an acknowledgement by Pope Francis. That, unsurprisingly, was not forthcoming. When our simple, but unwavering goal—revocation of the Papal Bulls of Discovery—no longer coincided with the broader policy concerns of the bishops and the politicians, they were quick to return to the more familiar ground from whence they came, but which is unlikely to offer them the refuge it had in the past. The cost was of course exorbitant—not only did the Holy See lose a unique opportunity to acknowledge the original infamy done to indigenous worldwide under the authority of the Papal Seal. In the strangest of twists, the Holy See coincidentally chose to dissolve the Pontifical Council for Justice and Peace—a creation of the Second Vatican Council and whose dual purpose was elegantly and succinctly defined by Paul VI as being "justice and peace." In its place, the bi-millenial tragedy of 370 million indigenous people worldwide would henceforth be dealt with by a body known as the Dicastery for Promoting Integral Human Development alongside supplicants from the ranks of refugees and migrants. Whatever the reasoning behind the act, the timing could not have been worse, and appeared to the indigenous to be the act of an absconding creditor. It's too bad, really, and a bit ironic. The sacrament of confession is also known to be the sacrament of reconciliation. An open acknowledgement of sin opens the gate for reconciliation between the sinner—in this case, the Vatican—and God.

But away from the fog of the Curia, and the fog of Ottawa, and the fog of the back channels of the powers-that-be, there are however several individuals whose name must be mentioned, because they brought an enduring dignity to our mission and imbued us with strength when ours was waning. The world is poorer for not knowing these extraordinary men and women, and by minimizing the event, the world has been deprived of their wisdom, courage and insights into the working of the ancestors and the Creator who governs all things here in the temporal world. They are:

Dr Kenneth Deer Secretary,
MOHAWK NATION at Kahnawake
Member — Haudenosaunee Confederacy
Chief Administrative Officer, Indigenous World Association

Dr. Oren Lyons
Faithkeeper of the Turtle Clan, Onondaga Council of Chiefs, Haudenosaunee (Six Nations Iroquois Confederacy)

Grand Chief Wilton J. Littlechild
Former member of the Canadian parliament, Vice-President of the Indigenous Parliament of the Americas, North American representative to the UN Permanent Forum on Indigenous Issues, and a chairperson for the UN Expert Mechanism on the Rights of Indigenous Peoples and the Commission on First Nations and Métis Peoples and Justice Reform.

ARIKI TOHUNGA TE WAIREMANA
Representing Aotearoa and certain South Pacific islands as ARIKI TOHUNGA as spiritual leader in the Spiritual realm of the Atua.

Chief Judge Emeritus Ted Strong
Yakama Nation, State of Washington
Former appointee — President William J. Clinton, President's Council on Sustainable Development

Chief Himko Kaps Kap
Great-great grandson of the Cayuse Warrior Chief Himko Kaps Kap, full brother to the Nez Perce Chief Toohulhulstoe, killed at the Battle of Bear Paw on September 30, 1877, member of the Cayuse Nation,
Confederated Tribes of the Umatilla

Australian Aboriginal artist **Herbie Marshall**

Keith Matthew
Former Chief SIMPCW (Shuswap) First Nation
Member, former councillor and former chief of Simpcw First Nation, British Columbia, Canada.

Charmaine Whiteface (Zumila Wobaga)
Oceti Sakowin (Great Sioux Nation)
Defender of the Black Hills
Spokesperson for the Sioux Nation Treaty Council of 1894.
For her prayers and compassion.

Glen Williams, Simogyet Malii, President, Gitanyow Hereditary Chiefs, for his generous invitation to Gitanyow and his sharing of his personal story and that of his people and how he became the youngest witness in the landmark *R v. Delgamuukw* ruling of the Supreme Court of Canada.

Steven Newcomb, Shawnee and Lenape, writer and preeminent scholar on the issue of Christian discovery, senior columnist with Indian Country Today and **Peter D'Errico**, Emeritus, University of Massachussetts Amherst, for their invaluable critical analysis of "Chains of Title: How the Vatican shackled post-revolutionary America".

Herson Huinca Piutrin, Mapuche, for his perspectives on the impact of the Papal Bulls in the Mapuche lands of Chile.

and the marvellous **Quetzal Tzab**, Maya Yucateco
Indigenous leader
Founder Indigenous Movement
Co-Chair: 2015 Indigenous Caucus of the UN Expert Mechanism for the Rights of Indigenous Peoples (EMRIP)
Expert/organizer/collaborator: Fondo Indigena, DOCIP Brussels, Decennial of the Indigenous Peoples.

The **Right Honourable Bob Rae, PC CC OOnt QC**, for stepping well outside the bounds of his comfort zone at no little risk and lending his vital support to a cause he knew to be a worthy one if trust were ever to be established between church, country and the indigenous peoples of Canada and worldwide.

Paul Barnsley, Executive Producer, Aboriginal Peoples Television Network, for his insights, his relentless, dogged courage in bringing indigenous issues into mainstream Canadian media coverage and for his coverage of the Haudenosaunee participation in the Long March to Rome during May, 2016.

I owe a special debt to **Mark Duiven**, Executive Director of the Indigenous Fisheries Research Institute, a man whose decades of experience, analysis and insights and most of all, generosity, created trust and support beyond all expectations and laid the basis for the success of the Long March to Rome. More than anything, I am particularly grateful to Mark Duiven for allowing me to make my own mistakes, and they were numerous, in pursuit of a goal we both agreed was a worthy one.

Although he may regret having introduced me to the Right Honourables Paul Martin and Bob Rae, I feel honour-bound to express my gratitude to **Michael Fekete**, an honourable and distinguished lawyer during an era when too many of the noble profession have forgotten the imperatives of the oath they have sworn.

For the record, it must be said that far from the musings and calculations of the Curia, there is one Catholic priest who sees the crime committed against indigenous peoples for what it is and is not afraid to stare into the evil while safeguarding the good. **Father John Tritschler** has also consigned his thoughts to paper and hopefully one day the Vatican will heed his words and acknowledge the true impact of the Papal Bulls of Discovery.

I also am indebted to the following people from the marvellous and boundless world of literature, who have tolerated my worst excesses and when my actions exceeded even those permitted under what is known as "artistic licence," they preferred silence to condemnation when the latter was richly deserved for my various torts and misdemeanours of lèse-majesté.

Olivier Rubinstein, Director-General, Editions Denoël, Paris, France.
Jean-Paul Caracalla, Chairman, Deux Magots literary prize, Paris France.
Miriam Cendrars, the mischievous and brilliant daughter of the great poet.
Michael Mirolla, Co-Publisher of Guernica Editions, for his patience above and beyond the call of duty and tolerance of

my non-compliance with even the most rudimentary canons of proper writing.
Jim Christy, the heir of Blaise Cendrars and the world's greatest living vagabond poet alongside the great Greek poet, **Yannis Livadas**, to whom I am also indebted for his recognition of my work investigating the life, times and works of Blaise Cendrars.

Credit where it's due, the uppermost echelons of the Curia can in no way be faulted for their impressive execution of protocol and ceremony, the presentation and receipt of letters of credence and other niceties of *courtoisie internationale* and more particularly, but without limiting the generality of the foregoing, the author wishes to express his appreciation and respectfully:

> To His Excellency **Archbishop Silvano Maria Tomasi** for the respect extended to the indigenous delegation on May 4th 2016;
>
> To **Dott. Alessio Pecorario** and his esteemed colleagues of the now defunct Pontifical Council for Justice and Peace, particularly for their sincere efforts to accommodate the visiting indigenous delegation;
>
> To **His Holiness Pope Francis** for granting a special status to the visiting indigenous delegation on this historic day, and receiving each leader individually with the utmost respect, asking each of them in turn to "pray for me";
>
> Also to **His Holiness Pope Francis** for subsequently declining the **Right Honourable Justin Trudeau**'s

request for a Papal Visit to Canada in the wake of the Long March to Rome visit and recognizing it for what it was — a staged piece of cheesy virtue-signalling for short-term political gain and pretty damn close to a rip-off of the 2016 visit of indigenous leaders, who sought a straight-forward revocation of the Papal Bulls of Discovery on behalf of 370 million indigenous peoples throughout the world.

Naturally, I shall forever be indebted to the members of the **MacKinnon clan**, to their millenial legacy as war heroes, upholders of our unrivalled clan history since the Siol Alpin, defenders of the little man and of the rule of law. I also take this opportunity to ask their forgiveness for trampling on the sacred ground of the ancient MacKinnon collective memory in pursuit of what will either be vain purpose or perhaps another form of the truth. Not even the dim view the clan holds of the author of this text can diminish the affection and respect I hold for their protection of the ensign to this day. Among those of the clan who fought so hard to preserve freedom so that others may live a better tomorrow, special mention must be made of:

Flt. Lt. Thomas Joseph MacKinnon, DFC and bar for gallantry in action overseas, RCAF fighter pilot, WWII, England
Angus G. MacKinnon, navigator and pilot, WWII, Shetland Islands
Eric T. Sherlock and **Allan Sherlock**, DFC and bar, RCAF bomber pilots, squadron 427, WWII, North Africa

And a final acknowledgement to my wife **Dr. Sandra J.T.M. Evers**, who, at incalculable financial, physical and moral cost, took decisive measures to ensure that eleven indigenous leaders would on the anniversary date of issuance of the infamous Papal Bull *Inter Caetera* personally meet Pope Francis, and then sit down with the former Papal Nuncio to the UN, **His Excellency Archbishop Silvano M. Tomasi** to explain, for the first time in history, how the Papal Bulls of Discovery had impacted tragically on the destiny of indigenous peoples worldwide by dividing the entire world into believers and heathen.

IN LIMINE

I HAVE LEFT too many casualties along the trail of this shattered dream to be blind to the impossibility of escape. I have betrayed my own flesh and blood until it became a habit. I buried secrets so deep within the catacombs of my heart, vowing that nothing but death and the Creator would exhume them. Nor was it fear of exposure that compelled my duplicity, but rather distaste at witnessing the desecration of the altar of my amorality by the vile.

But inevitably, my brazen challenges to the Almighty led me to gaze straight into a place which no man should ever behold — my alter ego — and thus to witness my past dissolve like a pillar of salt on a desert plain. In an instant, I understood that you either let what you have done and seen kill you, or you let it become part of you: There's no middle road. And, if this divided self is to be annihilated, then you must offer up your existence, just as Abraham laid out Isaac, not as a blessed act as the Holy Word would have us believe, but in the ultimate act of vile servitude. Yea, though I truly venerate the

Creator, this sacrifice of mine is nothing but macabre sport — solely to feed the rabble's insatiable lust for blood.

In full knowledge of this, I have now reached inside and torn this story out of my entrails. Ripped it from the wall of my reluctant soul. And now I leave it to you, with no hope of reconciliation, or comfort, or unity, but solely and exclusively because the fates inform me that it must be so.

REYKAVIK

Reykavik 4 am.

Keflavik international airport. 64°08' N.

Rush hour under the Arctic dawn. A lava lamp of distorted Ralph Steadman faces flowing through the corridors. The barometrics skewed. Kardashian replicants, Trump replicants, Botox survivors, butt-lift casualties. Wheeling, shuffling, drifting, scuttling, crawling, stumbling, racing up the concourse. Boozers in lime-green track-suits with their sons in black hoodies. Tattooed nuns. A wheelchair martial arts team from the Caucasus, waving pennants. Badger-faced men, Bjork clones, youths in army camouflage gear.

A cortège of men dressed in black shirts and pants. Corsican funeral directors? Authors convention?

Scum everywhere. PETA scum, Quaker scum, Papist scum, anti-vivisectionist scum. Confederate and Union scum. Alt-righters and Apneans. Deplorables and Democrats. Populists and preachers. Raelians and rat-trap vendors. Lavender collectors and allergy cases. Mothers and orphans. Doctors and abortionists. Opiate addicts who kill their pets for a fix. Fizz spewing from every orifice. An opaque turpentine of *homo excretus*, flowing and ebbing, clogging the estuaries. Users and abusers. S&Mers. Victims and predators, exorcists and atheists, UFC fighters and vegans, the incontinent and the constipated. Scum, glorious scum! Scum down! Scumeronis from Italy. Scumeux from France. Scumolskys from Poland. Scum from rivers and scum from the water supply system. *Eau non potable.* Brown backwash on the salty sea at the ebb tide.

Faces like mags, re-assembled families, dregs of the great global wandering trail of hunger, disciples of Avocado, New Delhi bodybuilders, Mongolian families wandering in tri-generational rags. No more priority class. It's all general boarding now, passengers from Hull, Kangbashi and Chisinau elbowing terrorists to the back of the line.

Sino-scum, Aryan scum, Celtic scum, female scum, trans-gendered scum, hetero-scum, infertile scum, groper scum and posh scum. Scum that won't salute the national anthem, alt-right scum, Antifa scum, macro-biotic scum, anaemic scum, testerone-charged scum, NGO scum, libertarian scum, me-too scummettes, scientific scumologists measuring scum volumetrically. Hedge-funders and short-sellers betting calls and puts on scum futures. Pensioned scum, pushing walkers towards departure gates. A single, multi-unit, subterranean lavatory for all genders, all races, all disabilities, one-size-fits-all lids.

A soapy, frothy, lathery, effervescent vile, fizzling, bubbling spume of scum. An ebullient, creamy, globular vesicle of *homo mousseux.* A social protoplasm of centrosomic waste. A terminal enema. This was the meeting point, the planetogametic sporocyst. This was the larval blastula. This was the fetal germ. This was the bacterial ovule that had spread to the warmer climes. This was the karyomitosic puke. This was the penultimate heave of the species before retreating again into stirpic backwash under the Arctic sea while the gods of scumology plotted their next gambit. I swivelled my head starboard, catching sight of my first mate.

"How do I look?"

"You look gaunt and ghoulish. What are you staring at, sir?"

Ah, salve for my wounds. My offspring know the words gaunt and ghoulish. Hope still there — two cerebral souls in a Gomorra of cretins. They shall be the twain, the threads of Terra Futura.

"I'm waiting for the knell
That summons us to hell."

"That's a crummy rhyme, sir."

My first mate is exceeded, exasperated and exhausted. I point a crooked, Grim Reaper finger at a uniformed pilot holding a Frappuccino with trembling hands.

"Over there. The Pilot of the Galilean Lake."

"Who?"

"WOW."

"Wow, what, sir?"

"WOW Airlines."

"We'll never leave here, will we?"

"Look. They're all transmitting signals from broken machines."

We'd been sleepless and in transit for a day and a half. Jet lag acting as truth serum, and admitting no lies. We were ravaged, but free again, no longer shackled. I gazed out the mausoleum of attendants, ushers at Loksins Beer & Brennvin and the deathless sirens dressed in black, handing out Icelandic change to the equally worthless Euros, I stared down the hall at the Blue Lagoon ice care, Elko Electronics, and the "great selection" of Icelandic cosmetics and Icelandic design. Sleep-deprived Vikings guzzling Segafredo espresso and double Kumensnadis. Anything to not cryogenically freeze to their stools.

"What, sir, what?"

Black, raccoon eyes perched on a face that had been perfectly tanned thirty-six hours earlier.

"This is ground zero. The celestial slime bucket of diversity."

"Stop, sir, stop."

"The world has been seized by a bottomless spiritual hunger. The more you feed it, the more it grows."

"I don't think I can make the next connection, sir. I can't go any further. It's just one too many planes."

"Do you know what they'll do with you, if you stay?"

"Leave me behind. I can deal with it. It was nice knowing you, sir."

My first mate is wild-eyed. Like he may suddenly run out of the airport or hijack a plan or grab a vodka cooler and swallow it in one mad gulp.

"Think of Sveinbjorn Sveinbjornsson."

"Swine-born?"

"He was just passing through. A man to the swine born. He didn't take his plane."

"I don't give a shit about Swine Benson."

"Look at these people," I said pointing at the bartenders at Loksun's bar, extras from *The Godfather*. "They were once like you. They didn't take the next plane."

"I don't care."

"They'll make you learn the Iceland national anthem. In toto."

"I feel sick."

"It's known to be a challenging hymn, Sir. It wrecks your vocal chords instantly."

"No disrespect meant, sir, but that's shite in spades. I'll learn it, or I'll write them a new one, but I'm not taking that plane."

Aye, the gift of exile. Your children may curse with impunity and no-one the wiser.

To die, to sleep ... aye but there's the rub ... there is a line-up of forty or fifty women outside the single loo open on the course, plunging into a subterranean chamber beneath the tarmac. Refusing to die. Mutating, secreting venoms without antidote, growing unspeakably hideous hides to battle the Arctic air.

"Here, take some Gravol, my man. That'll carry you through."

It is truly the reign of the mutants, but we — the four of us — have survived and that's all that counts. We have escaped the ring of slavery, and seen our place on the other side. Our escape route. Vancouver has been razed to the ground, and no-one exists. No family, no nothing, no past. We stand on the cusp of Arctic nothingness.

"Sir, promise me you won't sing. It's 4 am, and it's crowded."

"Birds flying high
You know how I feel ..."

"Sir!"

"Sun in the sky
You know how I feel"

"Sir, not in a Scottish accent!"

My first mate's eyes painted like a raccoon by the sleep gods. And, he's laughing, but he might cry. Poor cursed fellow, me as a father.

"Fish in the sea
You know how I feel
It's a new dawn,
It's a new day,
It's a new life,
For me,

And I'm feeling good."

The New Delhi weightlifter is smiling, nursing a quart of beer. I try a shot at Icelandic:

"O, guo vors lands! O lands vors guo!"

The WOW stewardesses are in a group of five standing at Loksins bar, guzzling water and following it up with espresso. Pie-faced and packed inside their Magenta cupcake hats, their skirts wrapped around their thighs like adhesive tape. Like Matryoshka stacking dolls, and when a similar group from Icelandic air wheels past, carry-on luggage in tow, they salute without stopping. Kveoju, or Saell or something else like that.

"This is the land of Omniglot. This is the land of Omniglot."

Suddenly I put my arm around my first mate, seized by infinite compassion.

"No worries. We're going home. This mission is done and dusted. Within hours, you'll be watching UFC fighting."

We have returned from the land of my ancestors, but we will re-depart again. We have endured life as settlers. For two decades, we gave, and we watched as the world was plundered. Plunderers on the right, inquisitors on the left, and us stuck in the middle with each other, and no-one else to protect us. And, now, under the daybreak of the Arctic sun, and in the midst of this scuttling bioplast of chromatic consumers passing through the Kevlavik Nordic roundabout, where no matter what direction you take, you're going south.

While some climb into dinghies and others hike barbwire fences, we also will uproot our past and look to the future. We seek a new homestead where we can put all of this behind us. But first, before all that, I have to remember. But then, we will move away. Forever. To the place where no-one will find us. It has always been so. Migration and the quest for a new land. To finally escape the curse of MacKinnon past.

PAST TENSE

HUIS BERGH

THE GUESTS WERE greeted upon arrival at the Rijksmuseum in Amsterdam by Natasha and Yvonne, two of the cousins, who were dressed in traditional kit—a knitted pouch, aprons, short shawls and clogs. Sherlock came in from Myanmar wearing a skirt. Michel's wife, a seamstress with *les grands couturiers*, designed the wedding dress. Throughout the hour-and-a-half trip to Huis Bergh castle overlooking the Rhine River from the Dutch side of the border, the two cousins narrated the history of Hannah's village, describing Kilder, a dependency of the Hanseatic town of Bergh since 1340.

The wedding itself was held in Huis Bergh, a thirteenth-century castle that was once the home of Count Willem van den Bergh, who in 1556 married Maria van Nassau, the sister of William of Orange. Later, Huis Bergh served as residence of the Hohenzollerns, the Habsburgs and, as it turns out, Hannah's grandfather, who was the live-in handyman at the castle. The Habsburgzal, where the minister celebrated the rite, was resplendent with oil canvasses of cross-eyed Habsburgs, Van Dyck canvasses and an array of wild game stuffed and stuck on the walls. Primitive, barbaric and lush, as only the Teutons can do it. Perfect for a party, and still five years before birth tourism and snowflakes and Australian cooking shows arrived to signal the final decline.

The reception was held in the *Teunissenzaal* on the Kelderweg, situated in the village centre, beside the church. Benny provided a colourful indoor fireworks display that briefly ignited a set of curtains but was successfully extinguished. Cousin Rob was the singer, a postman rightfully celebrated from Zeddam to Wiel for his commanding Righteous Brother baritone. Cousin Rob had placed a jumble-letter bulletin board advertising with asynchronous letters his next gig in Zeddam, where the old Tower Mill could be viewed. After persistent lobbying, he agreed to drop "Lyin' Eyes" as the opening dance in favour of "You've Lost That Lovin' Feeling," the second of his three-song English repertoire prior to reverting to his trusted series of *polonaises.*

About an hour into the programme, we were placed on two stools, back-to-back, bound in ribbons, and lifted by a cortège of male guests before the assembled invitees. Later in the proceedings, Sherlock would say: "I had no idea your in-laws were Jewish."

"They're not," I responded, "at least not officially," knowing that it hadn't escaped Sherlock's notice that my mother-in-law-to-be could be the twin of Anne Frank, and that the Anne Frank house is littered with photos of the Hollanders, one of whom appears to be Annie herself. But, Jewish, just because every uncle is a Mel Brooks lookalike? *Fuggedaboudid*—they go to church, don't they? So what if they don't know their family history back further than fifty years. So what if we were being hoisted in a traditional hora dance, surrounded by *achterhoekers* whose accents suddenly sound Yiddish?

The following day, there was a village parade in our honour, and a king and queen of the wedding were named. Then we proceeded onwards to the shooting gallery, where Duiven won the shooting competition. Benny conducted the

Achterhoek tradition of "shooting the girl out of the village," a ritual detonation of bombs in milk urns in the middle of a field to commemorate the event.

And then suddenly the three-day party was done and dusted, except no-one wanted to leave Amsterdam.

After another thirty-six hours, the phone would ring, and I'd find Raphaël crumpled into a psilocybin-induced paralytic ball under an Amsterdam hotel bed, locked in a fierce debate with a spider.

Within months, Jette would finally perform her final Houdini dive from a bridge too far.

Sid, out in the Tsilhqot'in wilderness, would fire off his favourite Winchester one last time and die an aboriginal legend.

Fred would disintegrate, beamed into thin air by the asbestos at Ground Zero, like Scotty, the *Star Trek* hero he loved imitating.

Gary would run away from Francis at the age of 78 and hook up with a black widow of indeterminate sex who would steal all his money and head for the Canary Islands.

Denise would contract lymphoma and yet somehow survive.

Hein's fall off his beloved bicycle would turn out to be a result of MS.

Sabrina would forge Bob's signature for opiates, and then in the cruellest of ironic fates, opiates would slay one of his own.

The Bataclan terrorists would narrowly miss Sylvie on *boulevard Voltaire*, and Michel in the *Petit Cambodge*, though the Charlie Hebdo killers would snare Cabu and Wolinsky in their infernal net.

It was a freeze-frame, a Kodak moment, of the 1934 Soviet Central Committee before the purges. Or the 8-ball scene in

The Deer Hunter, with Robert de Niro and Christopher Walken shooting combos on the pool table, while dancing and singing, "I Love You Baby." Which is strange, because that was the song that immediately followed the chair dance. And, just like in that scene of *The Deer Hunter*, everybody looked overjoyed and ready to cry simultaneously.

As Sam the waiter poured out Freddy's twentieth beer, Fred turned to Sid and said: "My wedding sucked." Nobody from Kilder could understand anyone from elsewhere. The Frenchies formed a clique apart — the Striches, the Marets, the Guillets — bringing an elegance to the proceedings.

Everybody just knew this wasn't the beginning of something. It was the end of something. Something that was finished, gone forever. For lack of a better word, it was the end of the twentieth century.

VOLVOS

IN LATE AUTUMN 1995, I found myself driving an early '60s, metallic-blue Volvo B18 sports coupe through a pounding rainstorm that was driving me as much as the car was. I was travelling along the flatlands of Vancouver's South-West Marine Drive in the Fraser River Delta, under the shadow of a dancing Ahalia statue at the Sikh mosque, dwarfing everything in sight between her and the sturgeon-grey flats of the delta. My sister Maureen had sold me the car for $500, and that sale was the primary reason I didn't take a final leap from New Westminster's Patullo Bridge into the river beneath. Over the past decade or so I'd been run through the gauntlet, had my children stolen, and been ruined by various agencies. But with a car and somewhere to work, a man like me had at least a fighting chance.

Like I said, the rain was torrential. I was riding the B18 hard, grinding the shit out of the gears, grinding the shit out of my teeth. I thought my jaw-bone was going to snap in half. My back was crouched into a fierce arch over the steering wheel. It was all because my homicidal Provençale wife had evaporated with my son and step-daughter, leaving nothing but a ragged, one-eyed teddy bear behind in a forlorn and empty basement suite to mark the remains of my broken life. A bullet can kill you, but if you want to kill a man like me *lente*, a teddy bear can do the trick as well as a stiletto, leaving the necessary signature of the perpetrator.

Reliving that vignette while driving through that storm suddenly unhinged me, causing me to involuntarily hit the brakes. The Volvo swerved right, hitting mud and gravel, then slid to a halt on the shoulder, somebody honking hard just behind. I switched off the ignition, stepped out onto the road, the flood from the sky and the flood of thoughts paralyzing me. I clenched my fist and pointed it at the heavens, and shouted: "You'd better have a reason for this!"

That obviously didn't do me any good either. The semitrailers raced perilously close, spraying an arc of water my way. Ahalia still visible through the curtain of rain, carrying a basket, as if gathering flowers, and carelessly throwing the petals of my life to the ground. This is life, I thought. Life as it is. Not just my life. Life itself. No more reflections, no more vows, no more illusions. Just the exposed gash of a soul.

I slumped inside the car, lit a cigarette and watched the windshield wipers squeak out their hemispheric trajectory against the crashing rain. I was at the vortex, the place where the general meets the particular, where your individual life crashes against external events, and the tectonic plates shift. It's a hard place to be. Perhaps the hardest. If I were to live again—for I was dead, dead to others, and dead even to myself, I would have to find out why. What lay rooted within me in my deep past that would eventually push me to embrace as I had, such a worthless, evil human being? If I compromised in the least, if I looked away from what I discovered, then it would be the end of me. No more dress rehearsal—this was the real thing. That's where I was. Lucky, said Jakob Boehme the mediaeval German mystic, is the man who dies before the day of his death. If so, I was a lucky man indeed, for on that day, in the shadow of Ahalia's generous outstretched hand, no man was less alive than me.

I turned the ignition key, rejoined the road and drove home. Once there, I cracked open a beer and sat down. I continued to contemplate a ruination that was beyond words, and to be honest, shed for the first time a real river of tears —for my fiasco of a life, for my lost children, for this utter debacle. My past had rejoined the present and both were empty, without value. A voice entered, Ahalia's it seemed, and said:

"It's a mess all right, but it's a mess you created yourself. You truly are the author of your own destiny."

There was no judgment in Ahalia's *pronunciamento*, no blame, but equally no respite. The crisis had been created out of my life, and the answer to the conundrum would have to emerge from the same source. It was what the French would call a *simple constat*. The ill-wind of *hery* seemed to lose some of its force, but not much remained of my will to resist. My life, such as it was, appeared like a Renaissance fresco peeling off the walls of a metro in a Fellini film, unable to resist contact with oxygen. There was an intense purity to that moment, but I wondered, as I have so many times in my life, how much fuel was still in the tank, and how many more times I could keep punishing myself for the commission of sins that were born of my incurable naïveté in believing Modigliani's words that a man's duty is to keep his dream alive.

SECOND PERSON SINGULAR

Blue

I

TWO DOUGLAS FIRS, as ancient as the Siol Alpin, rise heavenward at the eastern corners of the yard. For a thousand years they've watched over the bramble and rhubarb littering the rear lane, presiding over an empire of amnesia in a land that will never be yours.

"Blue! Blue!" you blurt, gazing into the sky. "Blue! Blue!" The sky responds, transubstantiating. The original memory loosening, then unhinging forever from its moorage. Your unformed mind a teetering raft of the Medusa, careening on a wild sea. Birth a terrorist act, a celestial aircraft crashing onto the Pentagon. "Blue, blue!"

Already a year old, your sibling is four. His grin widens, then collapses, exuding saliva. He spews out in imitation "Loo, loo!" and you respond in anger, Blue! Blue! You have only Blue! Blue! in your repertoire. The world is blue, the one, holy, Catholic and apostolic blue. The Great Schism looms ahead. Azure, turquoise, cyanine, indigo, jouvence, leucocyan, madder blue, wisteria, zaffer, calamane, ceruleum, hyacinth, indanthrene, syenite, still part of the sub-aquamarine future. Blue will become a thousand hues and shades, but now there is only blue. In the beginning was Beelzebub, and the blue was with Beelzebub, and the blue was Beelzebub.

The mezzanine lawn a riptide, moving from shore to

sea. The bark of the aboriginal towers a contorted record of what has preceded, inanely celebrated in present time by a shower of grass fluttering out of a lawn mower, a ticker-tape parade of confetti. You stare further into the blue, the terror abated, now yielding to an aftermath of doubt and division.

II

They are behind me now. The thought, inchoate, precedes its articulation into language, a residue from the other side, before you were rudely untethered from the wilderness. You are struck dumb by the instantaneity of your entry into this world.

Words splitting infinity and splitting infinitives. A fog of ungilded, technical plain-speak, bereft of emotion, flattening the image into distorted cuneiform. A pit and a pendulum. Something to swing from, something to fall into, something to slice off your parts. You hear a foreign tongue, a "Tower of Babble," words dropped from above, your path into this new reality. These words are ladders and drawbridges. They will take you inside this castle.

You have two recurrent dreams, both reflections of your captivity into the prison of silence. In one, you walk along the street, when suddenly you are snatched by an Oil Can Harry character, and forced to live within the confines of a cave, alongside a burly man confined to cleaning, a lowly creature. The other involves an ostrich-like beast that can remove your ability to laugh. You are terrified by this beast, and in the dream it has anesthetized your brothers and sisters and is bearing down on you as you awake.

Later, much later, you attribute your fear of authority and of relationships to these two dreams and to your inability to speak as an infant.

III

Your birthdate—September 11—is "humanity's other calamity." For the first eighteen months, you behave impeccably, some mewling, occasional random puking. Then the colic hits with a vengeance and when kin and progenitor declare war, you hit them back with air-raid volume, eardrum-shattering vengeance. You sense the presence of intruders in your pristine space-time continuum, and even then, your inchoate faculties declare the invasion a desecration of the altar of your life.

At the age of four, your world has multiplied exponentially. You spend your days in the kitchen nook, where you watch your mother bake bread, cinnamon buns, apple pies and lemon bread. She is not just beautiful. She is perfection itself. Your father, a decorated Second World War hero, returns from his law offices at precisely 5 pm daily, save Wednesdays and Saturdays, his days on the links at the Vancouver Golf Club, where membership can be procured for fifty bucks and another eleven for annual dues. His aviator's moustache is perfectly clipped to the nearest millimetre; even his leisure shoes are shined daily. His gait is measured, as is his speech according to a metronome designed by the Royal Canadian Air Force.

He changes out of his suit into clothes more appropriate to the day's end. You watch him move towards a cupboard in the kitchen nook, from where you monitor proceedings. The cupboard is at your eye-level, and is filled with neatly ordered, exotic bottles, with labels showing cutty sarks and sketches of anchors. You are sure each of these bottles contains a message sent from a distant desert island, and that each of the messages is meant for you and you alone. You are the Champollion called upon to decipher this cuneiform for all children under the age of five. You shall save them for the world.

Every day, your father marches in towards his cupboard, removes the bottle with the Cutty Sark on the label, carefully uncaps it and pours it into a one-and-a-half ounce glass, then empties the varnishy potion over three perfectly shaped blocks of Arctic-grey ice in a tumbler, and finally pours cold water from a pewter pitcher. He wears leisure clothes — a white golf shirt with a Lacoste alligator emblem, Bermuda shorts and high socks. He repeats the exercise with a second bottle containing a similarly resin-tinctured liquid and places each glass on a silver-plated tray. Then he and your mother disappear from sight into the living room, where you hear the sounds of the day. Sometimes Father Hennessey, rector of the local church, comes by and joins your father for a drink and a cigarette. You are certain that the reason for this ceremony is that your father is receiving messages from the seven seas, and that he will soon leave forever to fly across the Arctic Circle and save the Eskimos who are being held hostage by Khrushchev.

At the age of seven, you have waited long enough to cross the equator. You are alone, a solo pilot at the helm of your imaginary ship in the kitchen nook that has crashed on the desert island. No one is in sight. You are wearing a nautical sailor suit, with a nautical gold button, a shawl collar and an embroidered anchor, proof in your eyes that you are now a member of the League of Cutty Sark Spies. You walk to the cupboard and order it open. Open Sesame! You reach for the bottle with the varnishy colour and the Cutty Sark label. As you turn the twist-cap, the sky seems to be opening. Destiny calls. You pour out whisky onto the cubes in the tumbler and pour water out of the pewter pitcher à la *pater familias*. Adulthood beckons, a Sargasso Sea of moral ambivalence.

You swallow the nautical potion and gag, but the stomach, true friend, holds. After repeating this exercise several times, you have a vision. In the vision, you are in a longboat, containing a magical piece of timber from the sacred forest of Dodona. You are strapped to the keel, on your own instruction. Sixty oarsmen, Argonauts, slash through the water, and you are howling at the shore of a nearby island, because a group of mermaids are enticing you with a music so sublime and sensual that you would gladly give up your entire rich life for a minute with any of them.

The vision ends in darkness, and when you awaken, you are in a hospital bed at the same hospital where your father is a director, only four blocks from Hollywood Hospital where your grandfather has died exactly seven years previously, in a hallucinogenic-induced psychosis that might never have occurred, were it not for a diabolical weakness for the same liquid you have just imbibed. You are well and truly fucked, for you are a MacKinnon, and now your loyalties to the highest callings will forever be tainted, diluted, distorted and distilled by your love for a virtual reality that only alcohol can deliver.

IV

You are nine years old. You are watching Frau Nuesli's triceps jiggle as she chalks cube shapes onto the blackboard. Moon-faced, freckle-nosed Jonny Edwards, who the following weekend will fall off a cliff into Hells Gate, is spending his penultimate days on the planet picking his nose. Spastic Frankie

Johnson's face is twitch-twitching. Just outside the classroom, the two fire exit doors crash open. A man bursts through and runs down the hallway of St. Peter's, a single-storey primary school. A minute later, Sister Mary Lucille, Order of the Sisters of St. Anne, wimple and scapula tilting aeronautically, is racing down the corridor alongside the man. "He's apparently still alive, in intensive care." Sister Mary Lucille turns to Mrs. Nuesli, whispers loudly: "It's President Kennedy. He's been shot!" Mrs. Nuesli shuts the door and returns to the front of the class. Her face is ashen. She blesses herself, and then orders in her Westphalian accent:

"On your knees, class. Everyone on your knees. We do a novena for President Kennedy."

During the evening, you silently creep away from your basement bedroom, climb upstairs and park yourself under the dining room table, where you can listen to Mother and Father talking. Mother is smoking Du Mauriers and drinking a Presbyterian. Father has his Rothmans, and a Scotch in his hand. He is looking to the left at the Japanese wood sculpture on the fireplace mantel that depicts an old traveller drawing water from a bucket. There is a tear rolling down his cheek.

"Always the good who leave us behind."

"Nonsense, Gordon. You are good and you're still here. Of course, it's difficult, but we just have to sort it out and move on."

"Like always."

"Like always."

He smiles at his wife. He loves her as much as you do. But not more.

"I don't trust that LBJ. Too much bravado."

"I wouldn't be surprised if he was behind this."

"That's nonsense. But someone's behind this. No argument there."

"Without Kennedy, things are unpredictable. It will be difficult everywhere."

"Difficult is manageable. An Act of War will prove a different matter entirely. That will make things more than difficult."

"That's not all of it, Gordon."

"What then?"

"It's the evil unleashed. By the act itself. It will spread, like a cloud."

This is the cue for an entrance, stage right.

"Will there be a war then, Papa?"

"Of course not," he rejoins, without conviction, forgetting momentarily to chastise your impromptu arrival.

"But you have an air-raid shelter manual. And that poster that says 'Survival in a Nuclear War.' Will the Russians drop the H-bomb on us, Papa?"

"What do you know about H-bombs?"

You have no answer.

"David!"

"The manual says we need two weeks' food if the Russians drop the bomb. Plus a battery-operated radio."

The next day, you decide to become Pope. Only the Pope can stop this nuclear war. You draw a pyramid. At the apex sits the as-yet-unheralded Vicar of Christ, His Holiness David I. From the nadir, sits your first appointment as priest, followed by the natural ascent towards heaven, as bishop, archbishop, cardinal, and finally Pope. Choices have to be made. Death at eleven is no longer in the cards. Now, you only have to figure out how Jesus multiplied the loaves and fishes by the time the Russians drop the bomb.

V

You are an altar boy, serving 7 am Mass daily for Father Murray, an Orson Welles clone who can say Mass in nineteen minutes. He doesn't preach the liturgy; he machine guns it, mowing the words down as they stumble out of the trenches of the Holy Book onto the undulating plains of Leviticus, Deuteronomy, Genesis and Revelations. During the offertory, he slugs back a full chalice of house red—his fourth of the day, and these in addition to the pre-Mass shots he squeezed from the teat of a gallon box of Torres Red in the sacristy.

On Grove Tuesday, your 123rd consecutive Mass, everything goes black during the Confiteor. Ancient Father Forbes, he of the snotty *mouchoir* stored up his cassock sleeve, revives you with water and slaps you awake. Your adopted sister, also in attendance, drags you home by the arm. Your mother is angry, but not at you.

"That's it, Gordon. Over. This is nuts. He's just a boy. Have you lost your mind?"

"Maybe he should get a paper route. He has to bite the bullet some day."

"I've never heard anything so stupid in my life."

You have failed. You will never be Pope. You won't be anything. Your Calvary will start at the foot of a Mount of Olives of your own confection. While walking to school in the spring darkness the next morning, you offer up a prayer:

"I'm sorry about this, but I'm withdrawing my vow to die at eleven. I'd really appreciate it—scald me over the coals in the meantime—but I want to live for about ninety years."

VI

September 11, 1965. You are still alive, but your future as a clergyman is not. You have fallen in love with your sixth-grade teacher, Miss Chapman, but that hasn't gone far, since you have just accidentally punched her in the jaw during science class, while attempting enthusiastically to explain the width of a whale shark's mouth.

You are sent to learn drums at a studio near the docks after two failed attempts at mastering music, first in the choir group and secondly as a violinist, until the violin maker, one of your father's criminal clients, skipped town before delivering his Stradivarius. It is time for percussion. Your one-armed teacher, Tootie Carter, wears a beret, shaves weekly, and his breath stinks of cheap red plonk and the Drum tobacco he smokes while you pick at the snare drum as if it's chop suey. He growls that rhythm is impossible unless you listen to real music and learn to smoke. He one-hand rolls you a tailor-made and pours out a glass of Black Label beer. He begins to play his 78-rpm record collection: John Coltrane, Errol Garner, Chet Baker, and then drummers doing solos — Buddy Rich, Ginger Baker, Keith Moon, Mel Taylor of the Ventures doing "Wipe Out," "Baby Doods."

Now, you are corrupt, and one day Tootie Carter asks you over beer and cigarettes whether you believe in God. "Sure," you reply, "but I'm not so big on the church part." "Now, why would that be, dude?" he asks, firing up another smoke. "It's because of you, Tootie. You said never do anything through agents. I gotta be my own man." That day, Tootie Carter is arrested and your lessons come to an end. You swear to find a way to smuggle him beer and smokes inside the "joint," as he calls it.

As an ex-altar boy, you clean up wedding banquets in Dontenwill Hall, just down the hill from the church, and siphon the remaining wine with Kavanagh, Curtin and Flanagan, pouring the remains into empty bottles. You and your cronies drink your thirst dry in the church hall, and stumble around in the savage streets of the Fraser River Port like wild dogs, stealing from cheapo Smoke & Joke shops, the Army & Navy store, climbing fire escapes, hopping CN freight trains across the wide Fraser River. One day Kavanagh says he's got something to tell you, if you promise to keep your mouth shut.

"Sure."

"Tootie Carter's dead."

Kavanagh isn't showing anything; he's a tough read.

"No, he's not. He's in the joint."

"Negative," he rules imperatively. "He's somewhere else. Swimming with the fishes."

"You're wrong, wrong, wrong. He's doing time."

"They hung him upside down in Begbie Square. Right by the statue of the hanging judge. Check it out. There's still blood on the ground."

"He's a nobody; he had no enemies," you say, belief in yourself and belief in life running off a cliff somewhere, leaving only you behind.

"Whatever. He's dead."

The Crow who misses nothing, interrupts, says there's a show called *The Outer Limits* on the tube.

"Last night, this alien, who looked like a human, would meet humans, and every time he shook a hand, they'd turn into an alien. At the end, everybody in this town showed up at this church and they held hands in a ring, so they'd all turn into aliens at the same time. Then, after the show ended, this green alga came out of the television. It was pretty disgusting."

"Why didn't they just take off?"

"Cuz they're stupid, that's why. People are thick, MacKinnon. That's a rule. You better figure that out, I ain't kiddin' ya. Besides, everybody knows J. Edgar Hoover made *The Outer Limits* to get everybody ready for the H-Bomb, now that Kennedy's dead."

Late afternoon, you spend on the docks of the Fraser River, four short blocks from the New Westminster Courthouse, where *pater familias* is the local magistrate. Flanagan in his Mission Raceway shirt, Kavanagh in his paisley shirt, tossing a rotten orange up in the air, the Crow looking for frogs and snakes to catch and torture. Life has become tolerable.

School is bland — your uniforms blue, red tie, your tormentors head-to-toe in black and white, especially Sister Mary Lucille, tormentor supreme. Coif secured by the wimple, the veil and the long-sleeved tunice, the white scapular, like the dinner apron of an overfed Rothschild. Cross on her neck and that silver ring of the Sisters of St. Anne, the sign of a vow to squeeze the pleasure out of any child she ever laid hands on.

Kavanagh — one of a brood of fourteen — sings "Lucille" — the big hit by Eric Burdon and The Animals — as you scour the ports during the lunch break, prior to skulking back to class. Kitching is fifteen, and he's already flunked Grade Six three times. He flashes the bird whenever Sister Mary Lucille turns her back. Beaupré and Connell dominate the class, because they both have a rack that passes the pencil test. But nothing going on upstairs, except meanness. Beaupré has two dimples like Maltese crosses. Coke-bottle glasses. She's either twelve or fifty-two, you can't tell, but she's mean as a hairless Sphynx cat, and she'll use her claws whenever necessary.

One day, Sister Mary Lucille brings in a turntable, and puts on a 45-rpm. The song is called "The Eve of Destruction," by somebody named Barry McGuire.

The eastern world, it is explodin',
Violence flarin', bullets loadin',
You're old enough to kill but not for votin',
You don't believe in war, but what's that gun you're totin',
And even the Jordan River has bodies floatin',
But you tell me over and over and over again, my friend,
Ah, you don't believe we're on the eve of destruction.
Don't you understand, what I'm trying to say?
And can't you feel the fears I'm feeling today?
If the button is pushed, there's no running away,
There'll be no one to save with the world in a grave,
Take a look around you, boy, it's bound to scare you, boy,
And you tell me over and over and over again, my friend,
Ah, you don't believe we're on the eve of destruction.

You're watching Sister Mary Lucille, and you realize first she's forgotten the class, and second you spot something you never paid any attention to before — how young she is. She's not a penguin named Lucille after The Animals' song. She's somebody who is suffering because something is wrong with the world, and we'd better be listening, because the Russians are going to drop the H-bomb on us. Somebody like your father. Her skin is actually pretty nice. Maybe if she took that wimple off and the rest of her headgear, she wouldn't look too bad. Then she catches you looking at her, and instead of retreating into her penguin disguise, she lets her eyes well up. Then, you decide you're going to make what father calls "a bad move." You're going to write her a note and tell her to get the hell out of the nun business. It's not going to work, but you're going to do it anyways.

VII

Down on the river one day, the Crow and Kavanagh let you in on something.

"We think McCann is doing it to Schmitty's sister. In the rectory." That from Kavanagh.

"My sisters won't confess to him. It's that creepy look, the evil eye."

"Like *Night of the Living Dead*."

"Like *Wait Until Dark*."

"Like *Psycho*."

"Yeah, that's it. Like he thinks he's really his own grandmother."

"Yeah, and sits around in a rocking chair, knitting. And stabs beautiful blondes in motel shower rooms. With the needles."

"I say we cook up a plan to put him out of action."

The Crow says: "I got one. Let's organize a circle jerk at the rectory and cut his dick off. That'll calm him down."

"Too tough to organize. Plus, leaves too much evidence."

"No, it isn't."

"How about the confessional? That's how we get him, man. Through the confessional. The box."

"Yeah, the box. The box."

Flanagan is borderline mental. It's scientifically proven.

He once urinated on his brother while he slept. His father races Chevies at the Mission racetrack, and even did dragsters one year, and can do zero to sixty in less than six.

"We'll use the checklist for the sins, that'll get him worked up."

McCann isn't scheduled for confessional for three weeks. So, you wait and you map it out, and you volunteer for the mission, at 4 pm Wednesday confessional, because you're the only one who knows all the words, forwards and backwards. You go inside and survey the oldies, trying to get out of what's waiting for them for whatever they did. One has just entered the other confessional and two of the ancients have their heads bowed in prayer for whatever they'd done and couldn't tell the cops. Then it's your turn and the grill slides open.

"Bless me father, for I have sinned."

"Haven't seen you for a long time, MacKinnon."

"Wait a minute. You're not supposed to know who I am."

"An insincere confession is a mortal sin. Exercise your free choice but quit wasting my time. How long has it been?"

You figure he's got a technique. Like mind control to bend you to his will. Like *The Outer Limits.*

"Uhh, five weeks."

"Lying is venial, but during a confession mortal."

You wait, counting. One, two, three, four.

"Well?"

"Maybe it's better I just go."

"Not so fast. Stay where you are."

For a minute or two, he mumbles in Latin. It's like being in a medieval underground prison. Traps, secret doors, crypts, torture instruments.

"I have prayed for your forgiveness. But if you leave this sin within, you will develop a spiritual tumour. It will grow and multiply like a cancer, and slowly blacken your soul until evil controls everything within. Then you will die to God and become an instrument for malevolent forces. Is that what you want? God gave you free will! Now answer!"

"It's better I tell God directly. Nothing personal, you sound like you know what you're doing, but you might interpret some of this the wrong way."

You're thinking of Kavanagh coaching you to goad the shit out of him, get him turning his own techniques on himself.

McCann emits a long exhale. Kavanagh is a genius. His father was tortured by the Nazis and never coughed up the goods. Like father, like son. You're starting to feel comfortable in that dark box, but at the same time you're checking it out for *Outer Limits* green muck. Or possibly that a door might open and you'll fall into an underground prison.

"The road to God is steep, narrow and treacherous."

"I have to go. Maybe I'll come back next week."

You bolt out the door and run out of the church. Kavanagh, the Crow and Flanagan are smoking in the lower parking lot on Agnes Street, out of sight. You show them the thumbs up as you approach.

"Phase One complete. C'mon, let's go!"

You run half a block down the steep hill leading to the river and its sturgeons and the rest of the marine algae from a thousand years ago, then slow, continuing until you are on the docks on the Fraser River.

"He bite?"

"Hook, line and sinker."

Flanagan passes you an Export A. The Crow fires up a match, lights it, then slaps you on the back.

"I can't figure out why Schmitty's sister didn't come to us with this."

"Her pa's a Nazi."

"The Nazis are hiding out in Argentina, working with the priests."

"I'm completing the mission."

"Do it."

Kavanagh just points up at the street.

"Do the deed."

You look back at them one last time as you climb the hill. Flanagan stubbing out a smoke. The Crow throwing a rock at a seagull in the river. Kavanagh flashing the bird at an old guy cycling past, mouthing obscenities behind his back.

As you re-enter the box, the last penitent, Mr. Oakes, a beet-faced insurance salesman, is leaving. He notices you, scowls and blesses himself as he takes a pew.

You watch him kneel, say a few prayers, stand up and genuflect, and then leave the church. You watch the other side. Old Lady Doyle coming out. She hasn't sinned in fifty years. McCann'll be giving her 200 Hail Marys. You step in the box on the other side and wait.

"You again? Get on with it."

"I heard you're not allowed to tell my mom and dad or the cops."

"It's between you, me and God."

"Vow it."

"Watch yourself. I feel the mark of the malevolent here."

"Swear it," I say. "Swear it or I'm clamming up."

"You have my word."

"Swear it on your mother's neck, so help me Beelzebub."

You'd memorized your lines all week.

"Blasphemy," he hisses. Kavanagh was a genius.

"Do it."

"All right, I swear on my mother's neck. So ..."

"Circle jerks."

He bends over, as if in agony or ecstasy.

"Where?"

"Back pew of the church."

"Anywhere else?"

"A couple of times on the crucifix."

"Blasphemy."

"On Jesus' wound. Plus, once on the Virgin Mary."

No more sound from the other side of the screen. This is Rubicon time.

"Even a couple of times in the holy water."

"How often?"

"I dunno. A lot."

"How many?"

You count to yourself.

"Father, is it true you can go blind? What about hair on your palms? I heard a guy went crazy and killed a bunch of cats. Hung them in a barn with guitar string."

"You have made a pact with the devil. Come and see me Friday, early evening. At the rectory."

"What do I tell my parents?"

"That you're auditioning for the Christmas play."

"This isn't just me. The others sinned too. They have to repent, just like me. I don't want to go blind! I don't want to look like a gorilla! I'm scared!"

"Go home for now. You have transgressed the law of our saviour."

"You forgot something."

"What?"

He is so agitated, even forgetting his lines.

"What about penance?"

"We'll work out your penance Friday."

"Not my penance. Yours."

"How dare you, you impudent ..."

"For hosing Schmitty's sister. We got proof."

You're out of the confessional before he can grab you, and bolt for the doors. You notice McCann exiting via the sacristy at a quick pace, his surplice ruffling. You steer wide of the parking lot, as he climbs inside the Meteor belonging to the rectory. You hear it firing up and retreat, jump a fence as you take a couple of backyards and emerge safe, closer to the river, showing the thumbs up as you sight your accomplices.

That Friday, the mission aborts when Curtin, Kavanagh and Flanagan are stopped by the cops for throwing tomatoes at traffic from the sixth floor of the Army & Navy. Two decades later, you hear about Schmitty's sister. Kavanagh was right. Guilt, the real kind, moves into the soul, and parks under a long-term lease. Like forever.

> Father John E. McCann. Oblate priest. Ordained 28 May 1955. 1991 — six charges related to sexual abuse of girls under the age of sixteen in the seventies. CONVICTED. Served ten months in jail. Actively ministering in the Archdiocese of Ottawa for a number of years, both at St. Brigid's Church and, for the past four years or so, at Our Lady of Mount Carmel. Removed early May 2011 after publicity re his presence at Our Lady of Mount Carmel. (www.theinquiry.ca)

VIII

Your first attempts at fist-fighting — pantomime farces and parodies of what you imagine a fight to be — are not so much abject failures as absurd dances. Since the unwritten rules didn't allow for knives — they were for 'greasers,' as the language of the day went — fighting was different, and could leave someone maimed for life, because there were no limits.

Your first exercise in the manly arts takes place in the barren playground of St. Peters, when you make the mistake of taking on a sturdy but friendly boy named Davidson. You throw your idea of a punch at him, missing completely. Davidson returns the favour with interest, straight to the jaw, knocking you back a half-step, but more importantly teaching you that it is just as vital to avoid punches as to punch if you want to survive and that, guess what, some fat guys are tough as nails. You decide to give up on fighting, at least until you can find a user manual somewhere, but you have stepped over the line, like taking the first drag off a cigarette. You'll be back.

You don't pick your next fight; it picks you. Your daily trek to St. Thomas More High School is forty-five minutes each way, which means crossing through Moody Park, right by the public school. You have figured out by this time that to be a Catholic is to be a marked man, the blue uniforms and red ties of your primary school performing the same function as the yellow stars handed out to European Jews only twenty years earlier and inviting the wrath of the dregs of the dregs you have had to meet along your paper route.

You spot them from a distance — the diagonal of a baseball pitch separating you — the way you might spot a pack of mongrel dogs, and one sticks his snout in the air and turns, spotting you. Instinctively steering your trajectory wide, you head south in the direction of the river. One of the smaller ones, a mean-looking southpaw with a cowlick of sandy hair, grinds out his cigarette with a Beatle boot, shifts his posture forty-five degrees, ready, as the Hutu Interahamwe would put it, to "get down to work."

Anybody who has fought knows fighting is a dance, an

Argentinian tango — back, side, forward, forward, side, feet together; *uno dos tres cuatro,* you zag, and they zig, you zig and they zag in no particular hurry, in ever-reduced semi-circles, as if tethered into a crude maypole dance, drawing you together, and inevitably, there you all are on the same path.

"What the fuck did you say?" says the mean-looking southpaw.

"Nothing."

That word seems to rile him. He looks at his friends, with his left finger pointing at your pigeon chest; *you stay there 'til I tell you to move* being the message.

"Noth-*ing*. You hear that? Noth-*ing*!"

"Sorry."

You are about to learn lesson two out of the playbook. If the guy's got a tie, you grab it and yank it as hard as you can, to shoulder-level, then inflict maximum carnage on his face. Works every time. Except you're the one wearing the tie. And then, feeling the boots, eight, nine, ten kicks to the torso, head and guts, and time is slowing, and as each rib or tooth cracks and bruises, you have a new knowledge. *You deserve this*. You're the reason this happened. You agree with your tormenters, with your father, with life itself. This is the way it was meant to be. If you want to live and not become the pope, there's a price to pay.

That man who appears out of nowhere, who chases them away, is now looking at your cuts and bruises. "You don't look that good, but you'll be okay, you'll have a couple of shiners, but the nose is good." You don't say anything. "They teach boxing down at the YMCA. You should sign up." How would you do that? Nobody would believe it.

The next day, while delivering papers, Lionel Burnell and Kitching are standing at the paper box. Burnell is holding Robson from behind, in a choke-hold around the chest, and is counting aloud: "1, 2, 3, 4, 5, 6, 7, 8, 9, 10, hold!" Robson holds and then drops to the ground unconscious. A half-minute later, he is conscious but crying, sobbing. You decide to circle the block before picking up the papers.

Your route ends at Woodlands school and the federal penitentiary. Route 42. First close to Woodlands, the old bitch from the East, Slavitsky and her Doberman Pinscher. Then, walking past the crazy girl shouting from the fifth floor in Woodlands, "My mummy wears a red dress," while sprinkling the lawn with her clothes. And the ammoniac stink of the entrance. Then, running down the slope of the lawn, and climbing over the wrought-iron fence to the federal penitentiary, and delivering to the warden's houses.

Outside of the problem of your physique, which you would fix, and your Catholicism, which you will drop like an old skin, there is another problem — no back-up. Your closest friends are avowed cowards, while the public school enemy, trained in judo, and coming from families where the fathers worked on the tugboats or in the mills, have none of the ethical constraints that your father claims should govern your life.

Three times more you'll fight McFadden, bringing your record to 0-5. You're still not good enough, but the incline is no longer Sisyphean. You have grown fifteen centimetres in a year. You're finding a reason to fight, something else that wasn't there in the beginning. It's the desire to inflict the same damage done to you on somebody else, it doesn't matter whom, that will even up your record.

Childhood has taught you enough to chew on. If anything bad happens, you had it coming. If you're in a fight, you're on your own. And the last and best — just because you're born somewhere doesn't mean you have to stay.

KLAN AND COUNTRY

1973 PONTIAC GRAND PRIX—
400-FOUR-BARREL, MAGS, A GAS-EATER

IT'S HARDER TO be lower on the social rung than morgue cleaner. You pull on your green shirt and pants, grab your mop and bucket, head downstairs for a quick joint with Smith against the ambient hum of the laundry machines and the smiling face of bug-eyed Mrs. Allarie, a saint for the workers, and then it's limb-lugging time from the Operating Room, and the unlucky (or lucky) ones going for the big cover-up on their way to the cooler.

But, hospitals, you see, are filled with women—pre-digital women, sentient women—not #metoo, but #meneither. Who showed up to work looking like work was a lot safer than wherever they came from. The kind that save lives, or wipe grease or stand baking away in front of their ovens in subterranean kitchens, without anyone being any the wiser. We all end up seeing those women sooner or later, when it's too late for us to make up for our past sins. And the only people who see these women day-in and day-out are those patients arriving for their last days and hours on this mortal coil, and then us, the men in green of St. Mary's Catholic Hospital, the place of my birth, and the antechamber preceding the death of my father and no second chances, even if he was on the Board of Directors.

It also happens to be where my grandfather ended his

days, although he preferred the Acid Room up the street at Hollywood Hospital, if you judge the length of his stay—a year and a half—a lot longer than Cary Grant, or Mark Vonnegut Jr., or anybody else with $600 to spare and ready to undergo the "cure" of the day, unless that is, you were a CIA agent.

The only men in the hospital—outside of Harder, with his kyphosis, and Auclair, who weighed in at under forty kilos, and Igor Julien, bald but for those three sweet pea hair curls draped on his butternut squash-skull, and scrubbed-clean and starched Nazi escapee Bachman—were me, Smith and Philip. Philip the Dane, with his dense, innocent look and mincing lost orphan lisp that made women and the orderlies, old and young, coo; Smith with his conniving bad-boy DJ borderline smile; and me.

That left about two hundred women—nurses, cooks, tray-girls, cleaning staff, the dietary girls under the thumb of Miss de Haan who sang *achterhoek* ditties while driving the staff batty with her Dutch reformed maxims, the laundrywomen, the X-ray techs, the respiratory technologists. The two departments where oestrogen was bursting out of their barely buttoned uniforms was Dietary—the kitchens that had to crank out meals and snacks and drinks to everyone from the diabetics to the dying—and the laundry room, where the string of chutes emptied out piles of soiled clothing from the incontinent sick, and the hum of the machines, and the spin of the dryers, and the hardness of the older staff created a hybrid of oppression and defiance that drove the women's temperatures through the roof. And, us just like a small cluster of hard-shelled bugs moving from eugenic orifice to hive to nesting ground to feed the collective need, the crustacean men in green, scuttling and skulking in the corridors, then dragging the mops and squeegees, or dragging the amputated limbs or dragging ourselves, or ducking into corners until we could find our way back to the lounge and prepare for our 2:30 exit for life on the river.

One of the dietary girls, a biker Smith knew from Chilliwack, was friendly, and he'd warned all of us off her. Something about her whipping city councillors and living with a monster named Thos who took pictures for blackmail purposes. Smith called her "the black widow," and said she'd buried a couple of men in the backyard silo of her father, a pig farmer near Chilliwack. But there was another one, with a lazy smile and thick sandy hair to her shoulders, and a low-slung butt that moved nice and slow, with that country Abbotsford gait, a Mennonite girl named Louella who talked about nothing but horses, and who I'd caught looking my way in the cafeteria, so I took a shot. She was by herself checking the union bulletin board out in the hallway. Some guy dropped her off in the morning, but she looked sullen, shutting the door without looking back.

"Hey, Louella."

"Say hey back," she responded, smiling like she knew I'd say hi to her. She had that Valley Mennonite farm girl way of answering real slow, pronouncing every syllable as if she were opening a gate into her yard. Smith had told me, just keep saying her name, she loves that. Don't ask me why.

"Smith told me you liked horses, Louella. That true?"

"Don't like 'em. Love 'em."

"I'm going to the track tomorrow night. You like the races, Louella?"

"Sure. Can I ask you something?"

"Sure."

"You think I'm deaf or something?"

"No."

"Then, why do you keep saying my name? Havin' trouble rememberin' it?"

"Never mind."

"I'll tell you never. I never been to Exhibition Park racetrack."

"Nine-race card. Got a trifactor race or two."

She laughed.

"You can't make shit with those crooks. It's rigged."

"I got a system."

"Sure you do," she said, again laughing. "All those geniuses got a system. Why wouldn't you?"

"So, that's a yes?"

"Course it's a yes, cowboy. Long as you don't call me Louella every three words."

"Okay, Louella."

Just like that. Next day, I picked her up after my shift, and we left for Hastings Park in my 400-four-barrel Grand Prix, what I called the "conversation stopper." Girls loved that car, my family hated it. It opened up big possibilities, but it was a hell of a gas-eater.

"What's a judge's son doing driving a grease machine anyways?"

As an answer I just gassed it and let her feel the rude thrust of that engine. It was like the road was sucking us into space. That monster was the answer to all my problems on all fronts. It solved everything for the time being.

"Oh, this beast purrs, don't it?" she said, and I could tell by that smile what the beast was doing for her, what it did for me, making me feel things again.

"This beast is a moral outrage not fit for the decent, Louella."

"What's a daddy's boy like you know about horses?"

"This daddy knows shit about horses, and a fair bit about betting. That makes us a team."

"Sure, you got a system, right?"

"You bet. You pick the bad horses, OK? Just the bad ones. And there's lots of game horses at this racetrack. It's run by crooks. That should even the odds."

"You're on, cowboy, let's do it!"

Once up in the bleachers with a couple of sudsy lagers in plastic glasses, Louella checked the race card names I'd ticked off.

"Take Waikiki Willie off your list."

"I thought so. What's wrong?"

"His fekkin neck is gibbled, that's what's wrong. Willie's ready for just about anything except running. But lookee here. See that Salmon Ella, she's okay."

"She hasn't been trotted out yet."

"Don't care, I know her owner. She won't let you down."

So, I laid bets, backing Salmon Ella, Stud Squared and Humma-Humma on some straight ahead shows and wins, a quinella and the daily double. It was like walking into a Bukowski story. And now we were back in the Grand Prix, and Louella is pulling at my jeans right there in the parking lot. That afternoon came too easy. It was enjoyment on the instalment plan. Later she said:

"Oh, damn, you make me laugh and smile like I haven't in a long time."

This day felt like something new and different, like being let out on a daypass from the conventions of my past. I didn't hate my father anymore for trying to stuff me in a box of conformity while he golfed, curled, played tennis with his pals, or served on his boards while I was hossing body parts.

"That's good, real good."

"Girl like me doesn't deserve that kind of fun."

"What are you on about? Everybody has to have fun."

"Not me."

"Why not you?"

"I hear it every day and every night. Heard it since the day I was born."

Then she grew quiet, and started looking out the window as I drove along the 97 south towards the Valley.

"I shouldn'a done that," she said to the air outside.

"Done what?"

She smiled.

"Maybe we should run away, you and me."

"No, that's a bad idea."

Then, suddenly she became irate.

"What, you think somebody like me can just *do* this?"

"What do what?" I said stupidly.

"He is gonna kill me."

"Who he?"

"Thos."

"Thos? The Thos?"

"Insofar as Thos is Timmy's bro, sure, that Thos."

"And who's this Timmy?"

"He'd be my husband."

"That guy who drops you off in the morning."

"One and the same."

"You're married to him?"

She turns her gaze back out the window, and I'm starting to get that this isn't just pass go and collect your $200. More like you've read the Chance card, and it's straight to jail.

"Why the hell didn't you tell me you're married?"

"Don't look at me like that. You just *know* you wouldn'a taken me to the races. Zero chance of that."

"Just don't say anything. Play it by ear."

"Nothing! I'll say!"

"It's not like he'll kill you."

"No, he won't prob'ly. Thos'll beat me to an inch of my life, but he won't kill me. He's crazy, but he's cunning too. He'll want me to feel the pain."

"Good. Sorry, what I mean is not good, but it's a start."

"He'll kill you, though. Thos kills men, and he never gets caught. So, first he's gonna *know*, and second, he's gonna thrash me good, and third you're as good as dead."

"Shit. Shit!"

That triggered a funereal laugh.

"You know what Thos does, like one hundred per cent of the time to guys like you."

"Excuse, me, *guys like me*?"

"The toilet bowl treatment ... sticks your head down a toilet. And holds there until ..."

"Until what?"

"Just until."

The next day, I noticed Thos sitting in that canary-yellow Ford Fairlane convertible of his, with the push-button transmission, parked in the visitors' section — Thos long and reedy, with a curved back, and mean as a reptile, and I could see he was holding something in his hand.

I walked towards the convertible, couldn't take my eyes of that rhythmic metronome of his hand tapping something on his dashboard, his face ugly as a garter snake, sucking on a cigarette. When I was sure I'd entered his field of vision, I crossed myself and prayed: "Just get me through this, and I'm yours again. That's a promise." And, then, as if I'd just noticed him:

"Brother, may I share with you?"

He kicked the passenger side door open.

"In. Now."

"Peace and may the Lord be with you, brother."

I could now clearly see the billy club in his hand, and Thos with a voice like his nose was permanently plugged.

"Thuh fuck you doin' with Timmy's girl?"

"Louella has spoken to me of you, of your importance and of her suffering."

"Yeah, what the fuck you talkin' about?"

"Tell me, has her deaf cousin's condition improved?"

"Who'd that be?"

"Ah. Louella has chosen to spare you pain. I'm not surprised. Not in the least."

I noticed the billy club had stopped banging against the dashboard.

"You a goddam bible thumper?"

"Jesus needs no thumping, Thos. Our saviour is a self-propelling thumper."

Thos looked at me and spat in my face. A real goober. I didn't move and allowed the spittle to run down my face.

"God be with you, Thos. And, listen to the wisdom of the girl."

By my calculation, I'd bought about forty-eight hours. I dropped by the old man's for a visit.

"Dad, I've been thinking about law school."

"Good."

"About how I'm not ready."

"Son, no one is ready for law school. It's a form of ... don't take this word in the wrong spirit, but it's a form of indoctrination. It teaches you a new way of thinking. And it's invaluable."

"Well, there's more to it than that for me. I have to know what I'm using it for. And, I've got a plan."

I could see the disappointment, and it cut deep. But there was no way I could explain Thos.

"Dad, remember the letter you wrote me when I was in Leuven? About the great political philosophers in Europe? Well, I've been accepted at the Sorbonne. In history."

"Why didn't you say so? Hurrah!"

I'll say hurrah. Ten thousand clicks away from Thos the monster hurrah.

Smith lost his job, then went crazy a while after that. The mushrooms he engorged daily warped all his neural synapses. The Ponzi scheme he ran out of 4 North didn't help his case either. Mrs. Allarie, bless her beautiful soul, eased Smith out of his job and he moved to his natural habitat—Riverview Mental Hospital, and a full slate of antipsychotics.

Since that time, a lot of people have wondered what strange elixir or spell had pulled me over to Paris. Except that it was one hundred per cent push. The reason I ended up at Paris IV-Sorbonne was lurking in his canary-yellow Ford Fairlane convertible, with no end of time on his hands, waiting to do the toilet bowl treatment, free of charge.

About a decade later, I was lunching with Guylaine Drolet, the founder of the Agence Code advertising agency, when she said I reminded her of *The Big Lebowski*, a film popular then, so I decided to check it out. *The Big Lebowski* opens with two strong-arm dudes sticking Lebowski's head down a toilet bowl. That kind of brought me back to Thos. But, even going into exile at the Sorbonne didn't change anything. There's a rule about life. Either everything's a coincidence or nothing's a coincidence. Either there's a law of karma or there's not. Either way, sooner or later, I was going to get the toilet bowl treatment. I was starting to get toilet-o-phobic.

LEVITICUS

I AM EXCAVATING the dead. Soon, I too will be pushing up worms, but for now, I am the one doing the digging. The first corpse selected for exhumation is that of my paternal grandfather, a district court judge in far-off Saskatchewan, now dead for sixty-odd years. I never met him, nor he me, and until now, I knew little of the circumstances surrounding his life or death. Even with the current taste for historical crimes and misdemeanours, both imagined and real, my people far prefer the labyrinthine, cavernous realms of our self-willed amnesia. Mine is a clan for whom tragedy triggers an *omertà*, and none rest easy until the event is guided by complicit silence into the grey afterworld reserved for the unacknowledged. This perverse attachment to honour expressed negatively — to never tarnish the dignity of the ensign — has shackled us to a prison, the walls of which we no longer discern. At least until now.

My brother Haemish, who has discovered the death certificate of the grandpa we never knew, calls me on Skype. I have saved him on one or two occasions, and, whether out of gratitude or the decency that seems innate to him, he has remained loyal — although admits on occasion that he had "written me off" at one point or another during my own misadventures. I don't think this is my naiveté clouding my judgment again, but I see him as having the core integrity that is so lacking in the species these days.

Now that he has retired from his job as an insurance adjuster, Haemish has the freedom to pursue his reading of Vedantic scriptures. He has internalized his credo to the point that it emerges naturally and invites my mind to be sympathetic with whatever it is he's trying to convey. He delivers it through negative interrogatives on the reality of the external world, or perhaps more accurately on its inherent unreliability. It is thought, he opines, by virtue of the way it operates, that makes certain things appear to be true. Or, he might have said — not in reference to anyone but himself — that not even understanding necessarily gets you anywhere. But that it is still possible to experience reality in a different way, which naturally begs my question — how so? By not clouding perception with historical thinking, he responds, prior to both of us reaching for safer ground — his investigation into the skeleton of our former clan chief, Grandpa M., or A.G., as he was known. Today, though, Haemish's focus is on the death certificate and nothing else, or more specifically the initial without a name to go with it.

"You know the reason for the initial G?"

"Sure. First male heir is always given the initials A.G."

"Right. Except there is no tradition. He had no middle name. There was somebody named A. MacKinnon on his rugby team. So, they needed to distinguish the two from each other."

"Funny, I had always presumed that he had died in Saskatchewan."

That was one of the few facts I could glean from this desert harvest. And even that had proved false. It was unlikely — to have him die there and be buried here. Here being British Columbia, in the Ocean View Cemetery.

"I suppose a lot of things can fudge the memory lines. Particularly war."

"Don't forget drink."

Aye, drink. Chemical warfare. To be inflicted on the self. Our Celtic niqab. Not to be touched, sacred. No ceremony is blessed without Bacchus, who despite having erased all the Celtic saints from our pantheon, and replaced them with something else without a name, unless the name be dignified squalor. Something that embalms our suffering, the better to keep it swaddled for future reference. Haemish has left off with drink, *bringing dishonour to the ensign.* His exposure to the light of day doesn't seem to have harmed him.

"Strange though. We know so little of the man, *qua* man. And stranger still that no one should think a family full of cross-examiners and pontiffs would utterly fail to press the principal witness for an explanation."

"Well, I have something for you."

"All right."

"You see the entry 'Thirteen months'?"

"Yes."

I can see Haemish, and I know that the next words will change things, perhaps even the way I look at things, in a big way.

"He spent the previous twelve months in Hollywood Hospital in New Westminster."

Hollywood Hospital is the two-storey ranch house mansion, for affluent drunks and the crazed. From Cary Grant to Ethel Kennedy and Mark Vonnegut Jr. For the first two decades of my life, I wandered outside what felt like Boo Radley's house, oblivious to the fact that a secret of my clan was contained within and that somewhere in a time gone past, a mockingbird lay dead, and no one bothered to ask themselves why.

SLOVENIAN BEAR

I HAVE NEVER liked the word *lens*. There are a lot of words I've grown to dislike over the last years. Words that are worn like handbags, words that are intended to tar, words that are vested with ownership. Lens is definitely one of those words. That's why it's bothered me to see mine has been so out-of-focus for so long. That can happen when the instruction manual you receive has had a couple of pages torn out. Or when something you thought had happened never happened. Or when you have to find out on your own that what your Catholic mentors meant when they said "leadership" was in fact "submission." Or that there really was a reason you never heard a word about your father's father, despite the fact that he too was a judge, and that without having heard a word, you became what he had been — a rugby player and a writer.

Grandpa. Like us very soon, he is gone, and no one is any the wiser. Were it not for Haemish — Haemish named after the perverse tendency of the clan to adopt the namesakes of our vanquished ancestors. Haemish still on the run, this time towards Vedantic scriptures in the vain hope that the entire family will disappear into a Dhammapadian cloud of unknowing and finally leave him in peace to contemplate ... well, come to think of it, to contemplate nothing.

Aye, Grandpa, that's a fine photo of you on the 1905 St. Francis-Xavier University team photo. A fine photo indeed. And, despite the tendency of the family historian to adorn and flourish, I do believe there is truth to the fact that you taught someone, a loudmouth, a thing about the manly arts. Not that it would do you a whit of good later, when your own Conservative allies brought you down. No, I'm pretty sure that you did what I have done on one or two occasions and didn't just put the man down. You put the boots to him, is my estimate and that man-boy never walked again with the same swagger. And then it was done to you, by the backroom boys of your own political party, and you too were forced to submit, to grovel at the table until you were passed a bread crumb from Ottawa. A provincial judgeship, to underline your defeat, to embed within your soul that you don't publicly discredit the powers that be, or you become invisible. Not in a country like Canada, where executions are a backroom affair. No knitting *tricoteuses* in attendance there.

And then of course, there was always the great consolation, the fountain of all fountains, where all MacKinnons are reborn in the Corpus MacKinnon, and become great again as part of the collective imagination, and the sin of their individuality is expunged in defeat. Not in drink, although the nightly ablutions in whisky certainly offered temporary respite. No, the consummation devoutly to be wished was public service, fealty to the overlords. Lifetimes of service to prove we were and always will be above *all that*. Never tarnish the ensign. Aye, it is a great and glorious thing to be a MacKinnon, just so long as you don't append a first name to your feats of audacity or claim part of the ensign to your own vain purpose. Or particularly discredit the powers that be, with any Papist delusions of bringing moral purpose to the enterprise of governing this great land.

And, surely, Grandpa, if it all worked out that way, maybe we'd have heard a tale or two about you. Instead, a wall of silence. And now Haemish has revealed to me only days — or was it weeks ago? — that your end was in the most ironic and terrible way, being fed lysergic acid diethylamide in the Acid Room of Hollywood Hospital alongside the chiselled teeth and muscles of Cary Grant, and only blocks away from St. Mary's Hospital, the place of my birth, an entry into the world that coincided perfectly with your exit, thus allowing your curse to be transmitted perfectly into my nascent soul, corrupting it even before I entered stage left into the theatre of operations, where a Catholic nun applied the swaddling clothes to an undersized newborn with a protruding frontal lobe — me — unaware of the deeply hypothecated existence that awaited.

I recently read a tabloid "true tale" of a transplanted Slovenian bear that had run 199 sheep off a cliff, by selecting from the flock one particularly fearful sheep, and focussing his predatory instincts *in toto* on that sheep. The casual certainty of his loping gait as he descended upon that sheep accomplished its purpose, sending the ewe into headlong flight, and triggering a collective panic. Within a minute or two of grazing on that idyllic hillside of the high Pyrenees, the entire flock had rumbled silently over the cliff, and then it was over.

I'd like to be that bear. I'd like to find that sheep right now, and feel my strength course through my veins as I lope easily in its direction, triggering a mass exodus of the great and marvellous MacKinnons, mythologizers *in extremis*, and our perverse historic obsession for the common weal, honour and the ensign, the triple curse that has driven us time and again towards defeat, spoliation and exile at the hands of men not worthy to tie our sandals.

As I write these words, the trauma helicopter is passing over our home in the Dutch lowlands, as it does with increasing frequency, and I take the event as an omen that I had best be on guard against further trouble, even while I waste time trying to unravel what has preceded and how it conditions everything that is yet to come.

HOLLYWOOD HOSPITAL

LONG BEFORE THE advent of Dr. Timothy Leary, when the hallucinogenic became associated with hippies and the freaks, the Hollywood Hospital LSD programme was probably the leading LSD research centre in North America. Celebrities, politicians and anyone with $600 to spare could come here for LSD therapy to treat alcoholism, anxiety and other disorders. There was criticism and suspicion, the *Vancouver Province* informed us in 1975, not least with respect to the manner in which it was administered, but "LSD therapy proved an impressive remedy for 50–80% of the people seeking treatment for alcoholism," one of whom was my grandfather.

The LSD programme was administered by "Acid Al" Hubbard, a Kentucky hillbilly who successfully reinvented himself as rum-runner, supplier of uranium to the Manhattan Project, working from a Vancouver building on Alexander Street that had been built as a brothel. After his first acid trip, he was sold on its possibilities. He "... became a doctor by purchasing a degree in biopsychology from a Tennessee diploma mill." Acid Al experimented with and observed thousands of LSD takers, including Aldous Huxley, who would later write of his experiments in *The Doors of Perception* and *Heaven and Hell*, his personal investigation into hallucinogenics. And, like A.G., Huxley spent his last days tripping on LSD, although his was a self-driven detour from the usual neural pathways.

There were a lot of celebrity tourists sojourning in the LSD room, sampling the psychedelic in the way celebrity tourists take cures of Ayurveda and gem therapy. Cary Grant, crooner Andy Williams and Robert Kennedy's wife Ethel all survived, as did Mark Vonnegut, who had been brought in babbling and crazed, and emerged to attend Harvard Medical School, despite being bipolar. Al Hubbard didn't fare so well, spending his final years in a trailer park in Arizona, working as a security guard. He died on August 31, 1982, thirty years after Grandpa.

Until its demolition in 1975, Hollywood Hospital was located on Fifth Avenue and Fifth Street in New Westminster, B.C., five short blocks from the family home where I grew up. Yet I never learned that, within a ten-minute walk of my home, Grandpa had spent the final year of his life in that institution, possibly being treated with a drug that would become the starship of the psychedelic sixties. Until recently, in my sixty-third year, I had no idea that he had relocated to British Columbia.

The October 1905 issue of the *Xaverian*, the yearbook of St. Francis Xavier University, records that a degree of Bachelor of Arts was conferred upon A.G. MacKinnon of Antigonish. An exceptionally clever student, standing first in class and editor-in-chief of the yearbook. As a rugby player, his "series of sudden and characteristic rushes after the pigskin, winning for him later on a somewhat sinister but significant sobriquet." And "on one memorable occasion, proved himself an adept in the manly art by teaching a salutary lesson to one of his more dignified classmates."

In 1905, he becomes principal of a secondary school. By 1908, he has moved to Saskatchewan. On paper, the trail is perfect. Alderman, trusted politician, man of principle, devout Catholic, family man. In 1926, he stands for election as a Conservative, narrowly losing to the incumbent Minister of Transport. When the Ku Klux Klan undertakes a sudden, meteoric and vicious campaign in defence of white Protestantism, A.G. MacKinnon is front and centre of the battle to stop them. And then he makes a mistake, for all the honourable reasons, going public with two issues — rum-running across the border and corrupt customs officials, and the fight against the infiltration of the KKK within his own political party.

At the time, he is the chosen candidate to become president of the Regina branch of the Conservative Party, but what should have been an automatic endorsement at the 1928 Convention evaporates without explanation. Inexplicably, his name disappears from the ballot, and he is blacklisted as a result of backroom intrigue, led by a lawyer representing the Klan, with the possible collaboration of future Prime Minister John Diefenbaker.

By 1952, forty-two years later, he is on the Pacific Coast, in New Westminster's Hollywood Hospital, the last known institute in North America to use LSD in the treatment of alcoholics, and then transferred to St. Mary's Hospital after suffering a brain haemorrhage.

My father, A.G. MacKinnon, had filled out the death certificate. Two entries caught my eye.

Maiden name of mother:	**Not known**
Christian name of mother:	**Not known**

Length of stay where death occurred:	**Eight days**
Length of stay in province:	**Thirteen months**

No mention of Hollywood Hospital. I recalled a phrase my father occasionally pronounced when one or another of his seven children was out of order during Sunday dinner — one of the few anecdotes I had ever heard about that man.

"Children should be seen and not heard."

The next A.G. MacKinnon, my father, had learned the lesson well, and more than six decades would pass before I heard through my brother's investigations about the undignified end of a man with such promising beginnings.

ELEPHANT MAN

MY DESTINY WAS presumed—by others—from early childhood, and I have resisted that presumption fiercely. My family is immense in its stature, glorious in its history, grandiose in denial. Governed by a thirst for knowledge, a thirst for drink and a thirst for justice, each of the three intertwined, dictating the course of our lives far more than we dare admit. When tragedy occurs, as is frequently the case, we ratify the visit of fate *a posteriori*, as a familiar and recidivist intruder. My father defined life in his latter years as "a series of traumas." I am named after my uncle, who was killed with his wife in an automobile accident just five months prior to my birth.

At the time of his death, my parents had only my older brother, a handicapped, but brilliantly engaging child, who brought them joy and happiness only months after my father's father had died under circumstances that only came to light recently. Oddly, it was a cerebral accident at birth that would condition my brother's entire life, and medical accidents that would eventually take my parents back from whence they came. Then, while I slept in the womb during that spring of 1954, when my uncle David and Aunt Loretta lost their lives driving home one evening, my cousins instantly became my sisters. Now, I was the fourth of a litter that had quadrupled by the time spring turned to a bitter autumn. Even now, as I list off these seminal events, my mind refuses to countenance it as a factor in my life, as the chiding mantra enters my headspace—*get on with it*. For the MacKinnons, tragedy is a low-tech tweet, not to exceed 140 characters before *getting on with it.*

One of my father's other older brothers, Father Hugh MacKinnon, S.J., an Oxford man, and Chairman of the History Department at the University of Waterloo, was murdered in Mexico City during Advent 1981 under sordid and murky circumstances, just prior to my commencing my law studies at Université Laval in Quebec City. Within a day of his death, I was summoned by my father to report to Waterloo, *illico presto*.

By nightfall, I was lounging in my late uncle's bed, sampling his Campari and listening to *Carmen* in the luxurious confines of his condo, while I translated the police report received from Mexico, and prepared to take measures to settle his estate. There was also corruption to deal with from the south. It cost us 20,000 dollars to retrieve the body. We had to bribe the Mexican police. I recall drinking a fair bit of his stock and watching *The Elephant Man* on his TV. At one point, I called a few friends, one of them a former crony from San Francisco, via St. Louis and New Orleans, who had left the hallowed halls of Leuven's philosophy department to become a pianist in a New Orleans brothel and thereafter joined the lively San Francisco art scene where he was already making a big name as a sculptor. It occurred to me after a couple of minutes into our discussion that Rudy's voice had changed.

"Do you mind if I ask you something, Rudy?"

"Go ahead."

"You wouldn't by any chance be going in for that gay shit, would you?"

"Well actually, yes."

"Uhh, okay. Shit, sorry, Rudy, really. That wasn't very sensitive of me. You were my best friend back there in Leuven, you know. You were miles ahead of everyone, on every single level. Please don't explain anything."

"Well, actually, I wasn't trying to."

It was funny, even after surviving the Christian Brothers of Ireland, or maybe because of them, I still saw homosexuality as something priests and the brothers did due to a lack of alternatives, and their vague understanding of basic human plumbing outlets. It was 1981, and there were no instruction manuals available on anything except nuclear war. But Rudy being gay wasn't so much a surprise, as "why didn't I see this sooner?" It's like your next-door neighbour suddenly buying a scarlet convertible and, all of a sudden, you start noticing red scarlet convertibles and wonder why you never noticed them before. I briefly scoured my own historical template for some references. At age sixteen, I'd been hitch-hiking, drunk somewhere in Burnaby after a house party, and a beastly looking dude pulled over his car and offered to give me a blowjob and a ride home. I declined, so I walked home and an hour later was almost sober.

But, even when I later witnessed *Women in Love*-style scenes in high school, I tended to erase them from the mental template as temporary aberrations. None of this added up to anything for me, and certainly not some new way society would see itself. A few years later, and I'd be on opposite sides of the gender identity barricade, as Rudy would be at the forefront of the battle to publicize the AIDS epidemic, whereas I'd be putting my talents to service for the

Quebec Medical Association, covering up the misdeeds of the Quebec government, the Quebec Medical Association and a bevy of physicians in the blood transfusion cases killing innocent men worldwide. Until I couldn't take it anymore and said goodbye to all that.

And, with my MacKinnon denial template well embedded, my mind refused to delve into why Hugh would end up sitting in a chair, strangled, with his Roman collar mysteriously checked in at the hotel front desk. The answer to that uncomfortable truth was to reach for Hugh's Mahler collection and some sense bombardment. I placed the "Resurrection Symphony" on his RCA Victor turntable, finished the Campari and jump-shifted to the Glenfiddich, summing it up in a phrase.

"Hugh's dead, and now Rudy's gay. Turning into a big week."

The funeral was held the next day at the university —his colleagues were wretched with grief. There was no little intrigue. Uncle Hugh had founded the Faculty Club, and even now, almost three decades later, there is still an annual Rabelaisian dinner held there by acolytes who worship him to this day. He openly bragged that he had been expelled from the Jesuits—oh, I picked up a trick or two from you, dear uncle—but as a true MacKinnon, his expulsion had not been due to scandal, but due to his singular defence of a man—a fellow priest who had been falsely accused of something. I say as a true MacKinnon, because he, like me and others in the clan, never lose the opportunity to use the cloud of scandal to cover up a good deed.

Yielding to temptation was to be flaunted, but to come out of the closet as a clandestine Samaritan would ensure demotion in the pantheon of our moral imagination. Virtue to us is like women's hair to the Muslims—a fetish to be venerated while hidden from view. I recalled one particular single malt-laced evening in Green Park, in the West End of London. Hugh had perched his Glenfiddich at his side tauntingly.

"Don't expect any of this to come your way. There's beer in the fridge."

Hugh would bellow at me for questioning the tenets of the Catholic faith, and I'd wonder aloud about the Borgias and the pseudo-pontiffs. He'd berate me for my long hair and beard, only to suddenly flash his rogue smile while recounting that he'd recently been questioned as a "person of interest" in a murder investigation. I'd wondered aloud how he'd been scoring on the three vows, as he had yet to be expelled from the Jesuits. "One out of three isn't bad," he responded, wicked and as happy as he'd ever been.

We didn't really feel shame like others. We were the flamboyant and principled MacKinnons, up to our ears in shite and tragedy on a regular basis, body bags filled and nobody the wiser. And, Hugh and I shared a common trait — neither of us read history to learn, per se. History was just backdrop for our personal lives, something to explain and justify the intrigue and conflict we both attracted for the simple reason that we sought it out.

I suffer from Cassandra's curse — an ability to perceive the broad lines of history in advance, without being able to do anything about them. As a result, when it comes to historical developments — whether Quebec nationalism, the *fin d'empire* of post-Tiananmen China or the fragile and explosive nature of a Europe refashioned along the lines of the Middle Ages, I am like a moth drawn to the flame and cannot resist proximity of conflict. To me, my involvement in the sordid events that followed the death of my uncle was inevitable. However, coupled with this curse is another —

a sense of waste, and of dissipating the gifts that I have received, particularly those of history and of the law.

I have studied under the best minds of Canadian constitutional law at Laval, and my professors at the Sorbonne and Leuven were among the greatest minds of the West, and yet were utterly unknown in the way people are "known" today. I was mentored by one of Mulroney's inner circle and my father had lined me up to be an executive assistant to a former PM federally. This was in the natural order of things. The ensign could not be tarnished. As I was already on the University Senate while studying at the University of British Columbia, all of these things were on my mind.

At the age of ninety-five, my paternal grandmother summoned me to her deathbed and ordered me formally not to go into politics. Those were the last words she uttered to me. I had wrongly presumed that her deathbed wish was based upon a moral assessment of me, no doubt in part due to my burlesque approach to student politics on the UBC campus close by. But I have since found an explanation for all that — her husband's reward for fighting publicly and privately against the Ku Klux Klan during its meteoric rise and fall in pre-Depression Saskatchewan was to be ostracized from the party. And his final fate — utter obscurity in Hollywood Hospital. Of course, there was another reason, for Grandma did not issue her edict to other members of the clan — she had spotted a fatal flaw, something dangerous in me, for myself and for others.

Not that I disagreed with her decree. I had atavistic, Celtic urges burning within me that could neither be denied nor explained. Across and through all this, one conviction dominated — if I stayed around these Prairie Conservative Catholics for long, the results would be catastrophic, and all eyes would shift towards me for tarnishing the ensign. All of this at once — breaking the shackles of family, yearning to discover the ancient secrets of Europe at any price and a certainty that there was a woman of indescribable beauty waiting for me, somewhere in Provence or the hills of Tuscany, a Mediterranean. That image would lead me directly to disaster at a later time.

While others watched ice hockey, I was studying Jacques de Molay, the head of the Templars burned on a scaffold by the Church on the *Ile des Juifs* on the orders of Louis le Bel, after retracting a forced confession. And that image stuck as well. There was a fate devoutly to be wished. Crucifixion. Spitting in the eye of your inquisitor, just as the spike is being driven through my Celtic claw. *Eli, Eli Llama Sabachtani.*

FREE CITY OF DANZIG

AFTER MY RETURN from Leuven in 1975, I attended a French Catholic church near my parents' home with a man named Ernie Lonergan, where the liturgy was delivered in the broken French of Maillardville, a town of displaced French-Canadian workers from Eastern Canada. We were an odd couple, he well into his eighties, and me just twenty, but both of us on the linguistic fringe of New Westminster's main-stream Wasp society.

I learned over the course of the summer that Mr. Lonergan was once the owner of a textile factory in St. Petersburg, and that he had an outstanding claim against the Soviets going back to the revolution. He spoke nine languages and yet the only one I ever conversed with him in was French. For many years, prior to coming to Canada, he had lived with his family in Reading in south-east England, where I used to visit Thomas Cowper Johnson, a direct descendant of Edward the Confessor and of the poet John Cowper Powys.

I was introduced to Mr. Lonergan, because his daughter Gabrielle had married my father's oldest brother Joe, Distinguished Flying Cross and bar (shot down over Dover after dumping a load on the Germans, saved his crew and then bailed). Joe was later Canadian Forces Exchange officer to the Pentagon and Military Aide to three BC Lieutenant Governors.

Gabrielle, an extraordinarily beautiful woman, was born Gabrielle Josephine Sophia Dagmar Mousley Lonergan — in 1925 in Danzig, Free State of Danzig. Gabrielle's godmother was the Dowager Empress of Russia, in exile in Danzig. Her mother was brought up with the Tsar and Tsarina's children, and fled Russia in a hay cart in 1925, quite possibly with the knowledge that the Tsar's family had been murdered by Lenin's thugs in Ekaterinburg.

Looking at an old map of the Soviet Union, I imagine the trajectory. A young woman climbs onto a hay cart, and the horses plod forward. The year is 1925. First due west, following Napoleon's march into Russia, but in reverse. Napoleon, who had proposed to a MacKinnon in the highlands and was declined, yet retained the bond of friendship with the clan. The hay cart moves then south-southeast to Smolensk, then onwards to Polotsk. From there, they opt for a less-travelled road, one of three choices at the fork, and then to Vitevsk, through Desna, Drissa, Dunaburg. They are passing along the right bank of the Duna, onwards to Riga, and then back through Miga, Couland, Tilsit, before on to Wehlau where the road joins. They are tired and dressed in black, like a funeral cortège. In 1812, only a century earlier, Napoleon's advance bases were on the Vistula, right at Danzig and Warsaw. Now, in another century, I look from the canals of Amsterdam at this journey that would lead Aunt Gabrielle to Vancouver, the place of my birth.

Would they have gone west, towards Talinn in Estonia, and the Baltic Sea? Mr. Lonergan had mentioned something about Estonia in our conversations. In 1975, the Soviet Union was still shut off from the world. The thuggish oligarchs born of *glasnost* were not yet in the ascendancy. It was Brezhnev, *et voilà*. The Central Committee. Borderless travel yet to become the rule, and, entertainment-wise, only

Solzhenitsyn's dreary annals of life in the Gulag Archipelago to break the monotony. Russia was then, as it is today, a mystery, still locked in its eternal mind-split as to whether it is European or Slavonic. As if Tolstoy and Dostoyevsky, rather than liberating them, paralyzed the entire nation in a gyre of division as to its identity.

What with borders, and iron curtains, and people coming out of the closet, we've forgotten to look behind what was hidden behind in earlier times. But, gazing backwards, there must have been fear, because if that hay cart contained the jewels of the family of the Dowager Empress during that ride, the first plundering wayfarer coming by might just hit the lottery. Since Gabrielle was born on January 15, she was less than a year old, not that that would have protected them.

I'm not interested as much in the free city of Danzig as in the restless drift that governs our family, for it seems that we never find our rest. In any event, I had some decisions to make quickly, and looking back, it must have been my friendship with Ernest Lonergan that led me to reorient my studies, and take on a double course load in the history of Russia and the Soviet Union. Like anything else, my decision appeared to be a mad impulse to my family, but of course, none of them had even noticed that, as a twelve-year-old, while they frolicked in the sea, playing water sports, I read Pushkin, Turgenev, Dostoyevsky, Gogol, Gorky, Tolstoy and Chekhov. It would be another seven years before I discovered Solzhenitsyn, but he is not of the same class, while Nabokov is of another stripe. So, for me there was no break, no leisure as I constructed my own gulag with tools of my own confection. I would get to the bottom of these Russians in one year, and so it was that I enrolled in the following curriculum at UBC:

Geography of the Soviet Union
Slavonic Studies
History of the Soviet Union
History of the Tsars
Europe — twentieth century
Russian language

It seemed to make sense, and it posted another stake onto my mental map. But I had no knowledge whatsoever of the immensity of the task at hand, and I had elected to take only fourth-year courses, certain on the day that I could pull anything off.

For one year, I planned to douse myself in everything Russian, but then, as September approached and the reality of having imposed an impossible programme, I began having a series of headaches, and fearing the worst, I sought to cover it up by drinking, as heavily as possible. But, in the solitude of my thoughts, I was presuming that my time was up and that God had broken his bargain with me. Clearly, I had no choice but to leave town as soon as possible. The academic term had yet to start and I could already sense a churning within, and the imp of the perverse gnawing at my existential innards, refusing to let me free.

It was just as Haemish had said — wherever I went, things just tended to happen. This would all have amounted to nothing more than idle rumination, had a random event not intervened and placed me in clear and present danger. From a most unexpected cause, it would drive me right out of the country, unable to explain why to anyone of my entourage without risking utter shame and humiliation.

RATTLESNAKE ISLAND

EDDIE HAYMOUR WAS a Lebanese barber who arrived in British Columbia in 1955, and bought Rattlesnake Island (or Ogopogo Island, as some call it) near to Kelowna in Peachland, in order to construct an Arab amusement park, based on a vision he'd had of building a "Moroccan Shadou." Eddie managed to secure financing for the purchase, which he completed in June 1971, but the BC government opposed the project, and tried to force Eddie to sell the island for $40,000. Eddie refused, and descended into a spiral of threats and violence that landed him successively on the road to the Oakalla Provincial Prison facility, Riverview Hospital and financial ruin. Eventually, Eddie, feeling spurned by everyone, returned to his native Lebanon and took twenty people hostage at the Canadian embassy. This more or less confirmed in everyone's eyes that Eddie was nuts. His wife and children left him. He lost everything, until finally his case was heard in the Supreme Court of British Columbia.

I heard about the case because my father was the presiding justice, and against all the odds, he ruled in favour of Eddie.

Supreme Court Justice Gordon MacKinnon wrote:

> Senior government officials, including ministers of the Crown and with the knowledge of then-Premier W.A.C. Bennett ... no less than six departments ... were involved in the conspiracy ... The B.C. government's actions have been highly improper, illegal and even cruel.

Then he awarded Eddie two hundred and fifty thousand dollars.

But the Eddie Haymour saga didn't end with his release from Riverview:

> After a year in Riverview, he was released on the understanding that he would leave the country ... He decided to seize the Canadian Embassy in Beirut and made detailed plans with the help of six cousins. Lebanon was in the middle of a civil war and there were lots of conflicts in Beirut. Haymour bought submachine guns and rented an apartment near the Embassy to prepare for the assault. Haymour and his cousins waited for the right moment and seized the Embassy and took 34 hostages including the Canadian Ambassador. Then it was time to negotiate for release of the hostages ... After a nine hour wait an offer came from the Canadian government in order to avoid any bloodshed. Haymour was assured that he would not be prosecuted for the take-over of the Embassy and the Canadian government would pay his way back to Canada and assist him in pursuing his case for compensation through the courts. It was a victory for Haymour and he laid down his weapons and celebrated.
>
> Finally, in 1986, Haymour won his case for extra

> compensation in the BC Supreme Court. Justice Gordon MacKinnon agreed that the BC government had conspired to stop Haymour's theme park and called their actions, 'highly improper if not cruel'. Haymour was awarded $250,000 in compensation, but he didn't get his island back. Haymour used the money to purchase land in Peachland directly across the lake from Rattlesnake Island. He built 'Castle Haymour' a small hotel with an Arab theme, which he operated successfully for several years.[1]

It was a pretty surprising judgment, because my father was a member of the Conservative Party and many of his colleagues were in the B.C. government of the time—they weren't too happy with him. About thirty years after the judgment, my writer crony Jim Christy asked whether I was any relation to that Justice AG MacKinnon.

"Man, did he get suckered," he said, when I confirmed it was my father. "I did a *Saturday Night* magazine feature on him, and to do it, I lived with him for a while. He's a complete psychopath. You know what Loreen used to say—'With Eddie, never, ever, ever forget, he's always three steps ahead of you'."

Just to check the next generation's view, I asked Niall how he saw the whole Eddie Haymour saga.

"Well, I can see grandpa was a good judge, but ... well, you've got thirty-four assets under threat in Beirut. What's wrong with Canada's special services? Those guys just walked in and took over the embassy with submachine guns, right?"

"Yes, they did."

1. Hall, Eric, March 18, 2018, *Peachland News*.

"And they didn't take him out?"

"No."

"Grandpa would have taken him out."

"Actually, Grandpa gave Eddie a quarter of a million. But remember. He had done some jail time at Oakalla. That's a tough prison. Uncle Jack, remember, the pro football player, he was the Warden at Oakalla at the time, and cousin Art a security guard, until a half a dozen guards beat up some inmates and the papers got involved."

"Jeez, Papa, why didn't they get those Oakalla guards working at the Beirut embassy? They'd have taken those guys out."

"It's not the Canadian way."

"You always tell us Canada's about the rule of law."

"Not any more."

KLAN VS MacKINNON

SASKATCHEWAN, 1927. A small contingent of the Ku Klux Klan arrived on horseback from south of the 49th Parallel and attempted to sway locals to their cause. The core platform was on the issue of immigration. The previously British Wasp population was being invaded, not by sub-Saharan Africans or deluded ISIS aficionados, but by Ukrainians and Italians who, outside of the food they ate, were Papists, plotting a ruthless program of religious conversion.

An article in the *Winnipeg Free Press*, May 8, 1965, describes the extent of the phenomenon:

> Klansmen went from community to community on horseback to spread their word. They told listeners that people called one another 'Mac' at that time in the U.S. and Canada because it was a secret code word, symbol of a plot to 'Make America Catholic.'
>
> The Klan started with a campaign to clean up Moose Jaw, then a tough city where criminals appeared able to defy the law openly. It claimed support from prominent Americans such as Henry Ford (he denied it) and organized cross-bearing marches down the main street.

> Feb. 28, 1928, Dr Hawkins[1] told a Regina meeting, "The Jew is granted greater privileges in Canada than in any other country in the world. You can't become a member of his synagogue; you can't join his B'nai B'rith order."

As for the great Klan-Conservative link, the *Free Press* article describes the insidious plot in detail:

> Pat Emmons, a Grand Wizard of the Klan, once scheduled a public meeting at which he said he would expose the alleged Conservative link, but he couldn't make himself heard over shouts and jeers. The movement spread from Estevan in the south to Prince Albert in the north, having its greatest success in the heavily Anglo-Saxon Protestant south.

Not quite Mao's Hundred Days March, and the single incident of someone starting a fire at a Catholic shrine in Lebret doesn't quite add up to a *Kristallnacht*. Despite allegations of complicity with the Klan by the Liberal leader of the time, Premier James Gardiner, all of which were unproven, the Conservatives won the 1929 election and seized the moment of their victory to condemn the Klan. Shortly thereafter, the Klansmen, who one of its ex-members characterized as "a bunch of sharpies who figured Saskatchewan would be a good place to make a few fast bucks," disappeared into that good night and returned from whence they came.

The Klan, and its very ephemeral membership, were targeting two groups—Jews and Europeans—who, ironically, have re-emerged as pantomime villains in the small "l"

1. One of the movement's original founders.

liberal-left *commedia dell' arte* performed by snowflakes and millennials worldwide that all Europeans are responsible for all oppression since the beginning of recorded history.

One familiar with the styles of the Prairies, past and present, might be tempted to conclude that the KKK, as committed fashionistas, abandoned Saskatchewan as a lost cause because the residents were shabby dressers, and shrewd enough to refuse to fork over the fifteen-dollar annual membership fee. Or possibly, the real reason was that, as the author of the *Free Press* article put it in 1965, "because rural folk with a strong tradition of cooperative action couldn't support [the Klan's] divisive ideas."

That quiet rejection of the Klan as "a bunch of sharpies" resonates. It sounds peculiarly Canadian—it sounds like the people of the war generation, people whose first concern was that of the common weal. It rings true when you consider that only fourteen years earlier 619,000 ordinary Canadians with an average education of Grade Six volunteered to fight against the imperial ambitions of the Kaiser, and over sixty thousand died in order that others would know the fruits of freedom. It sounds like my grandfather, Judge A.G. MacKinnon, who sowed the seeds of his own political demise when, as a Catholic Conservative, he took a public stand against the Klan's attempts to infiltrate his own party in 1927-8.

It was a deeply moral stand, but what good did it do him? Blacklisted in his own party and with no one to defend him since he was a Catholic Conservative, a promising career with every ambition possible, was suddenly extinguished. Come to think of it, prejudice did play a role in instantly casting Grandpa out of the political arena, sidelining him and putting him in a dangerous position of economic precarity with ten mouths to feed, with the Great Crash of 1929 looming on the horizon.

BRAVEHEART

LAST NIGHT, I watched *Braveheart* with Niall, who is a real Braveheart himself. *Braveheart* is, of course, the story of William Wallace rallying the Scots, and laying the way for the great Robert Bruce's defeat of the English at Bannockburn in 1314. A MacKinnon chief was the marshal of the island fleet that transported Bruce during the start of that campaign. The MacKinnons of Arran sheltered Bruce while he was in hiding and assisted his escape back to Carrick. After Bannockburn, we were rewarded with lands on Skye. We held those lands until the infamous clearances sent us towards a forbidding land on the ship *Hector*, where many would die in the first winter. Here is an account of the fate of a MacKinnon who did not succeed in accompanying my family ancestor Donald, several years later, when the clearances hit their peak, recounted in *The Highland Clearances*:[1]

> John MacKinnon, a cottar, aged forty-four, with a wife and six children, had his house pulled down and he and his family, for the first night or two, had to burrow among the rocks near the shore. When he thought that

1. Geddes & Grosset, 2001 *The Highland Clearances* ('The Scottish Histories') adapted from the writings of Alexander McKenzie.

the factor and his party had left the district, he emerged from the rocks, surveyed the ruins of his former home and saw his furniture and belongings exposed to the elements and now almost worthless. The demolition was so complete that it was impossible to make any use of the ruins of the old house. The ruins of an old chapel, however, are near at hand and parts of the walls were still standing. MacKinnon took his family there and having swept away some rubbish and removed some grass and nettles, they placed a few poles up to one of the walls and spread some sails and blankets across. They brought in some hay, and laid it in a corner for a bed, stuck a piece of iron into the wall in another corner, on which they placed a crook, then kindled a fire. They put a pot on the fire, and boiled some potatoes and, when these and a few fish roasted on the embers were ready, MacKinnon and his family had their first proper meal since the destruction of their house.

MacKinnon is a tall man, but poor and unhealthy looking. His wife is a poor weak woman, worn down by disease and difficulty. The boys, Ronald and Archibald, are lying in their makeshift bed of hay on the ground, suffering from rheumatism and cholic. The other children are apparently healthy enough as yet, but very ragged. There is no door to their wretched abode. MacKinnon's wife was pregnant when she was turned out of her house among the rocks. Four days later she gave birth prematurely and this, and her exposure to the elements without shelter or nutritious diet, has brought on consumption, from which she will not recover.

There was something very solemn indeed in this scene. One would think that, as MacKinnon took

> refuge amid the ruins of this most singular, sanctified place, he would be left alone and no longer be molested by man. But alas, that was not to be. The manager of Knoydart and his minions appeared and invaded this helpless family within the walls of the sanctuary. They pulled down the sticks and sails set up within its ruins, put MacKinnon's wife and children out on the cold shore, threw his tables, stools, chairs, etc. over the walls, burned the hay on which they slept, put out the fire and left the district. Four times have these officers broken in upon poor MacKinnon in this way, destroying his shelter and setting his family adrift on the coal coast of Knoydart. When I looked in upon these creatures last week, I found them in utter dread, having just learned the officers would appear next day to destroy the huts again. The children looked at me as if I were a wolf they crept behind their father and stared wildly, fearing I was a law officer. The sight was most painful. The very idea that, in Christian Scotland in the nineteenth century, these children should be subjected to such gross treatment reflects strongly upon our humanity and civilization. Had there been famine or pestilence or war, I could understand it and account for it, but suffering to gratify the ambition of some unfeeling spectator cannot be justified and deserves the condemnation of every Christian man. Had MacKinnon been in arrears of rent, which he was not, even this would not justify the inhuman conduct towards himself and his family. No words can describe the condition of this poor family.

I would later work with the indigenous, and though I never referred to it, it was hard to ignore that the fate of my own family was strikingly similar to that of the indigenous, exciting a natural sympathy for what had occurred to them. Another passage of *The Highland Clearances* is evocative:

> The mild nature and religious upbringing of the Highlanders prevented them from the sort of determined resistance and revenge which limited the greed of landlords in Ireland. Their ignorance of the English language and the want of natural leaders made it impossible for them to broadcast their grievances. They were, therefore, maltreated with impunity. The clergy generally sided with the oppressing lairds, who were patrons of the church, sanctioning the iniquity. 'The foulest deeds were glossed over, and all the evil which could not be attributed to the natives themselves, such as severe seasons, famines and consequent disease, was by these pious gentlemen ascribed to Providence, as a punishment for sin.'
>
> The landlords, generally led by southern factors worse than themselves, were, in most cases motivated by pure self-interest, and they pursued their policy of extermination with a recklessness and remorselessness unparalleled anywhere else where the Gospel of peace and charity was preached — except, perhaps, Ireland. Generally, law and justice, religion and humanity were either totally disregarded, or, worse, were used as instruments of oppression. Every conceivable means, short of the musket and the sword, were used to drive the natives from the land they loved, and to force them to exchange their crofts and homes — originally built by themselves or their forefathers — for wretched patches among the barren rocks on the seashore. There they had to depend, after losing their livestock

> and having their houses destroyed, on the uncertain produce of the seas for subsistence.

Within my own clan, the preservation of our history is impressive, but we have slid a bit into the folkloric. With the indigenous peoples, I discovered a memory as alive as if everything done to them had occurred yesterday. Their entire sense of time is different from ours. Often, they claimed to have already visited the Vatican even before we arrived, to have lived through the entire set of events — and this was no mystical assertion, but an observation of things that to their eye, had already occurred.

JE *EST* L'AUTRE

—Rimbaud

KITURO VOLCANO

I WAS BORN during a historical interlude that has yet to be properly charted by the historians, in no small part due to its utter insignificance. What has been portrayed as novel and revolutionary from the 1910s onwards was born of war-weariness and a self-willed amnesia. Euphoria, *ekstasis*, the wind of inspiration, the fire of idealism, all of it had perished on the plains of Champagne, on the Somme, in Flanders Fields. Those who charted the paths of surrealism, cubism and all the artistic -isms that followed in the wake of the murderous political -isms and schisms, were the confections of sons of academics who knew nothing of battles, military or even professional life, and those who had tasted the bitter fruits of the assembly-line were few and far between.

Heroism was no longer *tendance*. Sacrifice was a con game, for suckers, and returning veterans from each of the great conflicts were honoured in their invisibility. Apollinaire and Cendrars were the last of the sucker soldiers. Even in the waning days of the Great War, when Apollinaire died, Cendrars, Raymone and Fernand Léger joined up to mourn the soldier poet. They stopped for a few glasses of rum on a grey and grisly Paris day at a small café on Boulevard St. Germain, prior to ascending to Montmartre for the funeral. Cendrars recounts the shameful episode of how his funeral began so dignified, and ended in ignominy:

> Let me tell you about the funeral. The priest had just given absolution. Just by the St. Thomas Aquinas portico, the coffin of Apollinaire emerged, draped with the French flag. We pushed the coffin inside the hearse. Guillaume's lieutenant *képi* was placed on the tricoloured flag, clearly displayed among the crowns and the flowers. The guard of honour — a demi-squadron of *poilus* regulars, weapons held under the arm — lined up, and the convoy rumbled along slowly, the family moving slowly on foot behind the vehicle. His mother, his wife were wearing mourning veils. Poor Jacqueline had barely escaped the Spanish flu epidemic herself that had taken away Guillaume ... But then, as the cortège turned onto boulevard Saint Germain, it was assaulted by booing and jeers coming from an out-of-control crowd cut loose of the most recent mob of protesters celebrating the Armistice, men and women arm-in-arm, singing, dancing, embracing each other and howling in delirium the famous refrain of the end of the war:
>
>> *'... Nay, ya shouldn'a done it, you shouldn'a done it, Guillaume, Nay, you shouldn'a gone, you shouldn'a gone to war.'*[1]

1. *Blaise Cendrars Speaks ...* (Ekstasis Editions, 2016) Translation of ten 1950 France Télévisions interviews, translation by David J. MacKinnon, introduction by Jim Christy.

I was never attracted to any art scene, and certainly not the Paris art scene. My experience of Paris was immediate, direct and carnal, and occasionally, when I got into serious trouble, it brought me to the ground, and to the knowledge that Paris didn't take prisoners. If you bought into its myth, you were likely to finish badly but fatally, still clinging to the conviction that you'd made the right decision. To stay there was like embracing a cloud of mist and in the long term would erode you into an insufferable bore with dental issues.

It still took me a year to get there. In '74, I played rugby for two Belgian sides. Avia-Kituro, named after an east African volcano discovered by the club's founder, was located on a Belgian air force field in Schaerbeek. Our team had travelled to Paris. I had nothing against buses, and liked my teammates, but I was like a helium balloon. If I wasn't fastened down with rope and lead weights, I'd be as likely to fly off into the cosmos first chance I got.

I managed to give the team the slip upon arrival, jumping on a metro and going into the Latin Quarter, where I knew my pal Kate had found digs on Rue Séguier just off St. André des Arts. It was a couple of floors up, accessible by a stairwell called "Escalier G." Her sister's name was Suzanne. She looked like Kirstin Scott Thomas. As I entered, a small cassette player was playing "Riders on the Storm," and on a small coffee table there were two hypodermic needles, cotton balls, a soup spoon, a shoelace and a cheap BIC lighter. Suzanne was unconscious but seemed to be smiling blissfully, her head propped up against the head of a bearded man in a similarly catatonic state. Kate was drinking a glass of Côtes du Rhône, smoking. She was the spitting image of June Miller but had nothing of the weird neurasthenic behaviour of Henry Miller's muse.

"Well, look what the damn cat brought in."

She reached for a scarf and her pea jacket, and we were out the door, and on our way to rue de Seine. We took up quarters in La Palette, in the rear room, and began a chinwag in the best of all possible neighbourhood bars, carelessly tossing back *demi-pressions* of Méteor, a local Parisian brew. Like being at home, except home was Paris.

"Give me a smoke."

"What about the rugby game?"

"Still another fifteen hours to go."

By 3 am, we were six sheets to the wind and rolling like tumbleweed down the rue St. André des Arts. The next morning, I had time for an espresso and a cigarette, then left to catch a bus for a rugby field somewhere to the north of the city, stinking of plonk. Upon arrival, the coach booted my ass all the way to the locker room. Then, oddly, I played the best game of my life, picking fights, making tackles, compensating for my bad showing.

I was for the moment redeemed, but the following week, I would be punished severely for challenging the gods. The team we played in Brussels was SHAPE, the British Army side, and the scurvy grunt opposite me at the number-two position in the line-out was a Sergeant Fury lookalike with a drooping red Fu Manchu moustache, about six feet seven with arms that hung to his ankles. It was to be his last game of rugby, as he was returning to the old country.

During the first half I found myself at the bottom of a ruck, and for a split second, I caught a glimpse of a set of steel studs, just as they smashed into my nose, breaking it in two spots and ruining my breathing for life. All because I found myself accidentally on the wrong side of the gain line. After the game, I was dumped off at Bruxelles Midi train station, and that was that. I returned to Leuven for another week of inhuman studies under the patriarchs of the history faculty, and life in a fourth-floor single *chambre de bonne*, with a single small sink, and only cold running water.

So, my introduction to Europe had nothing to do with the avant-garde. I had been parachuted right into life as a *petit Belge*, and in my miniscule apartment and anonymous place in old Leuven, I had never been happier, now having sighted for the first time Paris, the city of my dreams.

WOUNDED KNEES

IN AUTUMN 1975, I was walking inside the Student Union Building, University of British Columbia with Brian Ferstman, a journalist with the student rag, the *Ubyssey*. He was lamenting the quality of student politics, which was dominated by a Marxist clique, the product of the indifference of the leisure-seeking BCers and the affluence of the province then. So, I decided to run for the University Senate as there were five positions "at large" open. It was actually a fairly easy campaign to win, because most people privately agreed with Ferstman that anything was better than "Students for a Democratic Society," a barely veiled clique of Trotskyites who hadn't noticed that the Brit-dominated trade unions had the province by the short and curlies in the mid-seventies and that everybody, except for the forgotten aboriginals, was doing very well indeed. Unemployment was at virtual zero, tuition was virtually free, you could find beer at 10 cents a half-glass and gas at the same price per litre. In short, in the big picture, only a miserable Trotskyite could raise chicken-little arguments.

With that in mind, I ran my campaign on the "hidden problem of corruption in Caledonia and the shame associated therewith," as well as the need for free beer and prophylactics campus-wide. But from the outset of my nascent and soon to be extinguished political career, I encountered the politician's chronic nemesis — a scheduling conflict — as on the date and at the time of the all-candidates meeting, I was scheduled to compete in an endurance sporting event known as the Great Race. The Great Race was a five kilometre sprint across campus, punctuated by ten stops where contestants were required to guzzle a glass of industrial ale.

The Great Race began at high noon, as did the all-candidates meeting, but it was logistically feasible as the political contestants were presented in alphabetical order. I arrived in an auditorium with my stomach still churning, proceedings well-underway and somebody named Maartens concluding his pitch on his service in the Totem Park residence canteen and why that qualified him to sit on the Senate. Serendipitously, my name was called out just as I entered the room, giving the entrance and my allies in the crowd an opportunity to applaud. It was too late for preliminaries, and I jumped up on the stage and entered straight into the meat of the matter, delivered in my best approximation of a Hebrides accent:

> *Dia is Muire duit,* ... To aid in the further arrangement of removing the obstacles standing in the way of the people, who were faced with a similar problem to the one under review, an application was made to William Young, Esq. of Einverurie, in the county of Elgin, he who had been singularly successful in repairing a particularly troublesome fence at the edge of his lands. The northwest corner if memory serves me correctly. Captain John MacKay, late of the 26th Foot, the factor of Strathnaver, and Lieutenant Tibias Gunn of the Royal Marines, Chief of the Clan Gunn, factor of Assynt, and part-time prosecutor, has also been showing untiring zeal ...

At this point someone in the crowd shouted "get on with it!" but I wasn't put off so easily.

> "... untiring zeal!" I repeated, this time louder. "Having had the time to examine the audits that considerable amounts have been devoted to converting the mountainous districts into sheep walks and to remove the inhabitants to the coast or to the valleys nearby the sea!"

Blankstein, as campaign manager, had strategically placed supporters throughout the audience, who now stood up and engaged in some sustained and rhythmic hand-clapping. I persisted:

> "And, I ask you not rhetorically, but ovipositorially, are sheep walks a bad thing? No, not per se, an honest man might reply, but sheep walks — and we'll certainly not be calling them sheep runs under my watch! — like other contrivances devised by the authorities at the public expense, require an allotment of funds, maintenance, upkeep by able staff in such matters and not the appropriation of funds skimmed from the trade of cured and salted whitefish! *Sin agad e, ma tha.*"

At the back of the hall, I caught sight of something that immediately excised the pleasure I was taking in proceedings. The Judge. He didn't look too happy. It was going to be a repeat discussion, and this was just the latest pretext.

"What the hell do you think you're doing?" he said, after we were inside his Pontiac parked close by.

"Meaning?"

"Tarnishing the ensign in public. What purpose could that possibly serve?"

"The service of Oulipian humour," I said, but father wanted to keep me out of the Oulipian, a loop not fit for a MacKinnon.

The election followed shortly thereafter. I received over 3,000 votes, *for all the wrong reasons* telegraphed the condemning grimaces of clan elders when I crossed their path, and with the sheep walk issue still unresolved. During my first student council meeting, President Blankstein, older brother of my campaign manager, wisely resolved to defer the sheep walk issue until the following session in order to address a matter deemed more urgent. The Democratic Alliance for Students had tabled a motion on Leonard Peltier, an on-the-run Lakota from the infamous Pine Ridge reserve, the site of Wounded Knee. Someone had unwisely fired an AR-15 in the direction of two FBI agents in South Dakota, and the FBI agents being located at an unsafe distance, i.e. a few yards from that someone, their duties for the day were brought to an abrupt end, coinciding with the interruption of their heartbeats, thereby unleashing a thirst for revenge among G-men unassuaged to this day.

Peltier, who conceded that, although he couldn't take an oath on it, he may have been hunting that day in South Dakota, a perfectly legitimate aboriginal pastime, and as followers of the case would point out — Peltier having chosen discretion as the better part of valour — that it was neither unusual for him nor *ultra vires* indigenous rights since time immemorial to symbolically fire off a shot or two in the general direction of passing birds or trespassers in defence of Sioux territory, but certainly, and particularly given the number of firearms being discharged within the perimeter of the crime scene at the time of the alleged events, it was offensive in the extreme and a misread of rudimentary principles of causation to trace *all* 125 bullets that had riddled the cars of the two agents to Peltier's AR-15, solely because he had proceeded with haste to distance himself from what appeared to be an unsafe environment, in short by visiting some distant relatives at a Cree reserve in Hilton, Alberta north of the 49th.

Peltier had links with AIM, the radical American Indian Movement and some of its more radical adherents were interested in reviving the style of Crazy Horse. Furthermore, as the Communist council member pointed out, the fact that certain Weather Underground Organization enjoyed the hospitality of the Sioux on or about the date of the alleged events, and were admittedly one of the worst of the plethora of murderous terrorist groups extant, including Action Directe in France to Baader-Meinhof in Germany, Brigadi Rosso in Italy, and the Red Army in Japan, indicated there could have been white mischief afoot that day and no reason for Peltier to meddle in settler feuds. With no knowledge of the facts, and a vague recollection of my family-induced credo that hard cases make bad law, I advised caution to my fellow councillors.

"But, before we sign onto the cause, or the causa causans, I'd like to know what that cause is."

"Well, the cause," said the member for the Democratic Alliance, "is to protect Leonard Peltier from a fascist attempt to pin a murder on him he didn't commit."

"Isn't this a matter for the courts?" I wondered aloud.

"Dysfunctional," piped one. "Reactionary," piped another.

"Let's have some facts in support, shall we?" Then that mocking inner voice: "You sound like a Cape Breton politician."

"Get on with it! Too long-winded," grumbled another. But, somebody, some ancestral atavistic ghost out of the MacKinnon attic had taken over my vocal chords.

"… as I was trying to say prior to the last interruption, whether or not the entire US judiciary is dysfunctional is peripheral, and a determination for our Canadian court, not us. Certainly not me, anyways, it's my first day on the job."

"Fascist," from yet another anonymous voice. I was beginning to grasp the meaning of backbencher.

Marty, an engineering student, independent candidate, now took the floor, glancing my way, *I'll handle this.*

"Well, it's a budget allocation issue. Either we fund a killer on the run, or we get the J. Geils Band here for a concert next month and the planned Olympic-size swimming pool. President Blankstein has it all lined up and fully funded. So, what do we do? Bankroll a terrorist on the lam, kiss off our corporate sponsors, or get some rock 'n' roll happening?"

I held up my hand towards Marty, as if to calm him. We'd rehearsed it all in advance.

"We're not necessarily on the same side, friends, but I would remind my friends from the SDA that earlier in this session I was given short shrift on the sheep question, no doubt … ahem, for the surplus alliteration alluded anon on airing an albatross …"

"Get this clown out of here," shouted one.

"On a point of order, the sheep in question were born in Canada!" I underlined. "Leaving aside the sheep walk issue for today, I'm not necessarily against a group of students taking a political position or rally to a cause in defence of the little man, but *audi alteram partem* and all that, let's hear what that cause is, in fifty words or less, of course …"

"Go back to the Highlands, you fascist," chimed in somebody named Peter.

Vice-president Dougy Aldridge, intervened.

"This is a sensitive topic. I'm calling for a secret ballot. There's an atmosphere of intimidation in this place."

The Peltier resolution failed, the left went on to successful careers defending Aboriginals at the taxpayers' expense and the entire sheep walk issue was ignored by student council and the senate, which fortunately had no impact on my membership in the Faculty Club and free scallop and bacon appetizers during Friday PM happy hour. In midterm, for personal reasons, I resigned and left for Egypt. But for some reason, the incident remained with me. It was my first ever contact with the plight of an indigenous person.

A number of years later, around 1992, shortly after my return from China, where I'd been working, I was contacted by the Gitxsan and Wet'suwet'en First Nations, whose hereditary chiefs wanted to set up a joint venture with a Montreal acquaintance Peter McLaughlin, who ran the St. Ambroise real ale brewery. I then heard again about Peter Grant, who later would be lead counsel on the *Delgamuukw v. The Queen* case. By this time he was a champagne socialist and, whatever else that case was about, it was a money pit for the solicitors. As a Vancouver solicitor once remarked to me: "Aboriginal law's a great gig if you can get into it."

When I graduated in history, Uncle Hugh (Father to his friends & faithful) attended, *noblesse oblige,* and I invited him for a happy hour in the Faculty Club together, courtesy of my senate privileges. Prawns and avocado appetizers had been added to the menu, and they alone were worth four years of casual, dilettantish study. Five years later, the man sitting opposite me would be slain in a Mexico City hotel room, leaving us to pick up the scattered and insufficient remnants from yet another MacKinnon tragedy. By that time an American had become the Chancellor at UBC, and had ordered the fine old Faculty Club razed to the ground and built a parking lot in its place, then filled the soda machines with Coca-Cola campus-wide, instead of beer.

Ironically, the Faculty Club Hugh had founded ensured that the right to drink proper plonk was preserved *in memoriam at aeternam* at the University of Waterloo. After his death, his family and friends created a memorial dinner, and to this day, prestigious members of the historical community meet to honour his memory and to toast a man who had greatness in him, and whose life was abbreviated far too soon.

At any rate, as I was saying, the world was a different place then. The biggest risk was driving off a cliff if you fell asleep at the wheel. Or getting a finger chopped off working on the green chain. Or running into one of the local thugs when they were prowling the streets in your neighbourhood. But I didn't know anything about First Nations, let alone the Pine River reservation or Wounded Knee, and the killing of two FBI agents at what became known as the Jumping Bull Compound shoot-out. I would learn about that first during my tenure on the UBC senate, when Leonard Peltier was on the run in 76, but I would get to know the Lakota Sioux more intimately during the short and perilous days that shook the Vatican in 2016.

And then, four decades after his first appearance in my conscience, I was contacted by the International Leonard Peltier Defence Committee to join the cause for a presidential pardon for the convicted Lakota. Peltier had been wallowing in prison for forty-one years, and was now in ill-health. I contacted the Vatican, and they interceded on his behalf, but to no avail. Even Obama refused to pardon him.

A ream of white-collar criminals and drug dealers were pardoned, but Peltier remains behind bars to this day. I met many of his sympathizers through the Long March to Rome, and as happy as I am to be a long way from the Wounded Knee crowd, they left a deep impression on me. The Lakota Sioux are not afraid to hate or to go to war, and though I've flirted at the fringes of such people my whole life, they are in another league, cultivating the memory of historical wrongs, using it as oil on the flames of retribution and not afraid to speak of revenge. And something indefinable — that not even Barack Obama could bring himself to pardon Peltier. Something that I felt was rooted in fear.

There was a war going on between the Pine Ridge Sioux and the authorities in '76, and Peltier was a big part of that war. AIM was associated with the terrorist group Weather Underground, but its own were as hard-core as anyone from that group, including someone named Dennis Banks. The tradition being invoked by those warriors was that of Crazy Horse, and they were determined, resolute and ready to die if necessary. That was the knife-edge atmosphere on June 24, 1975, when FBI agents Ron Williams and Jack Coler came onto the reservation looking for another Sioux, Jimmy Eagle, wanted on assault charges.

During the days leading up to the Long March to Rome four decades later, Kenneth Deer, Mohawk, asked me to call Oren Lyons in New York. People outside the indigenous world don't even know who Oren Lyons is, but he enjoys a massive prestige and is one of the world's most admired people, respected and trusted as a Faithkeeper for the Onondoga Nation, of the Haudenosaunee, the former six-nation Iroquois confederacy. Oren Lyons spoke to me for two hours, tracing the story of his life, leaving the glory of Madison Avenue as an ad executive to return to his people. The struggles of AIM. Being thrown out of government offices during the 1972 Nixon re-election campaign. And so forth. And, he told me about a young firebrand named Steven Newcomb who returned from South America with a story — the origins of the conquest of the Americas, sanctioned by the Catholic Church via the Papal Bulls. I was aware of

Steven's reputation as a very hard man, but you couldn't deny his brilliance and his single-mindedness.

"Steven is a fiery, passionate man. Do not forget what he has achieved. We are indebted to him."

I was still somewhat under the spell of Oren Lyons, and not making connections to the tale he was telling in minute detail, and so this remark only returned to me later.

After we returned from the Vatican in 2016, we went to ground, just to recover. But, the issue of Leonard Peltier would return. Since Barack Obama was completing his tenure as President of the US, he would be commuting sentences and granting clemency to a select number of convicts come January. Frank & Anne Dreaver contacted me to see whether the Vatican could intervene on behalf of Peltier. I brushed up on the general facts of the case, recalling the murder of the two FBI agents, brutal and callous even against the acrimonious backdrop of relations between the AIM government and the authorities. And, I presumed for the sake of objectivity, that he was guilty but that it was worthy of mention to the Vatican. Forty-one years is a long time in a US prison.

I didn't feel like thinking about it too much. We were suffering from post-traumatic LMR syndrome. The Vatican had its own resources to make its own assessments. But, Archbishop Tomasi responded to my request, and someone followed up on it, as it turns out unsuccessfully. On January 17, 2017, the list of Obama's pardons was published. He had commuted the sentence of 209 persons, 109 of whom were serving life sentences.

I had done my part, but the case wouldn't leave me. I decided to consult the FBI file in its archives. For the most part, the events of 1975 point to a cold-blooded murder of the two agents by a group of Lakota Sioux who fired 125 rounds into two agents exposed in an open field with nothing but handguns to defend themselves. One of the guns was an AR-15, and the only person who had one of those was Leonard Peltier. Here is part of the FBI file:

> Soon after Williams' initial transmission, he radioed information that the subject vehicle had stopped and that he and Coler had come under fire. Williams began transmitting directions to Agent Gary Adams, who was approximately 12 miles away. Adams could not reach the vicinity of Williams and Coler due to gunfire directed at him as he approached. Contrary to some media reports that gunfire lasted four hours, trial testimony described the gunfight directed at Williams and Coler as lasting approximately 10 minutes. During this ordeal, a combined total of five rounds had been fired from both Williams' and Coler's weapons. The agents' vehicles alone had 125 bullet holes. This total does not take into account those rounds that hit the agents, glass, or were not recovered.
>
> At approximately 4:25 p.m., agents discovered the bodies of Williams and Coler lying beside Agent Coler's vehicle. Agent Williams received bullet wounds to his left arm and side, foot, right hand, and head. Agent Coler received bullet wounds to the arm and head.
>
> An examination of the physical evidence concluded that Agents Williams and Coler had been killed at close range by a .223 type bullet. According to witnesses, Peltier was identified as the only person in possession of a weapon that would fire a .223 type bullet at the time of the murders. The weapon was an AR-15 rifle.

> Peltier's AR-15, Agent Coler's .308 rifle, and an arsenal of other weapons were recovered from associates of Peltier on September 10, 1975, when a car exploded on the Kansas Turnpike near Wichita, Kansas.
>
> An examination by the FBI Laboratory made a positive match with a .223 shell casing found in the trunk of Agent Coler's car and marks produced by the extractor of Peltier's AR-15. No match could be made with the firing pin, because it was too smooth.
>
> On September 11, 1986, Federal Appeals Judge Gerald R. Heaney concluded: "When all is said and done, however, a few simple but very important facts remain. The casing introduced into evidence had in fact been extracted from the Wichita AR-15."

There was something else I'd read in another account. That the killers had turned the bodies of the agents face down, as the Sioux belief was that this prevented them from going to heaven. But despite the story, and my conviction that Peltier was involved in this, there was something that the FBI left out. Peltier has already served the equivalent of five life terms. How many times do you have to kill a man? And this land had been stolen from the Sioux under the authority of the Vatican. I had seen several of the Sioux in Florence — Loretta Afraid of Bear Cook, Barbara Drybones, and a Lenape man who shared their convictions — Steven Newcomb, who would leave an indelible impression.

But, when all is said and done, there is a core truth to liberty pointed out once again by the great writer, George Orwell. "People sleep peaceably in their beds at night only because rough men stand ready to do violence on their behalf." The Americans consider their freedom as synonymous with their governance of the world. Whatever anyone can accuse Leonard Peltier of, neither he, nor his coterie of AIM rebels can be accused of not believing in their cause. Had they prevailed, he would be a hero for the ages. The failure to extend clemency to this man is an avowal of weakness of the Americans, one rooted in the belief that "Indians" are in fact barbaric and cannot be tamed.

There was another event that flew under the radar during that wild and woolly 1975, when Peltier was on the run, and it's not one to help anybody anywhere sleep better at night. It is a very Canadian story, about a Miqmaq woman named Anna Mae Pictou Aquash, who became the lover of one of Peltier's closest cronies, Dennis Banks. Aquash was a principal in the AIM movement, whose militants occupied Wounded Knee on the Pine Ridge reservation in a 71-day standoff with federal authorities.

Aquash was radical and somebody not afraid of taking action. But, the women were jealous of her, and the political factions within the Lakota Sioux increasingly paranoid. Aquash was "bad-jacketed" by jealous Sioux women, encouraged by Peltier who was calling her a snitch, and was convinced she was an infiltrator for the FBI. Aquasha had found her way into AIM through an affair with Dennis Banks, the Ojibway radical. Around that time, Marlon Brando had lent Peltier and Banks a motor home and $10 000 cash, which helped facilitate their escape from Wounded Knee. When the police stopped them, Peltier managed to escape, and the women were arrested. Jail would only delay her fate, and in February 76, a body was found in a ravine on the reservation, a prescient sign of the Aboriginal women who would begin disappearing in the opening decade of the 21st century.

I mark the tragic saga of Leonard Peltier as the sign

that I have passed through the Looking Glass. A man cannot dictate the conditions of his birth and upbringing, but what he does with it is his own affair. That is the part that remains between him and the Creator. And of course, times change, and events leave footprints just as a man does. I now choose to share the results of my inquest in full knowledge that it will earn me nothing but even greater contempt from my entourage. But what risk? I shall soon be frittering away into dust, so hanging on to a reputation I never had in the first place is the least of my worries.

During the Long March to Rome, I heard countless tales of indigenous suffering. There was an atmosphere of ongoing volatility. Our proceedings were governed by the peace pipe, by the sweat lodge, and by the ceaseless reference to the Creator. Having lost everything they cherish, the indigenous have hung on almost ferociously to their belief in a higher being, to the idea of a happy hunting ground in the hereafter, and to the knowledge that our actions here on earth are in large part dictated by those who preceded us. Leonard Peltier also has that aura about him. I found it very difficult to immerse myself in things indigenous. But, I wonder who is the richer — we who deny the existence of God, or the indigenous who see the Creator in everything they witness, contemplate or do. We seem unable to see life without calculation, and in the end it has impoverished and pushed us out onto a spiritual desert.

THE ART OF RIGHTEOUS ANGER

I WAS ABOUT eight years old, driving my bicycle down McBride Road at Crescent Beach, zig-zagging beautiful patterns to my mind, when a car honked from behind me, nearly knocking me off my bike. It was my father, who told me to park the bike and get in the car.

"Are you trying to get yourself killed?" he shouted.

"But there are no cars on the road."

"I was!"

It never occurred to me that he was worried. The only lesson derived at my end was that I'd been thoroughly enjoying myself, without a care in the world, and that that was against some parental code — the anti-enjoyment code. The Christian Brothers also liked shouting, particularly the ones afraid of beating you. The Sisters of St. Anne liked screaming. It was just in their blood or their job description or their temperament.

During a visit to London's West End in 1978, Father Hugh, Dad's brother, was staying in a Green Park condo, on sabbatical from his duties as Chair of the History Department at Waterloo. We had dined at a very chichi West End eatery, along with my grandmother, and Justice D.B. MacKinnon, my father's younger brother. Hugh had put on a real spectacle, embarrassing the shite out of the entire table by ordering the waiter to return to the kitchen to debone his *truite amandine* while liberally pouring the Sauvignon Blanc down his gullet and pontificating on a range of medieval pontiffs, liberation theology or whatever else crossed his mind.

I stayed with him that night, nursing my beer while he continued into the Glenfiddich. At one point though, I asked him what his thoughts were on infallibility. For instance, during that period of the pseudo-pontiffs. "And your inference," he responded, his voice inflecting slightly deeper and louder.

"Well, all right forget them, but Pope Alexander VI, it's not the first word that comes to mind. I'd have thought fertile would be more appropriate, with eleven children."

"How dare you of all people, attack the tenets of the Catholic Church!" But then, just as suddenly, he went from apoplectic to breezily civil, as if he'd turned the hair dryer off.

During that evening, he alluded to a couple of things that he just might be—a murder suspect, a man who had only respected one of his three vows, a spy for the Soviet Union—and, as an Oxford graduate of that generation of Oxbridge students who were recruited by the Soviet Union, he well could have been. He was something all right, but the fool was so busy laying false trails that none of us will ever know what he was actually up to, perpetuating the MacKinnon tradition of trumpeting their public antics while concealing deeds of rare bravery, often in the service of the nation. And, whatever he was, it got him killed in Mexico City in December 1981.

In one of his non-tirade moments, Father Hugh actually saved me from wasting years of my life being indoctrinated in the mendacious blather of the lying lefties with a piece of advice delivered in one of his favourite octaves—churlish dismissiveness. The year was 1972, and I was summoned to serve mass at 6:30 a.m. at St. Mark's College in UBC. I showed up half-drunk after game six of the series between Russia and Canada. Hugh said Mass and then we went out for a stroll on the endowment lands, admittedly stolen from the Musqueam, but then preened to perfection and saved for posterity, or at least the posterity of the descendants of the Duke of Argyll.

"Tell me your curriculum," he instructed. I listed off a ream of lib-left courses randomly ticked off while nursing a killer hangover, ranging from sociology to theatre. And after each one, he pronounced "mickey mouse, mickey mouse."

"Listen David, let's talk straight, we haven't much time. I know you're angry about your father vetoing that job down at the refinery."

"It was a narrow escape, just about had a MacKinnon making coin. Wouldn't want that."

"Look, enjoy the bacchanalian delights of university life, but for god's sake, don't ruin your fine mind with psychology. Leave that to the Soviets."

It was funny he mentioned the Soviets, because he knew another Hugh, also a historian, Hambleton by name, and later arrested around the time of his murder. That would not prove his only gift to me—he conferred many others like the art of contrived moral anger, à la Jesus in the temple, and many a time I've privately sent up a prayer of thanks for that tool of the MacKinnon trade, essential to our survival.

RAMADAN '76

Les races n'existent pas
—Tahar Ben Jalloun

WHEN I FINALLY returned to Paris, it was via Egypt, during the Ramadan of 1976, with no information on the country, save the name of a hotel on Ramses Square, provided by a fellow passenger on our flight out of Frankfurt. It had taken a day and a half to fly from Vancouver, via Toronto and Frankfurt, and we landed in the early evening at Cairo Airport. The airport was obsolete, and as chaotic as a marketplace. Upon emerging from customs, we were crossed by a security person carrying a man over his shoulders whose head was covered in gauze, blood seeping through, the gauze purely for sanitary reasons, as the man was dead.

Once outside, we were faced with a crowd of over a hundred young men, pushing and jostling us. I grabbed my 112-pound cousin, wrapped my arms around him, and pushed through the crowd, through a turnstile medley of hands swatting, grabbing, mauling, trying to rip our money belts from us, laughing and shouting, but not forcing us to the ground, and so by pushing like a rolling maul, we found ourselves on the other side.

As we approached the bus platform, a bus, empty but for a couple of passengers, swung in front of us. The doors opened and the driver yelled something in Arabic, motioning us to climb aboard. The moment we had alighted, the doors slammed shut, and departed, driving directly to Ramses Square without stopping. The biggest taxi I'd ever been inside. We walked up El Gomhoria Street to number sixty-six, and there we were.

After checking in, we wandered down to Ramses Square, with no knowledge whatsoever of Ramadan. The day's fasting had ended, and a chaotic, joyous atmosphere reigned —flame swallowers, buses racing by with as many passengers without as within, thousands of revellers soaking up the nocturnal heat of early September. And, upon our return to the hotel, we headed to the basement bar, the sole patrons, with Mohammed the bartender serving us litres of Stella Artois.

After a day or two, we walked down to the square, found a cab and drove north to Alexandria. Nothing was planned in advance. The sky was cloudless, and for the next half-day, we ate dust, and felt our eyes sting as if someone had thrown burnt cumin into our faces, as we gazed out over the patched tartan of the lands leading through the Nile Delta northward. We rattled along in a dilapidated Mercedes-Benz with five other passengers, and I believe the cost for the trip was half a dollar. Upon arrival, we had no idea where to go and just jumped on a tram and began riding around the city, that was funeral-silent and not a European in sight, as we tried to figure out our next move.

A thirty-something man, notable in those days of 1976 because he was dressed in jeans and had long hair, introduced himself as Khalid. After learning we were looking for lodgings, Khalid offered to lead us to an apartment of a "friend." He led us down a series of roads in Sidi Bishr, past a sandwich counter, greeting and slapping hands with an increasing number of men as we progressed, and then took us up a flight of stairs to an apartment. An immense, broad woman answered the door, and she looked first at our new friend a bit suspiciously, no doubt due to our presence, and then shrugged her shoulders and allowed us inside.

The woman's name was Om Tity. She was morose. but kind. Chained to the house, she walked as if she were Jean Valjean pulling an ox-cart behind her. We paid fifty piastres per day, and lived inside a room with Mohammed, an engineer who occupied the third bed in the room and looked to be well into his thirties. Om Tity was diligent and washed and ironed our clothes daily, while her husband, a bald, round, friendly man, recounted a tale repeatedly: He had once inherited a fortune, and immediately travelled to West Germany, where his plan had been to become the heavyweight boxing champion of the world. An unscrupulous trainer had relieved him of his financial burden; he returned home in shame, and since, had been sitting at home telling his story.

The man who had brought us there had dropped by twice in our absence, inquiring as to our whereabouts, which we took care never to give, jumping *ad hoc* into taxis, and taking off to the Alexandria Yacht Club where we parked ourselves and drank beer all afternoon, gazing out over the Nile Delta, and wallowing in our self-designed squalor. The cracks seemed to be crawling up the terrace like spiders.

At the end of the day, Khalid, our friend from the tram, arrived at the door. Once outside, he laid out his plan for the evening.

"I have some friends who would like to meet you. Maybe you would like to smoke some good hash, no?"

Sherlock's eyes lit up.

"Agreed!"

We walked first back towards the tram tracks where

we'd met Khalid, then we kept walking, forever, at least an hour and a half, then the streets became smaller, and we turned into a dead-end road.

"Here it is."

We walked up a dodgy stairwell, knocked on a door, and a skinny dude welcomed us.

"Come in, my friends, you do what you like here!"

The man who welcomed us directed us towards the kitchen where hash knives were cooking. I took a long toke, and felt my head lift off and, within seconds, I could see everything was wrong. They were crowding Sherlock, and he didn't look aware, as if he were losing his bearings. I had to act and grabbed him roughly by the arm.

"Plan Z, buddy."

"Check," he replied, grinning, and I was furious. This was shit in spades.

"We'll be back in a second, gents."

I dragged him towards the door. We scrambled down the stairwell, and emerged onto the street.

I looked up to the window, and there was Khalid, waving. I waved back, pointed at Sherlock and made the cuckoo sign.

"Animated discussion, dude, as if we're arguing. Say anything, don't matter what."

As the day drew to a close, we found our way to a café that served beer.

"So, tell me, no disrespect intended, but we made a mistake back there, and you were digging a deeper hole."

He grinned, but there was a glare in his eye, something else, an anger to match mine.

The next afternoon, we caught a taxi to a resort area on the Nile Delta, and Sherlock relaxed, recounting stories of his father Eric and his uncle Alan Sherlock in the air force in the Second World War, as bombers flying for the RAF out of North Africa, and those of his grandfathers, both of whom were members of the legendary "Ladies from Hell" battalions, so instrumental in the Allied victories at Vimy Ridge and Passchendaele in World War I.

"I'm out for a swim, coming?"

He shook his head, and waved a man over for another beer, and I headed for the water, and swam out in the large bay, swimming crawl straight out into the deeper waters away from the crowd. I U-turned and began to make my way back, but noticed I was getting no closer, and that no one was close. I couldn't precisely feel the current, but I could judge by the two vertices of the parabola-shaped beach that I was losing ground and gradually going further away. I considered shouting for help but could see there was nothing approaching any kind of surveillance, let alone a lifeguard boat, so I coached myself, swimming laterally, with the current as it were, riding it, while attempting to reach shore.

After fifteen or twenty minutes, I could feel that I had been carried away from the outward-bound current, so I stopped to briefly tread water and gather enough energy to continue. I had another few hundred yards to go, provided no new current swept me oceanward. I recommenced my path, swimming on a diagonal, eventually making it to shore, where I half-crawled out of the water onto the beach. I then walked the several hundred metres now separating me from Sherlock who had consumed another bottle and a half, and looked pleased with himself.

"Beer?" he offered as I arrived.

"I think I just nearly drowned."

He grinned.

"Worse places than here to drown. Take up a seat and I'll order room service."

"No, let's go."

We found a cab and gave the man Om Tity's address and asked him how much.

"You pay what you like!"

"I'm cool with that," responded Sherlock.

"No, meter, put on the meter!" I said, gesturing.

"You pay what you like!" the driver said, smiling. It took us a long time, a very long time to cover the short distance to Om Tity's, or what felt like her neighbourhood. We had been circling for a good hour.

"OK, that's enough, stop here," I said. We got out of the car. Sherlock looked at him and flipped him a few piastres.

"Here, I pay what I want!"

"Just give him some cash. How much you want?"

But the driver was splenetic and waving his fists at Sherlock. A crowd of at least 200 men of all ages had gathered, attracted by the conflict. One of them walked up and said: "I speak English! What is the problem?"

"There's no problem."

"The driver says you won't pay."

"He says pay what you like! I pay what I like!"

"Look Sherlock, just give him the money, it's only about ten cents, have you done your math?"

"Have I done my math? I'll tell you I've done my math."

He turned to the driver.

"*Shurta, shurta*!" he shouted, at even a higher volume than the driver.

The men crowding around were already divided into sub-groups arguing our case, and I was getting uneasy. This mess was minutes old and looked to be degrading. Sherlock seemed to be enjoying himself. It had nothing to do with me or walking a tightrope. He wanted front-line danger. He'd been alive for two decades, it was high time to start taunting death. "Stupid," his father once said to me. "That's why we signed up to fight Hitler. We were schtooopid." Like father, like son.

"Look, just pay the bastard."

"Never. He gets forty-three piastres. That's it."

"Maybe I don't know you well. In my books, we could be dead right now. So, where's your goddam safety valves?"

"When Dad was flying bomber missions out of North Africa, his ground crew were fucking wogs. One day he's checking his reserve chute. Nothing but newspapers, dude ..."

"I don't see the connection."

"The connection is that taxi ride was worth forty-three piastres. End of story, MacKinnon."

"The war ended thirty years ago. Get over it."

"Not mine."

"Not mine, what?"

"My war isn't over. Just getting started."

"This isn't home and these aren't our people. Shit can happen."

"That's just it. Shit has already happened."

"Save it for another time and place. I mean it."

"MacKinnon, I have nothing to fear anymore."

He looked at me, and his eyes were red. He was smiling, but there was pain in the smile.

"I have no people, MacKinnon."

"What are you talking about?"

Four days previous he'd been in our family home. Dressed in a tweed jacket, with an ascot, gripping a pointer while holding court about our upcoming trip to the origins of our civilisation, holding the lot of us spellbound. And now this.

"I'm talking about — it's all shit, man."

"What is?"

"All of it. It's all lies, and shit. We're in no more danger here than back home."

"You're talking shit."

"You think it's safe back home? You're not looking, dude."

Alexandria melted away. I was looking at the son of one of Canada's greatest war heroes. He already spoke four languages at the age of twenty and had read history, art and philosophy at Aix-en-Provence, Salzburg and Madrid. And I was now looking at him, seeing him for the first time. Something was broken. Something that couldn't be fixed. Something, like he said, that had nothing to do with Egypt.

"Remember my big speech on the night prior to departure? Cradle of civilisation and all that?"

It was passing strange. His voice showed a sudden trace of bitterness.

"Sure, it was memorable. I was transfixed. We all were."

"I didn't come over here to remember anything. I came to old Europe to forget."

"To forget what?"

"Everything."

We both just left off with that, and it would take another two decades before I could make sense of this brief discussion. Too many other things were happening at once. Ten days later, we left on a flight from Cairo to Athens, utterly oblivious to the fact that we were on the same aircraft used for Egypt Air Flight 321, a Cairo-Luxor Egyptian flight that was hijacked by three armed terrorists claiming to be from the Abd Al-Nasir Movement, on August 23, only two weeks before our flight. And from there a string of adventures, through Mykonos, Brindisi, Piraeus, Rome, Berlin, Leuven and then finally to land in the city of light, Paris.

As for Sherlock, he would prove to me that Egypt was the safest part of the two-year string of adventures I'd embarked upon with that enlightened lunatic, as mad and brilliant a Celt who ever walked this mortal coil, but unfortunately for a samurai warrior of his ilk, a man born in peacetime, a temporal state utterly unsuited to his kamikaze wizardry.

Second World War panzer leader Feldmarschall Heinz Guderian often referred to the Canadian Corps as "having a reputation for offensive-mindedness" and "having a reputation for aggressiveness." These laurels would be continued by opponents into the Second World War, where famous general Erwin Rommel would refer to the Canadians as "along with the New Zealanders, the only soldiers in this war I fear." Rommel's experience was based not only on the appreciation of the Canadians as a general in the Second World War, but also as an officer in the trenches in the first.

SORBONNE

IN MY FIRST French class on boulevard Raspail in November 1976, under the shadow of the statue of Rodin's *Balzac*, and in the core of 1920s Paris, I fell in love with Martine Dubois. The fact that Martine Dubois, our professor, was in love with Rinsho, my Japanese classmate, was irrelevant. I had a ringside seat in my French class to watch Martine, her curled hair, the pearled necklace doubled over that she ran through her fingers, her cashmere sweater and, most of all, her voice. Thanks to the style of the times — long hair, long beard, basically hipsters without haircuts — you could fantasize, hope that Martine Dubois would fancy you as a renegade revolutionary, when in fact the dreams of a young Parisienne probably were for a Peruvian with Che Guevara looks.

It made no difference. She carried me along boulevard Raspail, through the Luxembourg gardens and back to the Sorbonne for classes in the Galérie Richelieu, with René Poirier, a semi-retired professor, who had been part of the notorious Oulipo group with Alfred Jarry and the word magicians of the 1930s. Poirier hypnotized me and the twenty other students who sat on the benches to hear about Pascal, Auguste Comte, Montaigne, France's greatest thinkers over time. Poirier was first at the philosophy *agrégation* of 1922, the year of my mother's birth, secured a degree in law, and taught at the lycée Janson-de-Sailly in Paris and the lycée de Chartres, later at the Universities of Montpellier and Algiers between 1932 and 1937. Sent to Brazil for the foundation of the National University where he worked until 1945, in '56, he was elected to the Institute.

Poirier is primarily known for his *Essai sur quelques caractères des notions d'espace et de temps* (1932) and *Remarques sur la probabilité des inductions* (1931). What he taught me was an anatomy of thought itself, as if the sum of knowledge worth preserving was like the human body, an organic infinite complexity of veins, arteries, glands, DNA, but yet worked as a whole. He called this complexity epistemology, a chart of the results of science, and he spoke of it as if epistemology were a living person. Here is a translation of his comments noted in my book, now fifty years old:

> It orders not only methods but the results of science, in a rational manner, distinguishing those that appear anchored and confirmed from those that are plausible and mere hypotheses. It investigates relevance and real value. It also contains a cosmology that determines the global properties of the spatio-temporal universe, properties of structure, limits, origins. It is even a philosophy of nature, an investigation into what lies beyond science.

As I read these notes, I see this marvellous man, bringing to life the genius of French thinking, rationalized by the revolution, that also guillotined as it were the baroque to ruthlessly embrace science as the primary value:

> To clarify our visions of the world, we have to unmuddle and break down the fundamental notions of time,

> space, matter, causation, probability, finality, body, spirit, soul, etc. (etc!!) This examination has two purposes: highlighting how our conceptions are formed based upon our experience allowing us to sketch out an 'intellectual anthropology,' but particularly, to attempt to discover whether there is a resemblance, a homology between the "second reality" that is comprised of our ideas, our models, our constructions.

To me, Martine Dubois and René Poirier were flip sides of the same coin, the binary quintessence of France, one I consumed daily through a mist of tobacco, wine and being utterly unshackled by the usual constraints of mortal existence. At that time, I had virtually no money and lived off the meals served at the subsidized university CROUS restaurants, where you could eat a five-course meal with one of their tickets, sold for three francs, twenty centimes, approximately sixty-five cents Canadian.

We walked through the rue du Faubourg Montmartre every morning, past the Folies Bergères, our one restaurant, Le Chartier, and onwards to the Sorbonne, crossing the Pont Neuf, into the Latin Quarter, convinced that we had found the source of life itself and of beauty — beauty of the city, of les Parisiennes, who ignored us utterly in their exquisite and distant mannerisms that we could only wonder at, as we struggled to decode them. And, then on the strength of a couple of bottles of Nicolas in our single room on the rue de la Victoire, heading out onto rue Lafitte, where we would hone our skills by attempting to seduce two middle-aged Provençales who ran a café nearby.

When I finally learned what I mistakenly surmised was the art of seducing a Parisienne, it never occurred to me that I was being lured into a trap, the confection of which I had nothing to do with. But that would be another decade later. For now, it was the life of a student, and when I walked past medieval Cluny or the Rue St. Honoré where Danton was led away in an ox-cart to his meeting with Madame Guillotine, Place de La Concorde, I thought I could see the shadow of the man against the façades of the buildings, and in the alleyways of the 1st, rue de la Grande Truanderie, François Villon's silhouette, as he prepared to stab a priest, and then contemplate the short coil of his own existence.

OTTO DIX

YESTERDAY, WHILE READING *The Spectator*, I fell across a painting of Otto Dix titled "Prostitute and War Veteran: two victims of Capitalism," a 1923 work that evoked in turn a reproduction of his "Portrait of the Artist Sylvia Van Harden" which hung ominously over my first marital bed on the *rue Champagneur* in Outremont, almost a harbinger of the fate that I would later inflict upon myself. This painting of the gaudy, monocled, knobby-kneed, thin-as-a-rail journalist was my choice — a reflection of my attraction to visual artists such as Dix who represented on canvas the garish sophistication of post WWI Berlin, as Germans tried to come to terms with the horrors inflicted upon them by Ludendorff. The Allies suffered an identical fate under the hubris-ridden direction of General Douglas Haig.

Nothing more symbolizes the senseless loss of life during that war than the Battle of the Somme, an Allied attack that was launched on September 15, 1916 and ended on November 11 of the same year. In that eight-week span, the Allies suffered 650,000 casualties, 200,000 of them deaths. That amounts to more casualties than those suffered during the entire Vietnam conflict every week. On the first day of the battle of the Somme, 30 million shells were fired by both sides into an area seven miles square, killing and wounding over a million young men in the prime of life, almost all of them volunteers. More than 24,000 Canadian men were killed, injured or went missing in that Armageddon.

British painters in the 20s expressed the holocaust of the youth of their nation — Over 19,000 British youths lost their lives — by depicting damaged landscapes, as if unable to come to terms with the bare reality that the greatest war crimes had been committed by the Generals against their own troops, even suspecting their own of cowardice and executing over three hundred for desertion.

But, it wasn't this context, rather an instinctive sympathy for the gaudiness and almost clownish baroque of Dix that caused me to make that the centrepiece of our home. Today, Dix's painting has taken on another meaning for me — the internalization of suffering by Canadian men I have known, each of whom can trace their own paths to these soldiers and the WWII generation, who commemorated their fates with a lifetime of silence, and their sons and grandsons left to piece together the puzzle.

Dix's portrait of a worn-out prostitute merged the two themes of the postwar period — retrospective and introspective — by expressing the human face as a shattered landscape. Otto Dix's expression of love through these damaged souls triggered within me a corresponding sympathy, and a desire to seek out the lost souls of the nocturnal underworld. I felt a similar emotion and curiosity when gazing at Bosch or Breugel or the Dance of the Macabre. When I later read Céline and Malaparte, the mind's eye would conjure up Otto Dix. Having lived in Paris during the final days when Pigalle and the Strasbourg St-Denis district still had the flavour of 19th century prostitution, these women were very much a part of my day-to-day life, and something that I cherish to this day. Each of them struck me as extraordinary and representing Paris in its quintessence. An intentional vulgarity, born of disrepair.

Our café on *rue Lafitte* in the 9th was run by two retired hookers, a place we dubbed *chez les femmes*, where we spent our time tossing back démi-pressions at a doubloon a glass while playing pinball and listening to *Lay-lady-lay* by Bob Dylan, one of only three English tunes on the Wurlitzer jukebox. Otherwise, it was the Pink Floyd tune, *Money, Kung-Fu Fighting* or the great French *chansonniers* of the times — Brel, Léo Férré, Brassens, Barbara — or cornball pop like Mireille Mathieu, a pretty, but extremely hoaky triller popular in the provinces and a bombastic dance tune, *Gigi L'amoroso.*

Later in the evening, we'd drift up the *rue des Martyrs* and talk our way into the bordellos on the upper reaches, where one or two of the madams allowed us to nurse a single beer and observe the theatrics as clients moved in and out of the bawdy houses. From our vantage point, it looked like the bordello had the upper hand in a game of chance rigged from the outset. The johns were played as marks, and even mocked as suckers with open derision, and the johns played their roles as foils to perfection.

One trick I never forgot was how — without putting out — the bartenders and hookers worked together to keep clients purchasing drinks at ten to twelve times regular bar prices, constantly spilling them, pouring them out the second a client had his back turned. I'm convinced this was the most lucrative part of the trade. It was a brilliant execution of a make-work project, worthy of a technique deployed by Silicon Valley shysters in later times. *Nobody works but the work gets done.* Dangling out an enticing promise of nirvana while constantly keeping it just in sight, and just out of reach of the client, while you skin the poor bugger of every last cent he was stupid enough to stick in his wallet before embarking on his evening of relief from a useless and anonymous existence.

Our lack of funds kept us from sampling what was on offer, but it also gave us a somewhat privileged position as spectators of the *commedia dell'arte* being played out. Pigalle whores were part of the neighbourhood — just as the butchers, the dice-rollers and the pickpockets were part of the neighbourhood — rather than being corralled off and auctioned as in Vegas or Reno or the Dam district of Amsterdam where I now live. The hookers were guardians of the Pigalle nocturne, and for us they symbolized more than anything our own escape from the New World.

It was the seedy banality of off-Pigalle that I found endlessly fascinating and irresistible — a real-life moving portrait of dodge, sleight-of-hand and *escamoterie*, tawdry, cheap and garish, a one-ring circus. In those days, prostitution did not have the stigma of cross-border slavery it has acquired in our era of parroted virtue. Simenon, the famed Belgian crime writer, was almost casual in claiming to have slept with ten thousand women, including 8000 "*professionelles*" as he referred to hookers.

A decade and a half later, the practice of prostitution would make an entry into my life unexpectedly. A recent calculation brought me to the realization that I had had somewhere in the order of 2731 trysts with a *professionelle*. The fact that it was always the same *professionelle* — my Provençale ex-wife — doesn't make it any less venal. Nor does my ex post facto discovery of her vocation excuse me in the least. I could see from our first meeting that she was an expert in arts with which I had only a passing acquaintance and that she was trouble in spades. When she was not throwing objects my way, threatening me with ruin, confiscating my passport or introducing me to dubious cronies,

Rachel could weave tales that left me entranced, or confused, or looking for a possible escape route. And once in her trap, I discovered a new companion — boredom — for there was nothing she executed with more passion than a refined *fainéantisme*.

Oddly enough, despite her recidivist tendencies and chronic sloth — and the fact that at least six other men shared her bed whenever I was absent — I am convinced to this day that she was in love with me. Such are the skills of that profession. Even her sloth drew me closer and closer to the flame. Which goes to show the extent to which a man can wallow in his own delusions, even after extraordinary suffering.

Rather late in life, I have come to the conclusion that more of my acquaintances than I realize envy my existence and particularly my close proximity with low-level criminals. I have been characterized variously as unmanageable, disloyal and on occasion, utterly mad. From a distance, my adventures and my discoveries, already extravagant and erratic during the time I led my vagabond existence, exponentially increased and reached a zenith when I encountered Rachel, who coupled her usual recipe of *sexe à l'outrance* with a taste for mocking death, and even courting it. And, despite it nearly costing me my life, and most certainly costing me lifetime friendships, career and the esteem of my fellow man, I imagine that very few men have experienced what I have — *d'aller jusqu'au bout* — to take things to the end, when you stare into the abyss of your mortal soul. Most leave that for the final act of their lives, but I was impatient, anxious to push the envelope, as they say. So, that leaves you with what is left after all of this.

On the night of our catastrophic marriage in Vancouver, a good friend and physician who had been my best man dropped by for a post-nuptial drink at our West side basement suite. I cracked a bottle of Veuve Cliquot, courtesy of Blankstein. Nobody but Robert knew the reason for the marriage was even more cock-eyed than what it looked to be. I would learn before long what a fool's game that was. But for the moment, I was just feeling darkness after this pantomime farce of a wedding, and the city-wide embarrassment I'd brought upon my family. By the time of our farcical nuptials, I had acquired a dangerous and near-suicidal fatalism, clinging only to the thought that, if she brought me down, I would ensure that she wasn't far behind. It gave me in the short term a form of impermeability, but one that was unsustainable.

The Veuve Cliquot was top-notch, and I set to work getting drunk to forget the day's antics. About ¾ of the clan was in a state of shock. I think now, and with no little regret, that if I had consciously set out to cut a swathe of disrepute across the clan's heritage, I couldn't have chosen a better path. Beware exposing your child to the *Memoirs of Casanova*! But I wasn't on the path of redemption yet, far from it. I was trying to expunge the memory of my existence, and I still had a pit viper in the next room, no doubt plotting her next move.

"This is damn good swill, MacKinnon."

"I'll say. Listen," I said, motioning towards the other room, "why don't you go in there and sample the goods?"

"On your wedding night? I think I'll take a pass on that one."

"Don't let that stop you. Just sit down beside her, and don't say anything for a minute or two. Start petting her. Like a dog," I added to underline the nature of the enterprise.

"No fucking way," he whispered, pouring out some more of the bubbly.

"I know you. C'mon, go for it. Tell her how good she looks. You'll see. She won't say anything either, and she'll give you a look, man, then you slip your hand on her thigh. I'm telling you ..."

I could see he was mulling it over, but just then we heard my *bride*'s voice from behind the closed door.

"*David, je t'attends.*"

"To be continued," I said, pointing him towards the door, outwardly cool, inwardly feeling like a canvas of degenerate art being stomped on by the Gestapo.

The next day I had to go to work up on West Boulevard, just across from the school where my older brother worked with special needs kids. Incredibly, I had a healthy contract lined up with Berlitz Language Schools — a quick twenty grand, but that required the fierce concentration and endurance of a monk to properly execute. The phone was ringing as I entered in the office, a haven of peace, and a brief respite from the madness. I picked it up, and the shrieking started.

"I'm going to kill you."

"Look, just calm down."

"Calm down, calm down? I'll show you calm," she shrieked. "I'll never forgive you."

"For what?

"For what, he says. I'll show you what a *française* is made of, my friend."

"Just, err, relax a bit."

"I'm leaving you. We're going back to France."

I knew she was playing me. There wasn't a chance she'd leave without doing something big. Something to dwarf even the previous evening. What I couldn't predict."

"Give me an hour. I'll come home and we can discuss this."

Patrick, my lessor, colleague and patient friend, waited discreetly for five, six minutes, then peeked into the office.

"How's the newlywed?"

"Sorry about this disruption. You shouldn't be catching all this collateral flak."

"Oh, don't worry. You should have met my grandmother. This type of thing was her stock-in-trade."

"Maybe I should call her up."

"Bit late for that. We buried her only this year. But not before she had survived four husbands. She's one of the reasons we are doing well today. Which brings me to you. How are *you* doing?"

"Rather distracted. She's a bit of a full-time preoccupation."

"Probably doesn't bring more clarity having the judge within proximity."

"Actually, I think she's trying to seduce him."

"You don't say. Hmm. One of those."

"One of those."

A phone call interrupted. The person on the line was Dmitri, a Russian acquaintance involved in the illegal shrimp trade in Poitou-Charentes.

"David, I'm glad you're there."

"How did you get this number?"

"Never mind that. There's something you need to know."

"Sure, what?"

"Rachel, she looks innocent, but you don't want to stay close to her. She is big trouble."

"Yea, she keeps reminding me."

"Look, I'm from the milieu, all right? She tell you *that*?"

"No."

"Just ask yourself, *mon ami*. If she's calling me all the way from Canada, it's strictly business. I like you, but I got to make a living, you understand. A contract is a contract."

"Sure, I understand. Man's got to earn a living. Don't worry; I'll be all right."

"You seem all right, but you should understand, it makes no difference to me either way. Course if you're nowhere to be found ..."

I wasn't ready for that.

"I appreciate the call, Dmitri."

"Don't say I didn't warn you."

I spent the next hour preparing a collective email for all my clients, explaining that a long-term mandate meant I would not be available for six months. I knew I needed every ounce of my energy to survive as a human being, and thought if I wanted to keep my business alive I would have to suspend operations for the time being. I was up against something big, somebody who wanted to destroy me. There was no more wiggle room, no breathing room, no nothing. I had wrapped myself in the clutches of a human predator.

A couple of days later, I was found wandering alone at Third Beach, nearby Stanley Park with nowhere to go except into the ocean, and a few big bridges close by. I recall clearly being there, but I don't recall what got me there. I was just there, staring at the water, and realized I was a man with very few options left. I managed to find my way to VGH. After the usual precautions, suicide watch and the like, I was left in a room. A personable young doctor came in and, after some tests, began speaking more casually.

"Your brain is functioning."

"That's of some solace."

"You don't really *a priori* belong in this place."

"It seemed like my only option."

"You seem to have found yourself in a bit of a pickle."

"Indeed. Feeling a bit marinated."

"So, whereabouts is *this woman* now?"

Those words came as unexpected relief. I had been foundering on an open sea, fettered to chains of slavery. But now this wasn't my bride, or the woman to whom I owed a strange fealty through her manoeuvring. She was "this woman." You're thrown off a ship after being beaten to a pulp, keelhauled and you find your way to a desert island. There's one other man on the island. He looks at you, and says: *None of this was of your creation.*

"She wants to return to France."

"Presumably with you in tow."

"Yes."

"What do you think will happen if you decide to get on the plane with her?"

"That I get on the plane."

I needed to hear those words suddenly. To hear myself utter the words aloud in order to take in their full significance. I liked how he stated it as one scenario of many options.

"I'm fairly sure that one or both of us will die. Perhaps not right away, but before long."

"That's kind of what I thought."

"So ..."

"I don't think that waiting on this one will do you any good. It's either or."

"I'm not getting on that plane."

"Sounds good."

"What does that mean?"

"But there's still all this ..."

"All this other shit."

He set down his clipboard.

"Do you have any friends left?"

"Not many — one or two."

"Good. Let's try to work with that. If you can find one, tell him to come by and pick you up, pronto. And to keep his mouth shut. Then get out of town. Go incognito for a while. That's my call."

I think this doctor's name was Paul. The friend who picked me up was another Paul. Every Paul I've ever met was a saviour. I stayed with Paul for a night in North Van, and then we were on the road, first to Lillooet on the Gold Rush trail, where an awaiting glider took me up in the sky. While up in the air, I thought of Otto Dix and Quebec and Cri-Cri who I'd left for this worthless whore. And the thought of what I'd done to Cri-Cri made me, for a fleeting second, contemplate jumping out of the glider. At that very second, we were hugging a cliff formation, and an updraft shot us skyward, lifting me also as it were out of danger. On the ground, Paul brought me back to a motel in Lillooet, where we set up shop, cracked some beers and played poker.

"How do you feel?"

"The same way I did in the oil fields. That I'm not made for this rough stuff. Some people are just harder than me."

"Most people, David."

Shortly after that trip, I moved up to a Benedictine monastery nearby Mission. For ten days, I lived the vow of silence, staying in a dormitory cell, alongside monks who didn't speak a word, save one who was very friendly, an old codger sweeping the foyer and common areas of the monastery.

"You have had a rough time, haven't you?"

"No worries. I'll be all right."

"It's perfectly understandable. A young man like you, out for adventure. Sometimes it's just a question of luck. If you ever want to drop by my room and share about how it has affected you, I'll set aside some time to listen to more of your story. Sometimes it does one good to just let it all hang out. Don't worry, I'm not judgmental."

"Thanks for the sympathy."

At one point, I phoned Tom, an acquaintance specialist in psychopaths and personality disorders and whom I'd been consulting via telephone to get a grip on what I was dealing with.

"This is going to sound pretty insane."

"Let me guess. You miss her."

"Yes."

"It's the warm body, isn't it?"

He knew.

"Yes. It's the warm body."

About a week after I returned to Vancouver, I was watching a news program on television, announcing the arrest of a 67-year-old monk at the Benedictine monastery, a serial predator who targeted seminarians. As he was being led away in handcuffs, I caught sight of him — my friend and confidante from Mission. Seeing him arrested didn't really change my opinion of him. He was a friendly old pervert, and being arrested didn't seem to bother him one way or the other, at least judging from the benign smile on his face as the police led him away. And, me with lots of time and no friends, and six free visits with a shrink, courtesy of the Law Society.

"I'm not really big on talking about myself."

"Not many people are. Just tell it as if it's somebody else."

"Somebody else, like who?"

"Somebody else like *you*."

NOTHING BUT STRAW

ON THE DAY that I was to meet with France's greatest living historian, Pierre Chaunu, I felt once again reaffirmed in my destiny. I had completed what I was convinced was a seminal work on early-nineteenth-century Quebec. I had just finished a double espresso and a smoke while contemplating the statue of Auguste Comte from my window table inside the Café St. Louis on Place de la Sorbonne. Comte, the much-beloved philosopher taught by René Poirier, nearby the other two pillars of my Sorbonne life — the statues of Voltaire and Louis Pasteur in the courtyard of the Sorbonne outside the Galérie Richelieu where Poirier shared the fruits of his exquisite mind.

If you had submitted a word-association test as I continued down the entrance hall of Paris IV-Sorbonne towards Escalier G, leading up to the *Institut de recherche sur la civilisation moderne* and the office of Pierre Chaunu, and proposed as an opening query "destiny," I would have responded, "inevitable," *instantaner.* If you had followed up with "genius," I would have replied, "crowning." I had used Regine Robin's techniques on *Histoire et linguistique* to create a quantitative semantic model decoding the mandements, sermons and pastoral letters of Joseph Plessis, Bishop of

Quebec City and Jean-Jacques Lartigue, Archbishop of Montreal. It occurred to me, dizzy with hubris, that Plessis, from the Latin *plectare*, signified intertwine or weave branches. Like a crown of thorns. It most certainly didn't cross my mind that the (Du)Plessis family would hold my captive attention for fourteen years, until the demolition of the entire Duplessis clan, and simultaneously, the eradication of the great Quebec dream of a nation-state.

My step was sure and I was governed by the conviction that I had played my cards well. After years of research and the completion of the corpus of my study, I had torn off a brilliant thirty-page introduction, positing my work in the line of Bourdieu, Barthes, Foucault, Febvre, Bloch, and, of course, my mentor Chaunu, despite only having had a single one-on-one and, truth be told, not having read a single page of his prolific works. I perhaps hadn't given sufficient consideration to the fact that Pierre Chaunu was the avowed enemy of Barthes and Foucault, the leading Protestant conservative in France, the man emblematic of the fight against abortion, a Huguenot and friend of the right-wing Abbot of Nantes.

Chaunu's office was a small, nondescript room, decorated with a chair and desk, two fold-up chairs opposite. Chaunu began the interview from his side of the desk, pointing to one of the fold-up chairs wordlessly. I modestly awaited the garlands of praise, and at this proximity, could see he really was the doppelganger of my Uncle Bob, a Whitehorse weatherman and the nicest guy on god's earth.

"*Qu'est-ce que c'est que cette foutaise*?" he began, stunning me with a verbal uppercut, holding the thesis downwards like a soiled handkerchief.

"*Quelle foutaise*?"

He stood up, rounded the desk, and sat down beside me, breathing into my face.

"*Quand même*!"

For a minute he continued staring at me in apparent disbelief.

"Have you been enjoying your extended holiday in Paris, Monsieur MacKinnon?"

"Yes, err, non, *monsieur le professeur.*"

"And, tell me, Monsieur MacKinnon, at any point in my 150 published works, my work with Febvre, my 400 doctoral juries and 400-plus supervisions of Maîtrise degrees, have you ever once heard me cite Bourdieu with approval?"

"Err, no but given the linguistic ..."

"*Et Foucault! Et Barthes! Quand même*!"

My hair blower treatment continued for twenty-five minutes, "Uncle Bob" really giving it to me. Finally, he paused. He was still only fifty-five, and full of spit and vinegar, but unbalanced. I felt if I didn't appease this rampaging Huguenot, my plans for greatness were dead in the water.

"So, if I understand you correctly, I'm sorry to be blunt, but how do I salvage this work?"

"That's more like it," he said, immediately adopting a more civil tone. "The corpus isn't bad. But get rid of that introduction. It should be less than a page ... this is a study in two parts. Respect the forms. *Classique.*"

It took me less than an hour to toss the introduction and rewrite it. Chaunu awarded me the *maîtrise, cum laude*, but his biggest gift, like that of Father Hugh, was to flush out any left-inspired BS with a furious intellectual backhand, a salutary slap to my intellectual face.

Fortunately for posterity and the nascent paper recycling trade, when my mother died, large sheaves of notes I had carefully stored were trashed along with my Masters thesis under the direction of Pierre Chaunu and some off-colour sketches inspired by *Hare-Kiri*, the original anarcho-leftist predecessor of *Charlie Hebdo*.

But looking back, I cannot help thinking that, for his encyclopaedic production of more than 150 works, Pierre Chaunu became lost in the details of his polemics, and he must have reflected upon his deathbed, like Aquinas, that all of his writing was "nothing but straw." That one song, "Avec le temps" by the poet Léo Ferré would imprint itself within the immortal firmament of human memory with far most lasting depth than the entire work of Chaunu, because it expressed in a few words, the quintessence of man — our ephemeral nature. Perhaps his greatest gift was his prescient fear that with the decline of demographic vitality, France's political decline was sure to follow.

But, oddly enough, here again there was synchronicity, for I would eventually discover his tome *Seville et les Amériques* and use it, and some obscure Portuguese scripts, and some chess strategy to bring eleven indigenous leaders to the doorsteps of the Vatican, only forty years now from the date of my first enrolment at the Sorbonne.

NEMESIS

SUDDENLY, EVERYTHING WENT wrong, and all at once. I had left Paris in June, without a cent, but equipped with a gift of a hand-woven hammock from a Greek friend, Michaelis Mamalingas, and more importantly, a plan for my new frontier of conquest — Cape Bogador. Charles was a friend from a Gabonese diplomatic family, and had promised me that, upon completion of my Masters thesis, I could fly to Gabon where a helicopter would await me, and from there a position in a local university.

The thesis was more than doable. After reducing me to a crumb, Chaunu had offered some practical advice that saved me — stay away from Barthes and Foucault! The big issue at the time was loyalty of the French Canadians, in the wake of two American invasions in 1775 and 1812, and the Church was in thick with the negotiations — because they feared more than anything the Enlightenment, a creation of the French intelligentsia, and that was the ideological spark alongside Thomas Paine's *Rights of Man*, for the American revolution. In Quebec, democratic institutions were tentatively making their way. Voltaire and particularly Rousseau were considered as seditious writers by both the Church and the Château Clique, led by a bishop named

Jacob Mountain, and a governor called Murray, whose tenure has been referred to as "the reign of terror."

I chose the material because it fit my destiny as a future prime minister coming from Western Canada, an utter fantasy considering my own vagabonding tendencies, but one that consistently had me on the rails as far as my formal trajectory went. My paperwork was always in order, and in the end, that would save me.

Seven weeks after my return, I visited our family physician Dr. Yelland for a quick check-up prior to my departure for my African adventure. Doc Yelland was a charming man, an Edinburgh Scot. He nearly killed my mother with an allergy shot, and she ended up being a Botox pioneer, taking botulism injections to keep her eyes from closing. He used to travel to the old country to watch the annual Edinburgh Rugby Sevens. I'm a great believer in synchronicity. Doc Yelland only poisoned two of us, leaving seven members of the family intact. Unless he recommended that Chinese doc who killed Dad. That would defeat the theory, but that was probably just coincidence.

He greeted me with a conspiratorial smile: "Still on your French fixation, are ye," in his Edinburgh brogue, and added a non-sequitur that I didn't fully understand yet: "*Chercher la femme.*" Then, after a quick look-see, he said: "Sobering news for you, lad. You're not going anywhere." I had to check into the hospital for the removal of a cyst. It was a straightforward operation, but proved unsuccessful, and involved two further interventions, a serious inconvenience, but one further complicated by a notorious painkiller — Darvon — that has since been removed from the market, and probably the cause of my contracting atrial fibrillitis later on.

The problem of Darvon is due to the fact that the majority of the drug is converted into a metabolite that is even more toxic and has a longer half-life than its parent compound. From 1981 to 1999, 2,110 accidental propoxyphene-related deaths were reported. In the year I was taking it, there were 221 reported deaths.

To sum it up in a phrase, it triggers heart failure. The FDA finally called upon the pharmaceutical companies to stop making propoxyphene (PPX) in 2010, based upon a clinical trial in which electrocardiograms demonstrated that the drug altered the heart's electrical activity, potentially causing serious or life-threatening arrhythmias. In 2009, I was finally diagnosed with atrial fibrillitis, a condition I have to this day, and which I trace back to that casual prescription. Atrial fibrillitis can be described as an electrical firestorm in the atrial chambers of the heart that confuses the entire physiology of the body. I cannot dissociate what followed with this condition and its chaotic properties with the desires of a soul aching to find meaning in today's world, and indeed, part of the curse that has governed my life since.

While I popped Darvon, and occasionally blacked out, I stopped none of my excessive activities and was unaware that I was risking becoming another case of Darvon roadkill. But I had Gabon on the mind. However, my body had a different take on events, and by February I was bedridden after a third operation, and was rapidly becoming desperate. It was during that time that a friend dropped the copy of *Moravagine* on my table side, and my reading of that book indebted me to Cendrars forever and allowed me to finally escape the confines of a clan I was finding oppressive, and that was personified by my father. Whether that feeling was subjective or not was irrelevant. During every waking moment, I thought only of escape, no matter the price, setting the stage for the next big mistake of my life.

If a young man from my background then does what I did after reading *Moravagine* — i.e. on the strength of nothing but anger and desperation leaves his sickbed, moves into a basement suite in a house owned by Sikh immigrants, and spends his days in a hellish toilet factory as a kiln loader, six on, two-off, operating within metres of that 2,400-degree furnace, it can only be for one reason — that the alternative was worse. And, so for the next year and a half, I moved from the Crane Pottery Works to the Alberta oil fields, and finally to the relatively forgiving climes of city construction work, before once again striking out, this time for Quebec, in the hope that my cherished dream of returning to Paris would finally be realized.

154 HI-MOUNT

I HAVE BEEN saved by Jews more times than I can remember. The first was Zsuzzanna Gati, daughter of Laszlo who at the time was the conductor of the Victoria Symphony Orchestra, while I was a lowly toiler at the Crane Canada Pottery Works. While Laszlo was bringing Yehudi Menuhin, Van Cliburn, Jack Benny and Mstislav Rostropovich to the people of Victoria, I was spinning and stacking glazed 297 Seneto toilets into the kiln for baking at 2,400 degrees Celsius and listening to the constant berating of my supervisor, oddly enough a man with the same name as the TV dinners I ate—Bob Swanson.

The Crane works were about two city blocks long, adjunct to the Canada Pacific Railway line out that way for easy shipping. Twice per shift, the company secretary, a blonde who wore scarlet miniskirts and pumps and resembled Martine Dubois to a tee, walked from one end of the factory to the office with the shift report, and during that long walk, work slowed to a crawl, and every man's suffering increased a notch as we watched her continue her way back to payroll. She drove a bright orange XKE Jaguar 1963 convertible. That car was a piece of work all right, especially with her in it. But from my standpoint on the assembly-line, the 154 Hi-Mount was a sculpted masterpiece with a functional design, specifically customized for the institutionalized. It was hellish, but nobody could argue that my job wasn't essential for society.

One Friday, after a treacherous shift when two workers were taken to emergency, one with a broken back, another with chemical burns to his face, I booked off at 3 p.m., showered, and caught a taxi directly to the Bayshore, where I could catch a Twin Otter to Victoria Harbour and start spending my hard-earned cash. There were friends waiting for me in the harbour, and we moved quickly up the hill into the closest bar, and things got rolling. Later in the evening, we insinuated our way into a house party in the Oak Bay quarter, and I saw Zsuzzanna for the first time, and, since I was wearing a top hat at the time, she saw me.

She was living with a CBC producer, but that didn't stop her showing up at my sub-basement suite in Coquitlam in a Mercedes-Benz the following week, an event so unlikely that she appeared like an angel from the celestial realms. I managed another six months at the toilet factory and moved out to Kitsilano. Returning home after shift, I'd get funny looks as I rolled into granola-land in my 400-four-barrel Grand Prix. But, when I went on afternoon shifts, the CBC producer would leave for his job, and then Zsuzzanna and I spent our hours together when Kitsilano was an indolent layaway, one of the best neighbourhoods on the planet.

I hated my job, although I liked the workers, slaving on the assembly line. Inside those works, there were moulders, glazers and kiln loaders like me, and then the foremen, whom we all hated, and would have killed if we had the chance. For food I cooked Swanson TV dinners at the edge of the kiln, and it was ready in a minute and a half. So, when I arrived home, I looked fine, but my head was still shaking off the effects of seven months of Darvon, so from the outside, no surprise that people thought I was a bit crazy. I read a lot of Bukowski and Cendrars and Miller and also Lessing's *Briefing for a Descent into Hell.* That to me made sense—I'd been torn to pieces, I felt, and forced into this, but I accepted it.

Zsuzzanna told me during one of those lazy afternoons about her father. How he was the head of the symphonic and chamber music department of the Hungarian radio station in Budapest when the revolution broke out. How he had emigrated to Montreal in '57, in much the same way my Hungarian brother-in-law had, with Zsuzzanna on his back, and then began working with Zubin Mehta as violinist and viola player at the Montreal Symphony Orchestra. How charismatic he was, how loved he was, how he mesmerized audiences with a natural *joie de vivre* and his conviction that music was for everybody. When he passed away, in December 2014, the *Globe & Mail* recalled him in their "Lives Remembered":

> For several years, early in his career, he was a violinist and conductor of the Hungarian State Philharmonic. When the Hungarian Revolution broke out in 1956, he was head of the symphonic and chamber music department of the Hungarian Radio station in Budapest. He had already survived a war, several tumultuous governments and border changes, so when the revolution began he decided it was time to leave. In 1957, he and his wife Agnes immigrated to Montreal with their baby daughter, Zsuzzanna ... For the next ten years, Laszlo played violin and viola with the Montreal Symphony Orchestra and also acted as assistant conductor to Zubin Mehta. Concurrently, he was a highly acclaimed guest conductor at dozens of

> orchestras across Europe and Mexico. He loved the stage and people were attracted by his charismatic joie de vivre. Audiences were mesmerized by his stories and his high-calibre soloists and entertainers (such as Yehudi Menuhin, Van Cliburn, Jack Benny and Mstislav Rostropovich) as well as his passion to make concerts available to every person, not only to the elite.

Like her father, Zsuzzanna had a mellifluous and enchanting voice. If I remained even partially human during those days in the inferno of the Crane Pottery Works, she is the reason. I am forever indebted to her for bringing me civilisation when I spent my waking hours largely in an inferno. And her tales of Laszlo Gati renewed my desire to tap into the fountain of Europe and to find at the source their genius and how it had come into the world.

I decided to check out what had become of her. She was last seen in a fashion show in Pasadena, California, "Hats Off To Fashion," a tribute to *My Fair Lady*, which oddly my wife and daughter saw in Dutch only recently. She, of course, was thirty-nine years older, but she had saved the essential — that modesty, her old-world timidity, and somehow even in the tacky costume of the hats off to fashion week, she seemed to embrace something, for lack of a better word, Hungarian.

Not all of her good manners rubbed off on me, because finally, when I couldn't take it any more, I told Bob Swanson where he could stick his 154 HiMounts and to go find himself another slave. And, then found work that was even worse, and switched a kiln oven for the Arctic cold of northern Alberta.

WRECK BEACH

1972. THE YEAR Canada beat Russia in hockey. The year Idi Amin expelled 60,000 Gujarati Ismaelis, and the year Budden was sitting on a Liquor Board carton in the dead centre of the one-room shack he'd built in the cedar forest leading down to Wreck Beach on the UBC endowment lands peninsula. The place he called his "off-grid hunting shack." The box contained sixteen bottles of dollar-a-bottle Baby Duck, a cheapo, oversweet Canuck bubbly made by a winery called Andrés. He'd taken over a squatter's hut, the only one granted a non-conforming use status on that prime piece of Musqueam land confiscated by the university.

Budden came from Fernie in the Kootenay mountain country in eastern British Columbia. He was broad-shouldered, blond-haired, his eyes were like gun turrets. I'd met him six months earlier while shooting eight-ball in the Cobalt, one of a string of dead-end bars on Main Street near Hastings. Since neither of us was really out to make friends or influence people, six months had gone by in a flash, but we were still spending all our time shooting pool and drinking together.

One of Budden's Kootenay friends turned up for a few days. Larry Arishenkoff was a Doukhobor, born into an offshoot rebel sect called the Sons of Freedom who were into pyromania and public nudity. That made him sort of a son of a son of freedom, since he'd left the sect and made his money as a faller for Crown Zellerbach. He had a Fu Manchu moustache, and was pleasant to have around, because he just drank and didn't say much, while Budden and I did all the talking.

Budden uncoiled the wire wrapped around the neck of the Baby Duck and popped the plastic stopper.

"Still down in the mines."

"Pretty well."

"I made a lot of money down in that Crowsnest Coal Field. How you doin'?"

"I'm doing okay," Larry said.

"Up against the cave wall, baby."

"You said it."

"I'm done with that, just moved down here. That money doesn't come in easy, so I ain't giving it to a landlord. I'm just sitting here doing the Wreck Beach squat for a while, maybe drift down to the Eastside, pick some fights with the city boys?" Arishenkoff smiled, and Budden continued. "I love fist-fighting, man, it's in my blood. Fucking, boom-boom, baby. You see old peaceful looking Larry here in a brawl? You don't want to be on the receiving end."

While working our way through the wine, Budden explained to us some of the strange customs of the Kootenays.

"There was this guy — they called him the monk. He was this short, curly-haired motherfucker. There was something wrong about him. He laughed too loud at the wrong times and took showers three times a day. Sometimes, at parties, he would disappear for two, three hours at a time. So, one night, he stumbles through the door, and I can smell something rancid. So, I followed him next time right through Gizzard Linch's cherry orchards, past Longacre Ravine, and into Barry Wilcox's stables down by Lizard Creek. I creaked the door open, and ..."

He shrugged.

"There's not a lot going on up in Fernie. We live under the curse. Bill Fernie convinced the daughter of an old Indian chief, Chief Red Eagle, to tell him where all the coal was in the Kootenays. But her mother put a hex on all the white people of Kootenay. Said we'd all finally die from fire and water. Nothing changes in Fernie; we all live under the curse."

At some point in the middle of the black peninsular night, Budden reached down, and not one of those sixteen bottles had a drop in it and he said again: "It's the curse."

"Let's go down to the water, welcome in the new day."

We stepped outside his shack and walked the trail down to Wreck Beach. It's a good twenty-minute hike down cedar trails, right in the middle of the rainforest. If you're born in paradise, you tend to more or less presume that's just the way it is, and you don't believe people who tell you you're lucky to be there. But, after sixteen bottles of Baby Duck and a couple of hits of white blotter, the mental walls cave in, the trees breathe, and the sky talks to you.

We continued our walk down to the ocean. A Cunard ocean liner was crossing the inlet from the city harbour in a southerly direction towards the Juan de Fuca Strait and the Pacific Ocean. The first B.C. ferry of the day was coming in from Active Pass, steaming towards Horseshoe Bay. Just as the two vessels crossed each others' wake, the first rays of the Pacific dawn struck the water like a rose-tinted laser, lighting them up against the morning sky. Arishenkoff was quiet. He claimed he'd shaken off the fanaticism of his family, but there was something religious about him. You wouldn't be surprised if one day, he just disappeared and moved into the forest somewhere.

Wreck Beach was all kelp, driftwood, and sand thick as clay. Everything lay ahead. We had no ambition, and our minds were bending with the curves of Burrard Inlet. After a while, Budden broke the silence.

"We used to go to these football games — my girlfriend and me. Back in Fernie. Or we'd take a bus down to Creston to watch the Creston Cougars Junior Varsity team play. I was only twelve, but she was thirteen and the whole football team hated me they were so jealous. We'd bring this thick, woollen blanket with us. I'm telling you, it gets cold already in October up there. We'd nestle down in the bleachers, pull that old blanket over the two of us, and you don't want to hear the rest ..."

Budden never talked about love, except in the past tense.

"I loved her, and she betrayed me. So, that's it for love. Over."

He meant it too. Arishenkoff traced out a pattern in the sandbar with a loose piece of driftwood, creating a gutter, which immediately filled with water. We walked along the beach towards Spanish Banks, a stretch of beach where you could see the whole West End of Vancouver, curving into English Bay and Stanley Park. Arishenkoff shivered.

"This is Icepick Willie zone, folks. When the screech is wearing off and your teeth grind and your eyes frazzle like scorched eggs sunny side down."

We turned upwards and hiked up to Fourth Avenue and stopped in at Mildred and Gloria's Sizzlin' Hot Mexicali-Tamale Diner for some breakfast. When you do things like this, a high, invisible wall divides you from the so-called "normal," so the three of us decided to more or less stick it out together for the time being. Without actually putting it into words.

Later that day, we moved back to the Cobalt on the

Main, and started drinking and playing pool. The game was eight-ball, and not everyone plays call pool the same way, and usually the disagreements would lead to some kind of a fight. This time, it involved a Vietnam veteran with a head like an ice cube. He and Budden were about to square off, and he pulled out a handgun, and levelled it at Budden. Budden smiled.

"Oh that. Go ahead. Pull the trigger."

The Vietnam vet smiled.

"I just might do it, motherfucker. Send you down with the gooks."

"Do the deed, man. Get it ON!"

Cube-head stuffed his gun into his suede Aussie jacket, spun around and walked out the rear doors into the parking lot. Like he was still thinking, do I use it or not?

A couple of weeks later, Arishenkoff contacted me by telephone.

"Budden's dead."

"What happened?"

"Electrocuted."

It took me a while to get over Budden dying. But, then it dawned on me that, if he'd survived, he would've ended up in a bad place. And he must have known that too. So instead, right up to the day he died, he remained whole, unified, sexual, violent, natural, animalistic. And I'd chosen to stick around. I wasn't sure why. Probably just that the other part could wait, I'd get there sooner or later.

THE LAST WORD

Greetings from Hell,

By the time this falls into your hands, I'll be busy snatching sparks out of my ass and shaking hands with some former acquaintances. The torture of these waiting games and parallel trials has proven even worse than I anticipated. I am on the planet at the time of writing, because I want to ensure that my personal affairs are in order. I will do the honourable thing and see my family moved into their new house. God knows I didn't build that log house for profit, but every damn German and his uncle wants to buy one these days.

My children do not deserve to have a dad charged with a criminal offence. Based on what the shit-eating fascists have told them, they are now ashamed of me. We have not spoken of the allegations; I hope to do that before I leave this place. Before I depart, I want to address the issue of shame. Every action I have taken in my life has been motivated by love and a desire to overcome the circumstances of my own birth and early childhood. If and when the truth ever emerges — but what are the truths of love, my friend, incomprehensible to the world? — you will see that my trial has been imposed by others with their own agendas. That being said, they couldn't have found a better target.

I have been haunted as long as I can remember by the fear that I am a fake, and the conviction that I am worthless is only magnified because of what I used to do for a living. Every kid to whose life I made a difference, every award I have given out, every team I have taken to the finals, every kid who says that I was the best teacher or principal they ever had, every crummy little year-end gift, every assembly where I either had them laughing in the aisles or weeping or just plain worshipping me (the list goes on) now means nothing. Nothing. I have been accused of being an impostor, and in my case, the charge had only to be levied for me to wholeheartedly agree.

Oddly, the man whom I most admired, my stepfather, is the one who set me unerringly and irrevocably towards all of this. I live under a double curse, my real father dead of a self-inflicted wound, and his successor ready to make me pay for it. I've always known I could never escape it. None of this has been relieved by the ugly and public taint of these cruel accusations. You are different from others, friend. You know that, when I have had enough, I will act in no uncertain fashion. You have always respected my right to do so. For that, I am grateful. But I know that doesn't relieve you of the pain I will cause you, and so I would like to apologize to you for what I will have probably already done by the time you read this.

—*Wick*

"I'M BACK"

I AM A great believer in synchronicity, and think it no accident of fate that Sid's last name was "Wick." And that was his very interior nature, that of a kerosene lamp burning up within, and fuelled by a passionate nature destroyed by the disrepair of his congenital fate. And this fate turned a Homeric hero into the myth of Sid, the man who others built up by creating a monster, and then forcing the man to live up to the myth. Everybody was afraid of Bad Sid. Even Turk, who reigned supreme as a professional defensive back and as Second Row supremo on the British Columbia rugby pitches until he was cut down like an old Douglas fir, told me a long time later that Bad Sid made him nervous.

People are still afraid of him even now, seven years dead. You get that feeling he might just walk around the corner in that quiet way of his and say one or two words. Something like: "I'm back." Or: "Hello." In a way that would cause whoever caught his attention to crumble, the way an impala's legs crumble in immediate surrender when a leopard has driven its teeth into its thigh, operating the cull necessary for group survival, or the way a rabbit might start running after a death adder bite, zigging and zagging, and then as the adrenalin causes the poison to work its way into the system, slowing down, moving towards consent and resignation, to the place where we all end up sooner or later.

Bad Sid understood that, in the end, predator and prey become one. That look came from a place he feared far more than the alleys and bars and forests that he could track like the Chilcotin people who knew him well.

Most people don't consider evil until it's too late, but it's out there, always waiting. It's a cloud. A cloud of dust and particles. The wind carries it, and it tends to blow our way when we've been weakened. Zoé got sick right around the time that Bad Sid stuck that Winchester into his guts and pulled the trigger. This time, goodbye. I'm gone. I was in Manjary that day, a place where you hear voices, and see things. I didn't have to ask anybody what time his finger moved towards the trigger, and that he said goodbye to himself. I heard it from our outpost on the Strait of Mozambique, and strangely, at the very time where the curses of the locals were taking on tones thick with meaning. And I didn't have to be there in the outback of British Columbia to know what Sid was thinking about when he pulled the trigger. He was thinking about Dee. Dee Wickes. Damn Dee.

Mean Dee. Motherfucker out of the navy, eyes like slimy oysters, bristles on a half-shaved chin, done nothing since but drink Old Navy rum in that rocking chair while Sid's Mom, Mary the red-headed Witch, always pinning a Welsh leek onto her white blouse, watching her son lay waste to all and sundry on the pitch. Then Dee and his simmering hatred for that blond boy with the Adonis build for not being sprung out of his own seed and squinting while he issued his thousand-day mantra: "You'll never amount to anything. You're nothing."

Bad Sid so convinced that mean Dee was right that he burned the message into his body—Death before Dishonour.

In those times, and in those savage regions, the world was divided into two groups — those who fought and those who submitted. Me, a skinny Catholic boy with an oversized frontal lobe stuffed to the cortex with thoughts of the Russians and memorized chess moves and the Latin liturgy, I found out the truth at the age of twelve. Then I found it out again and again, serving as a punching bag for a series of public-school thugs, and then watching the Christian Brothers of Ireland do the same thing. If you were in the wrong place, you were in the wrong place. You got in the way.

Then, that day arrived in the Cariboo Hill Hotel, the meanest bar in town in a time when fighting was the pastime of choice of morons after hitting that punch clock. That was the night that changed everything, that started the era of Bad Sid. No, not that day. That fresco, because that's what it was — Italian Renaissance, Fra Filippo Lippi, Raphael and Caravaggio — a fresco etched in my mind, a triptych on those folding doors you see on the Hieronymus Bosch paintings.

Everything in it in infinite detail, but falling under three parts — pre-Bad Sid, the Bad Sid era, post-Bad Sid — when we all had to learn to survive on our own again. That was another hard lesson, learning that his superhuman strength in the end weakened us all. That fresco, like I say, was embedded, coloured in *sepia-unione*, like Red Dead Afternoon, or a Tin Tin movie, a series of celluloid frames.

The waiters were doing the segue in the moving fresco — dropping sixteen twelve-ounce glasses of Molson Golden near a frozen, cryogenic urine draft that'd dissolve the chrome off your camshaft. Hardly a woman in sight outside of two Musqueam girls slashing at each other with broken glasses. And Bad Sid, presiding over the table, exuding nobility, and only exacting small tributes from the table, a mere kowtow in exchange for his esteem. But not making the angle of the bow a condition precedent; it was always principle with him.

"Honour to meet you, sir," he said during our introduction, knowing full well the honour was mine. Bad Sid looked around the expanse of the Cariboo, Greater Vancouver's best rumbling palace, attracting men to their sure perdition, just as the bears can't stay away from honey, or flies from shit. Bad Sid looked at me and smiled and there was charm, and sadness and disappointment in that fathomless smile.

"Look at this. This is what remains when all is said and done."

We were drinking the beer too fast to taste it, looking for that *déclic* that would snap our brains and make unreasonable acts seem reasonable. Bad Sid had caught sight of a large curious looking copper bass embedded into a frame in the wall behind me.

"This piece belongs in your home."

Two doormen were moving at a face pace towards us.

And during those long, frozen moments when everything had been silenced, and Bad Sid moved up and down between the tables, much in the way you see ultimate fighters moving in the octagon these days, in a simian gait to underline the animal in them, I recognized one of the bouncers, no other than Thos, the owner of a canary-yellow Ford Fairlane and I realized I was indebted forever to Bad Sid and could walk the streets again.

After his death, I took a drive up the Gold Coast trail in British Columbia, where he had toiled two decades earlier as a foreman on the railway. Spences Bridge is a town fifty kilometres north-east of Lytton, at the end of the Kettle Valley Railway, a spur line marked by nothing more than a rail bed, and the one-lane truss bridge that gave a name to this one-pit stop at the crossroads of the Trans-Canada and the number eight to Merritt. Population 138 and still the main rancherie of the Cook's Ferry First Nation, a Nlaka'pamux band of the Nicola Tribal Alliance, with my wife, daughter and son, outside a dilapidated A-Frame, and in sight of the Nlaka'pamux Church. In 1892, the population included thirty-two people of European ancestry and 130 indigenous people. There were five general stores, three hotels, one Church of England and one school. So, the population had dropped by twenty-four, four of the general stores had closed down in 122 years.

At the top of the triangle, where the road splits, there is a cemetery. The place where Bad Sid conceived his first off-spring — who later would ratify the Hemingway curse on the male blood line by attempting to take his own life at the age of seventeen — not far from the rail bed where he'd once put a Portuguese man into the hospital for six months for trying to knife him when he was a foreman on the Canadian Pacific Railway.

People look at cops differently in the north, and they look at Aboriginals differently. Holes-in-the-wall like Spences Bridge attracted a particularly dangerous and deranged type of individual, for the most part people who either can't live with anybody else or are cemented to the ground by the paralysis of their forefathers. But the thing is that those 138 people in the hamlet aren't the same 138 as a generation ago. Bad Sid could take three years of the place, and after he'd beat everybody up, he moved down Cache Creek way, and that's where they found him.

Nobody knows to this day who the "they" were, but there were nine of them, and obviously one of them had seen him working as a gas jockey on the afternoon shift, out on the number eight halfway down to Merritt. So, they waited, and they came in with their bats and chains, nine of the "they." And, after he made the first four pay heavily for being brave, the fifth one caught him in the back of the legs with a bat, while a sixth had whipped a chain around his head. And at the age of nineteen, the strongest, most fearless fighter throughout the Cariboo Chilcotin Gold Rush region went down, the first time he'd ever gone down.

Probably that eighteen-wheeler pulling into the station stopped it all. Bad Sid wasn't yet dead, not even unconscious. There were parts of him broken, and a good chunk of his teeth on the ground, and even though he wasn't blind, he couldn't see too well. And that same low growl of a voice, the one he'd always heart, the mantra from early childhood.

"You'll never be nothing. Worthless bastard."

It's only today that I realize in all those years, I never had the opportunity to ask his real father's name, having presumed that Dee was his dad. Since he had taken his own life during Mary's pregnancy, he had in fact erased himself from history. The Malagasy say a person without a tomb has "no tale to tell" and is lost to the hereafter. Sid too would be erased from the history books and would become a man with no tale to tell, confined to a limbo, deliberately assigned to a wilful amnesia by many who, like me, were indebted to him for his tragic magnificence.

THE END OF CHARLIE MAGGOT

1980. HAVING COMPLETED a winter out on the Alberta tundra moving oil rigs, just learning to speak like a human being was enough to keep my mind occupied. A couple of months doing banal construction work back in Vancouver had helped me lick my wounds, after a family of seven animals in human disguise had found a way to drive me and my brother out of a gulch known as Drayton Valley. That mess was caused by a brawl, and that brawl was triggered by a sewered eight-ball during a game between me and Jack Sugar in the pub of the Drayton Valley Hotel.

Anybody who thinks that Canada is or ever was filled with innocents hasn't moved through the graveyard of its winter during a stint with those hard men. My co-driver on the eighteen-wheel Kenworth tri-drive picker boom truck where I parked my butt for those twenty-hour days, twenty-one on, seven off, was a scavenging badlands dog known in trucking circles as Charlie Maggot. Charlie Maggot's idea of time off was beating the crap out of anybody within striking distance in the Drayton Valley Hotel bar or who got too close to his Kenworth or who just got too close period.

The only thing separating me from permanent maiming by the Sugar brothers turned out to be Charlie Maggot, and it wasn't because he liked me, but because no matter what kind of shape I was in, I always showed up to stick those chains on that eighteen-wheeler, or climb on the back of the picker truck in that Siberian cold to guide the derricks pieces onto the flat deck, or just to watch Charlie Maggot sucking on dishwater coffee out of his thermos cap and his latest dumbass tale about how he liked to kick down the door to a toilet cubicle in the pub, while a fellow patron was mistakenly thinking it was his "god-fucking given right to shit in peace," and then just kicked the victim in the head for good measure, "to see that fucking gook coming out of every fucking orifice in his shit-head!"

One morning I showed up in the yard and the truck was on blocks, and no Charlie Maggot. Sean Walcott, the dispatcher, was in, looking past me, not even a good morning.

"What's going on, Sean?"

"Sweet fuck all, that's what's going on."

He looked pretty pissed about something.

"Where's Charlie?"

"I'll tell you where Charlie is. Charlie's driving his pickup the other day, and spots his mother-in-law up ahead, walking down the sidewalk on 50th Avenue, down by the Dollarama. So, Charlie gets the dumbass idea to fucking drive up on the sidewalk and mow her down from behind."

"Not wise. Is the mother-in-law okay?"

"Outside of being dead, sure she's fine."

"Where's Charlie then?"

"In lookin' out, is Charlie Maggot."

So, that wasn't just the end of Charlie Maggot, it was the end of me and my brother, protection-wise. I'd set out to prove I was a man, and all I'd learned was that I'd never gain the kind of hardness that came natural to the Alberta hands in ten lifetimes. I was pretty sure I didn't want that hardness, anyways. The men who had it seemed to be missing something else, something human. Being bushwhacked, I didn't look much different, and being temporarily unfit for social purpose, I went on a binge, driving from hole to hole in my 400-four-barrel Grand Prix, inflicting upon others what had been done to me.

But, then, my luck turned, when a Vancouver cop picked me up unconscious off the pavement of the parking lot of the Cobalt Hotel on Main Street, keys in the ignition of the beast, engine running, and me with a cut across my head. He dragged me to a café and poured a coffee into me. When he learned I was straight out of the oil patch, he decided not to charge me with DUI, and I decided that the gods had been kind, and it was time to straighten out a bit. I followed up the next day on a tip for a construction gig inside city limits and bingo—I was back in business.

It was like nothing bad had ever happened. My foreman was a gentle soul named Colin Campbell, a reader himself, who liked to roll his own Drum tobacco tailor-mades as he laid out our work chits for the day. Doing a regular day-job at first was passing strange, laying forms, pouring concrete, hossing beams and gyproc, or just pushing a wheelbarrow without having to worry about someone taking your head off the second you turned your back. And, while I pieced together myself physically and socially, and under the influence of Campbell, I turned back to the books of those times—Herman Hesse, Brautigan, the great Ken Kesey, Harry Crews, John Fante, Charles Bukowski, and the books on vagabonding, from Villon's poetry to *The Autobiography of a Supertramp* to the wanderers to Asia, like Thomas Merton and Alexandra David-Neel. In the wake of my defeat, I was only hunting down one thing—other men who had been possessed, like I was, by the itch to run away.

During that time, I took a stab at reading some of the Canadian writers — Robertson Davies, Margaret Atwood, Farley Mowat. I was looking for something different and, to my unsophisticated eye, they were putting on an act — costume drama without the name. But I didn't know then that you had to dress up to mix with that crowd. I had grown up amidst savage animals at the mouth of the Fraser River and found plenty more everywhere I worked. The jobs I'd picked up — longshoring, the oil fields, factory work — were filled with men either maimed in the home or maimed on the ships or maimed on the assembly line. It didn't build character; it built whatever was needed to fuel the greed of the project managers. And then, I discovered a vein of ore that had to be explored — the multiple, labyrinthine works of the great Blaise Cendrars and his hero, Rémy de Gourmont, who had led me to the low Latin poets, to the world of physiology and the sexuality of all organisms.

My aim, even prior to departure, was to empty my mind and empty my eyes of everything I had seen and been, a self-imposed amnesia. The sale of goods for the West had been that of a land of promise, freedom and natural beauty. What I'd seen was savagery and brutality that meant, out of nowhere, your life could be changed in a second, and that just because it snowed didn't mean it wasn't the law of the jungle.

But now, things were looking up. Short-term, my cash-flow problems were solved, and my arrival coincided with a Quebec autumn, when their monopoly on maple, balsam and birch, and the sheer beauty of the Quebec City girls wandering on the Plains of Abraham overlooking the Saint Lawrence River, and the dirt-cheap rent, and the plethora of bars, and residue of old taverns with Black Label at a buck a quart, made it an unknown hideout, where I could size up my next move. "Bite the Bullet," my father's life axiom, had been proven wrong out on the tundra. I had gone to Alberta to emerge from the physical and metaphysical shadow of my father, but all it had done was leave me bushwhacked and broken, and by the time I'd worked it out of my system, I'd run out of money again.

STEINWAY PIANO

I WAS TAUGHT by my West Coast culture that nothing mattered, and for a time I took my culture at its word. I would pay a price for that too, but only much later, after I had inflicted casualties of my own. From the thugs of my neighbourhood, to the literary icons of restless freedom I worshipped—Miller, Cendrars and Bukowski, the leitmotif was not to learn about fellow humans, and ultimately not even to care about your self. My particular brand of the great Western narcissistic quest for freedom was in fact a form of cultural self-immolation, born of my contrarian nature.

When I learned that you couldn't trust anybody over thirty, I distrusted the man who said it and began to harbour a closet affection for my parents, who obviously made a hell of a lot more sense than the paranoid schizoids of the hippie generation peddling their false wares. There was no getting around it. I held my freedom because others had sacrificed theirs and that knowledge was the only thing that kept me awake at night. But the idea that our benefactors couldn't be trusted was a farce. That said, if anything, that realization made me feel even worse about my inability to escape their shadow. Ergo, Quebec.

The only chink in the Canadian armour—since in 1980, the indigenous still didn't exist in the Canadian mind

—was Quebec. Quebec was unhappy, and wanted a nation. But, more importantly from my standpoint, Quebec was fifty per cent young. And, since the money people had pulled up their tents and relocated to Toronto after René Lévesque's separatists came to power, rent was dirt-cheap in the old city, an abandoned, but impeccably beautiful fortress virtually untouched since the 1774 Quebec Act, its rooms being monitored by local notaries and rented to slouches like me until the property market got back on its feet.

My own family and friends viewed my choice of destination with bemusement and wariness. Ironically, the man whom I most disagreed with where it concerned my own life, Justice A.G. MacKinnon, didn't issue his usual dissenting obiter. We had a brief, sad, and somewhat humorous discussion during a visit the night prior to my departure. In the usual place—his living room, with the same Japanese wood sculpture of the man drawing water. Same throne of a chair beside the Steinway piano. Same impeccable view of the millennial Douglas firs in the backyard.

His choice of Scotch had been elevated at the same time as his nomination to the judicial bench. The Cutty Sark had sailed off over the horizon, and had been replaced by Talisker, James Bond's whisky, the peat-heavy single malt from Skye. He wore his addiction with elegance; it was something you didn't want to see cured—it contained the Channel Dash, the flying under the radar, the standing up to the filthy Krauts. The understatement. The things you could never emulate, because he had brought it to another level. The only choice was war. The plebeians, being represented by me for the occasion, were allowed to nurse Lucky Lager.

"Have you spoken to your grandmother?"

"Yesterday."

"You are aware that E. Davie Fulton sits on the bench with me? The former Justice Minister. A great constitutionalist."

"Well, Dad, pass on my best to the Right Honourable, etc."

"After the war, he made some real efforts to build bridges with the French Canadians."

Father had a lazy eye and a sea-blue iris that could intimidate a man thrice his size, and if that didn't do it, his language would. But, this time I was slightly surprised.

"Why do you think we're here, David?"

"Well, it's drawing board time, I suppose ..."

"Meaning ..."

"... our interim review of my chequered life?"

"Not entirely. I can't very well blame you for your recent medical condition, can I?"

It was a concession, and made me uneasy. The last thing I wanted from my father was sympathy.

"MacDonald was wondering aloud why my son would consider such a thing."

Walty was the second of his golf foursome.

"What was his take?"

"Something vintage Walt. Probably best not to repeat it."

"Do you share his view?"

He said nothing for a moment.

"Of course not. But, that's not why we're here."

"Then why are we?"

"If you don't bite the bullet, son, the bullet will bite you."

"You think it was a cakewalk out there in Drayton Valley?"

"Well, what did you learn there? Assuming you went there to learn something."

It wasn't enough for him to do something. It had to be for a reason. But he wasn't going to hand me that without a price.

"Look, I'm moving to Quebec. Is that all you have to say to me?"

"Now, you're angry."

"No, I'm not. I guess it doesn't look that good. Look, it's a big world out there. I'm not sure what I'm looking for, but I'll pay my own way."

"You'll pay more than that. But don't misread me. You might find you can do something useful out there. Something for the country."

"I'll give it some thought."

"Do that."

Quebec beckoned. It would be a pit stop, but an enjoyable one, as I fought my way back to France.

In 1995, by a stroke of fate, I would cross paths with Fulton and we had several discussions at the Vancouver Club about the country, and the best way to defeat Parizeau and the separatists. He still retained the trace of a posh accent from his Oxford days. He never cared about himself, or his reputation. It was country that counted.

Donn Downey said this about Fulton in his May 24, 2000 obituary tribute in the *Globe & Mail*:

> Edmund Davie Fulton might have, and maybe even should have, been prime minister of Canada. Yet fortune and his own shortcomings conspired against him to take him first out of the political mainstream and then to jail. On pedigree alone, he could almost demand the office. Two of his ancestors had been British Columbia premiers and his father had been a provincial attorney-general. He was a Rhodes Scholar and served in the war as a major with the Seaforth Highlanders.
>
> Mr. Fulton initiated some far-reaching legislation

> as justice minister, including prison reform and steps to patriate the British North America Act, devising the Fulton-Favreau formula in collaboration with the later Liberal justice minister Guy Favreau. 'We were within an ace of doing it before [Quebec premier] Jean Lesage opposed it,' he said.

If Fulton had prevailed, and that had been implemented, Canada would be a different country today. Trudeau Senior would not have been able to graft a republic onto our history and provide a perfect framework for the identity politics that are crippling the country today. And the fates would turn on Fulton and ruin his career, when he sat on the BC Supreme Court bench, alongside my father.

> He had been a drinker since his days at Oxford, but the pressures of being a judge took a toll.
>
> "I found ... the pressures during the first two or three years surprisingly great because of my concern for the individual," he said.

In 1979, he was behind the wheel of his car after drinking and caused two minor accidents. He apologized to the Chief Justice and the police, was fined $500 and was allowed to remain on the bench. He abstained for a year but then a prostitute's published memoirs suggested that he was one of her customers. He sued for libel and took a leave of absence from the bench. As the trial neared, the prostitute publicly apologized for mistaking another man for Fulton. However, these headlines were overtaken when Fulton was charged with drunken driving.

LA HAINE

MY LIFE IS composed of a series of jagged frescoes, torn from the canvas as each successive plan for conquest crashed to a halt, plunging present time into an amnesiac zone, and making it impossible to see the whole. On bad days, when I yielded to drink, I allowed the past to cloud the present, the collateral damage far in excess of my importance in the scheme of society. When reason returned, and with it moments of dark lucidity, I cut away the moorings of one life in favour of another, and when I executed these cathartic changes, I did so with an uncharacteristic cruelty, leaving casualties when I brought each episode of my life to a radical close. I saw it as inevitable, an overripe fruit falling from a tree branch to the ground. If a man chooses to lead more than one life, he must be ruthless in dying to his past lives, no matter how recent.

Despite my cruelty in the execution of this rule, my demons of guilt and regret were grappling irons on my conscience and refused to release me. It is only now that I realize that you are tethered to your fate until the gods decide to release you for having purged your sins in other ways. No other issue is possible. Even in the turmoil of the nascent, secular nationalism of 1980s Quebec, and long after the disastrous epilogue which made my return to that land I so love and respect impossible, my destiny was tied to my wish to leave my mark politically, to fulfil a vague search for meaning and completion, and to assuage my relentless need to betray my own, to consummate my betrayal by a debasement, a descent into the venal.

Technically, I'd picked a bad time to show up. The 1980 referendum for independence had been lost by the separatists, and an apolitical gloom hung over the province. Families had split right down the middle — on the one side, the old and the frightened and on the other side, the rest of them — fifty per cent of the population — who were young, beautiful, revolutionary and ready for an untimely rip of the nascent republic right out of the womb of its unworthy mother. They saw themselves, to use the phrase of radical separatist writer Pierre Vallières, as the *White Niggers of America*.

But then Quebec woke up in May 1980 to a nightmare. Their dream had been scuppered by a con-job — engineered supposedly by one of their own, Pierre Elliott Trudeau ... aye, but there's the rub. Because nobody was less Québécois than the Canadian Prime Minister. As René Lévesque knew from experience, and as the young separatists sensed viscerally, the English were only a nominal pantomime villain. Pierre Elliott Trudeau was the devil incarnate. Jesuit-trained, rich as Croesus, a renowned playboy and contemptuous of this new culture born of the soil. But certainly no Canadian either. He was Canada's first global media star, a man with no discernible personality traits.

Under the microscope, if he was charming it was a cold form of charm. Maybe a bit of the sociopath in him. Feeding on the unexpressed fear of a rather generous, naive and friendly Anglophone population operating under the illusion that they had no identity, when in fact they had the finest identity in the world. Everybody agreed on that, except for the Québécois, who saw us all as agents of the Queen. *God kill the Queen* as my brother-in-law Eric used to put it. We were the Israelis and the Québécois were the Palestinians. End of story. If you could handle the flack coming your way in the short term — as a bloke, *un hostis de tête carrée*, or any one of the myriad venomous epithets an Anglo received in those days just for crossing the border into enemy territory — then you walked into heaven.

I arrived at 8:10 a.m. at Quebec City airport, and then cabbed into the city, right down a street called the Great Alley, as if you were a bowling ball, sliding right down the strike lane in Championship Bowling. Those people back home — that place I came from — those were the last phrases sliding through my hedonistic, curious, adventure-seeking brain, as we wheeled through Saint Louis' Gate, swung south on rue Ste-Ursule, and I looked into the future and saw nothing but swimming straight into the arms of the first Québécoise I had the luck to charm and start putting some clear distance between the self and the former self.

The focus of my research and my pretext for coming to Quebec was an unfinished Masters thesis on Church-state relations in Lower Canada during the early nineteenth century. My digs in the old city were right across the street from the Ursulines Convent at number forty-two, rue Ste- Ursule, just inside the old city. So far, so good.

After recreating myself as a Sorbonne-educated Quebec historian and solicitor, I would be hired at the largest francophone law firm in the world, founded by Claude Ducharme, a prince of a man who also negotiated the exit of René Lévesque from the Liberal Party. While in their employ, I worked on a top-secret file for the Bourassa government — in fact, I produced the English version of it — examining the contingencies involved in the event of a Quebec separation in five key sectors. It was not lost on me that Premier Bourassa, the eternal fence-sitter and Machiavellian, was not only considering the inconceivable while publicly selling himself as a federalist — he was preparing for it.

At the same time, we had been left with the results of the former separatist government decision to nationalize the asbestos industry. When Jacques Parizeau brought the asbestos industry under government control, the vendors ensured that the government had signed indemnification clauses assuming present and past liability for asbestos cases. Our firm was left to pick up the pieces of over twelve thousand cases launched in the USA by those suffering from the effects of that lethal mineral. One of the claimants happened to be the World Trade Centre Twin Towers in New York City. And when those towers fell under the onslaught of the terrorist attacks of September 11, on my forty-seventh birthday, it unleashed a cloud of that asbestos dust that entered the lungs of my best friend, a Vancouver fireman who had flown to Ground Zero in the aftermath to dig up the remains of his dead comrades, who had fallen honourably while saving others.

The fear at the time was that a US attorney would ask a judge in a class action to lift the corporate veil and start seizing the billions in Hydro-Quebec assets in the United States. I was privy to the sins of a government and could have stepped outside and made a fortune as counsel for asbestos litigants.

But, by the time I worked for them, my loyalties had been confused enough that there wasn't a chance in the world that I would betray the Québécois, even while continuing to naively believe in the greatness of my own country. I had set out to better the world, only to discover that the Québécois not only were independent; they had an identity. And, besides, you can't betray the Québécois when you are proposing marriage to one of the notorious Duplessis family.

Some Anglo-Canadians stayed in Quebec permanently, but most were gone within a year or two. When I finally left, in the tumultuous year of 1995, also the year of the second referendum, Matthew Fraser, author of *Quebec Inc.* and I had a couple of drinks together in Paris' 2nd arrondissement and toasted those years.

"Tell you what, MacKinnon, what we did was fucking authentic!"

"We were cultural freeloaders."

That brought a smile to Matthew's face.

"Diversification, baby."

"You got it, baby. Turning *brand power* to our own purposes."

"Fifth columnists."

"Working in the service of Queen and country. Pawns of the federalist Trojan horse of multiculturalism."

"Spot on, baby."

"I ever tell you my uncle was a spy?"

"No shit. Anthony Blunt? Kim Philby? That circle?"

"Possibly. He was Oxon, but it wasn't mutually exclusive. But Hugh went his own way. Jesuit priest. "

"Let's call him up."

"That'd be difficult. He was strangled to death in Mexico City. In 81."

"Priest you say? Not a fucking SJ?"

"On top of that, a mediaevalist. Did a thesis on Pope John XXIInd I think."

"Hey, that's good. No shit ... strangled, you say? Where do you strangle a priest?"

"Around the neck."

"Situs, man. Did he have his Roman collar on?"

"He was seated in a chair. And, no. He'd checked in his collar at the front desk."

REVENGE OF THE CRADLE

THE OLD CITY itself was an enclave, walled in fortifications, the modern reminder of the military garrison of the French forces in North America until their defeat on the Plains of Abraham in 1759. On the second street after coming through St. Louis Gate, you arrived at rue Ste-Ursule, the street of the Ursulines, a steep-banked two-block-long road coming down from the Plains to rue St. Jean. At number fifty-two, you entered into a tunnel, fifteen metres long, into a courtyard, where we dwelled. At the other end of the tunnel, from our vantage point, we could see the outer wall of the Ursuline convent. At the top of the road was the "bunker," the political arm of the Parti Québécois, the faction sworn to tear off a massive, tectonic chunk of Canada to form a new country under the symbol of the fleur-de-lys, the ancient ensign of the royal houses of the Sun King.

Rent was easy, $42 per month. Alongside the exodus of "smart money," another silent exodus, intra-Quebec was underway, parallel to and sometimes coinciding with the other gap in their society. This one was from the Catholic Church, as the Québecois, pretty well overnight, left the Church in droves, something amazing when you consider that only a decade or two earlier its nationalism was built upon the bedrock of a Catholic priest's philosophy—Lionel Groulx's *Revanche du Berceau*, or "revenge of the cradle."

But the priests hadn't figured that youth would have its own ideas on how to dispose of its new sense of power. The new, smart, educated and completely disillusioned population, after the referendum loss, turned their energies to culture and education, and a whole new class of urban planners, architects and engineers was born. Churches were being converted into condominiums and swimming pools that were becoming the set pieces, first for the gentrification of the old neighbourhoods, and also for the colonization of areas of Montreal and Quebec City by the gay community, antecedents of the hipsters. Quebec turned completely secular.

Everything was dirt cheap, and you could find a cottage in the countryside for $20,000 or even less, and farmland for $100 per acre in the Eastern Townships. But Barnes and I were hacking it out in our ten-bucks-a-week flat in the old city. Somebody we'd met, an Anglo girl from Upper Canada named Janice, had said there was a language institute up the road taking on professors with zero qualifications, run by a man named Henry Abbott, who Janice had described as a serial pervert. The next day, I awoke early, showered and bused to a nondescript ground floor office inside a six-storey grey concrete building in the suburb of St. Foy.

Abbott looked the part of serial pervert—a slovenly, half-bald skinny dude who combed the last strands of hair on his side over the scalp, with a disagreeable leer, and a pantomime Clouseau accent.

Within a month, I was teaching forty-three hours per week. Ninety per cent of my students were aged between twenty and fifty, with a sprinkling of a few older ones. Most were professionals sent and paid for by their company—

munitions companies, accounting firms, schools. To break the ice, I'd always ask them about their home town, their background, and their families. Most of them had one or two children, many none at all. But, if you pried a bit and asked how many brothers and sisters they had, the answer was between five and twenty-five.

One of my students was a munitions worker named Jean-Yves who came from St. David-de-Falardeau, in a class of half a dozen workers from a munitions factory, all men. It was a good class and you could talk about things we had in common — the Montreal Canadiens, the beer they drank, their jobs. His co-workers came from large Catholic families, so I put the question to him.

"So, Jean-Yves, how many brothers and sisters?"

"At last count, twenty-five."

"Not your clan, your brothers and sisters."

"I'm telling you, twenty-five. Same mother."

"Well, how did you survive?"

He laughed.

"Yeah, survival, sure, we were good at that, weren't we? I'm still here, aren't I?"

"Good, so tell me, what did you do during the long winter months with so many children?"

"Yeah, man, what'd we do? Played in the fucking barn, OK?"

I glanced at the other students, who looked morose. One of them, a middle-aged man, spoke up.

"Leave him alone."

"Sure, no problem."

The class went on, uneventful. After the class, Jean-Yves approached me, speaking in French.

"Nothing personal. I don't like talking about my family."

"That's okay. I don't like talking about mine either."

"I'm just a loser making bullet casings. It's what I do. I don't want trouble."

"But, the Canadiens is your hockey team, right?"

"Sure, Guy Lafleur is my hero."

"Okay, we'll stick to hockey from now on."

"Thanks. You don't want to know about the games they play in St. David-de-Falardeau, *hostis*."

"So, I'm just a loser teaching English, right, *un hostis de bloke*. And you don't wanna know about the games the Christian Brothers of Ireland played, do you?"

I was starting to get the hang of these people, and I had a feeling I knew where they were coming from, the same social tundra as me.

PURE LAINE

FIRST DAY IN the abode of the Duplessis family in Trois-Rivières, Québec. Cri-Cri's mother is making pea soup in the kitchen, looks up with a wicked smile. She scoops the ham bone out of the pot with a ladle and throws it to the floor, sending it skating up to my ankles.

"*Tiens, mange ça, hostis d'anglais*!"

Everyone laughs. La défaite, 1759, has been avenged, and the beast can sleep for the time being. Her sister enters the room. A gorgeous Amazon, twin of the Belgian singer Viktor Laszlo. Nathalie. Indifferent, blasé. She examines me, head-to-toe. I'm a reptile.

"*C'est ça ton hostis d'anglais?*"

Next is brother, Eric. A mad savage, *coureur du bois*, who spends six months of the year as a civil engineer. Two seasons in Quebec: winter and road repair season.

"*Hostis.*"

He walks past you. The mother, named France, performs a U-turn and takes pity on you.

"Don't worry about Eric. *Il est fou. Cinglé*!"

She makes the cuckoo sign with her index pointing at her temple, and suddenly sends you a complicit smile. We're all nuts here; get used to it. It's all the shite that's been served up on our plate.

Later that weekend, you find yourself on the terrace in front of their grandmother's cottage on the Saint Lawrence River. Her name is Simone and she was once as beautiful as Marlene Dietrich, but a long tryst with heroin wears on a woman's charms. She has tasted all the good things in life, from morphine to fur coats to fast cars. She has brought six kids into the world, and it took her another five miscarriages to get there.

Simone's voice crackles hard, and she can be vulgar and venomous, but it is a vulgarity she bears with elegance and her venom is administered with art, because she had known what it was like to be filthy rich in a land of peasants, before the big emancipation. Simone scrutinizes the watercolour depicting a woman on bowed-knee before a man who looks to be examining her with disapproval. She is pointing at the patriarch's hand placed on her head. Something ritual. Not just in the painting but in her decision to show this to you now. It is an explanation.

"What's that about?"

"People talk about the wonderful *bénédiction paternelle.* You didn't receive it if you weren't pregnant or had not given birth in the year."

She fixes her eyes on you.

"I had five miscarriages before my first birth. All because of them. *C'est eux qui m'ont baisé, ces prêtres, et ça, royalement.*"

She then points her finger upstream outside the window, in the direction of a gated property.

"They still own the land from here to Donnacona." Then pointing mischievously between her legs, she adds: "Them. *Comprends-tu ça?* They owned our vaginas. They still own the land. Even today. But no-one listens to them anymore. The churches are empty. Ha! Do you know they have a swimming pool there, and no-one even swims in it? The fools! In Montreal, they are buying up the churches from the Grey Nuns and sticking swimming pools in them!"

She stops for a moment, gazing out over the narrow stretch of the St-Lawrence outside her cottage.

"They're old, like me now. It's strange. Soon we'll all be six feet under. But one thing I liked about Church was Sunday mass. When I arrived in my fur coat, every head turned to look. Even Father Dumont would look up and smile. I wasn't just anybody walking in there. I was Madame Léopold Duplessis!"

Before long, you have the pleasure of knowing all their children. First her eldest, Maurice, named after the dictator. Maurice who had stuck his greedy paws onto the heritage, squeezing it out of his father while on his deathbed. Then beautiful Anne and Pascale. And Uncle Jean, the *benjamin* of the family, Jeanno, an accountant with slippery fingers. And, Colette, the King's wife. Like a vicious Siamese cat. Then crazy Renée, dressed like a cheerleader at age 60. Married to Dick the New York attorney. And their son, Richard. Who would rape his mother and stab her to death. Just like that. And, then the car accident, killing cousin Anne, and injuring Pascale. Colette, the wronged wife, perched like a kitten, waiting for her moment, and when Maurice suddenly dies, the entire fortune passes to her.

They were hard, those Duplessis. I could see how they might get their hands on power and I could see how they could lose it. A family of carpetbaggers, crooks and sex kittens, but when it came to the women, a family of creators, engineers, brilliant administrators, archeologists, and urban planners. A great family that finally survived because they knew how to laugh at themselves and bust their ass working.

I suppose that since I saw Quebec society and its politics from the inside, I should make a comment on how I see them. Despite the fact that I was nominally the enemy, I was utterly accepted by the Québécois solely because I took the time to learn their language and trained in their legal system. I had no lessons for them, quite the contrary. They showed me what a complete society is — a nation-state built upon a deeply-rooted indigenous identity, derived from the peasant instinct that land is the source of identity.

There have been many who have used the term "peasant" to describe the Québécois condescendingly. I cannot think of a higher tribute to this extraordinary people. In comparison, the fluid, top-down qualities of Canadian federalism appear to be incredibly bland. The Duplessis showed me the lay of the land in every possible way and whereas their eloquence was more rough-edged, their realism made fools of the mythological MacKinnons who have yet to shed their atavistic folklores.

The Québécois revealed to me a culture of incredible beauty, and I remain attached to the singer-songwriters of those times, from Vigneault to Richard Desjardins, who are poets unsurpassed in the world today. The mental landscape of my years when Quebec emerged decisively from its colonial cocoon is a fresco of weeks out in the forest of the Vallée de la Jacques Cartier, maple syrup time in the Mauricie district, skating on Québec's St Charles River, chanting slogans alongside separatist pals at Parti Québécois rallies held in Montreal's Centre Paul Sauvé or drinking apple cider with the Cistercian monks.

All of this paradise only interrupted by an utter delusion — Paris — which would deliver up a real taste of hell on earth, and then miraculously, unexpectedly, undeservedly paradise from a most unanticipated quarter. As the old cliché goes, be careful what you dream for. There are still days I regret not having stayed to fight alongside them for the country they so richly deserve. I have always come too late to the truths I cherish, and despite holding fast during my sojourn to the notion that Quebec should remain part of the Canadian federation, I now believe that it should not be at the expense of their language. *Vive le Québec libre*!

ONLY DOGS SHOULD PAINT DOGS

WHEN YOU DON'T charge people for services rendered, you can fall across some of the best, most interesting cases. I don't recall how she found me, but one day in 1992, a Quebec artist named Lyne Robichaud walked into my seventh-floor office in the Cooper Building on the Main, Montreal's Alphabet City. She had painted a beautiful canvas, somewhat evocative of Gauguin, titled "Woman with Bananas," depicting a Caribbean woman carrying bananas on her head and inspired by her interest in the day-to-day lives of the women in those islets close by the Sargasso Sea. So far, so good, you would think. The Concordia University Women's Centre, however, didn't see things that way and banned two of these paintings from an upcoming exhibition.

The Women's Centre then issued a formal statement, accusing Robichaud of "reproducing derogatory, condescending stereotypes of women of colour and of all women," and claiming that it was their "responsibility to refuse to display images which could be read as reproducing—whether intentionally or unintentionally—racist, sexist, homophobic, and/or violent images and stereotypes."

Neil Bissoondath, in an April 11, 1992 letter to the *Gazette*, wrote on the issue. Bissoondath, originally from Trinidad, has written extensively on the boomerang effect of multiculturalism that has solely succeeded in creating cultural ghettos in the country:

> Two months ago, Quebec artist Lyne Robichaud had her painting 'Woman with Bananas' banned from exhibition at Concordia University Women's Centre: the depiction of a black woman by a white painter was deemed unacceptable. Calls were raised for artists to restrict their imaginative explorations to their own culture and gender. Not long after, Canada Council director Joyce Zemans waded into the issue of 'cultural appropriation' by suggesting that before exploring lives or cultures different from their own, artists should seek consultation with, even permission from, such groups. Implicit in her stand was that failure to do so would have an unhappy effect on Council grants to artists.[1]

One member, Shira Spector, said that one of the paintings was "racist" because the artist, Lyne Robichaud, "was exploring primitive and mythical imagery of women."[2] Putting another spin on the painting's rejection, however, Robichaud was informed over the phone by art committee member Sue Goldstein that "because you're white, you should stick to making paintings of white women."

The story hit the media, particularly in Canada, but also internationally. Soliciting calls to their "Info-Line," "Is this picture racist?" appeared as Question of the Week in

---

1. The *Gazette*, Montreal, Saturday April 11, 1992, p. B6 Article: "Not Correct: Padlocking the Minds of Writers" byAuthor: Neil Bissoondath.

2. Quotes from Michael William *The Sad Truth: Femme aux Bananes* (Woman with Bananas) in *Anarchy: A Journal of Desire Armed* #33—Summer '92.

the *Montreal Gazette*, thus marking them out as willing to engage in the lowest possible smears, anything for a by-line. They must be knee-deep in click-bait by now.

I helped Lyne with her case before the Canada Human Rights Tribunal. We developed the argument based upon the notion that according to this new "*dog*ma," only dogs should paint dogs. It was amusing, and Lyne's feisty personality won her the sympathy of most commentators. But that's the whole point. The smear, despite all that, stuck, and Lyne felt bitter about being unjustly accused of racism.

One day, she dropped by the office and took a photo of the two of us, the woman with bananas together. I periodically dropped by her loft in old Montreal, but she drifted away from the art scene and went into another line of work. It's hard to fight those battles alone. But I had learned my lesson. The entire artistic and political establishment, these so-called progressives, were mediocre non-talents with political agendas, and ready to use the threat of withholding subsidies to enforce this new conformism in a country where imagination in official circles was already in short supply. And the worst thing you could do would be to curry their favour — then you'd have to suck up to the civil servants. I would curry their disfavour, and discover that in the end, they were all toothless. No sound, no fury, but in the end still managing to signify nothing. With the notable exception of the Italians.

FEEDING THE CROCODILE

IN THE 80s, Montreal was a marvellous bric-à-brac of clearly demarcated ethnic boroughs and ramshackle neighbourhoods. There was chicanery aplenty up in the towers, rampant corruption at city hall and the odd *bavure policière*, or police blunder, but for the time being a woman could walk home alone at 3 a.m. and arrive in one piece. But, if you were watching, things were changing, and the indolent corruption of days past when the whisky barons and the bordellos ruled the city was taking on a new flavour.

On the street, crack had arrived five years earlier, and in the scuzzy sides of town, the effect was immediate. The urgent need for another hit after the radical downs led to something hitherto unknown — young men punching old ladies and grabbing their valuables, that type of impulse crime. But much bigger crimes were being prepared off the streets, in the high-rises where I plied my trade as corporate solicitor and trial lawyer. This alone bears mention, as it was a key turning point in Quebec history and one undoubtedly replicated worldwide, as a generation of ravenous wolves, the sons largely of the war generation in the English-speaking world, and the disappointed heirs of the apostles of separatism took over the boardroom.

When I first started the practice of law, I had the immense privilege of meeting Claude Ducharme, founding partner of the firm and a prince of a man. Ducharme had negotiated the departure of René Lévesque from the Liberal party when he founded the *Parti Québécois*. There was something of an old-world charm and a friendly generosity in his mannerisms, traits entirely absent from his successors. What I essentially witnessed during my tenure at his firm when the next generation of wolves succeeded was a cover-up job and a wide-scale collaboration with banks to ensure the new francophone corporate class had a firm foothold in the world of mergers and acquisitions and intellectual property, and the financing of global ventures through lender consortia of Japanese, German and Canadian banks. The race for the new world order was out of the blocks and picking up pace at a tempo that would soon become exponential.

In the trial division, we were defending the Quebec Medical Association from a new and potentially crippling form of claim—blood transfusion cases leading to death from the recently traced AIDS virus. Our mandate was clear—general deterrence. Individual cases were opportunities to eradicate the illusion that Quebec was fertile terrain for suing doctors. During that time a homosexual flight attendant named Gaetan Dugas, mistakenly identified as "Patient Zero," had died in early 1984. Dugas had had, by his own admission, somewhere in the vicinity of 2,500 sexual partners, but he was far from the sole out-of-control hedonist at a time when gay culture was a frenzy of sexual promiscuity—if its practitioners were to be believed on the stats—that would have shamed the decline of the Roman Empire. I was working for Desjardins Ducharme by 1986 on a case involving one of the first AIDS victims—who also happened to be gay—who was suing because he claimed he'd received tainted blood in a transfusion.

I had just returned from a chambers application involving the plaintiff that had left me shaken. I was stunned that he was even able to stand, emaciated and wearing thick glasses, because he'd gone blind in one eye while driving and crashed his vehicle, and had unseemly sores on his bone-rack of a body. Later, I sat at a table of attorneys who were shaking their heads, laughing in disgust, so I asked what the source of their humour was. One of them passed the file over to me.

"Check the medical report."

I looked at the documentary profile of the man I had just seen at the Palais de Justice de Montréal, living out his last days under the cold gazes of the men in the room with me and now considering his condition with a mixture of disgust and nervous laughter: He was suffering from gonorrhoea, syphilis, two strains of herpes, haemorrhoids and crabs—every form of the dose imaginable.

"Who's opposing counsel?" said Dupont, lead counsel on the file. "Somebody out of Anjou, sole practitioner." "They've got a fucking dearth of real-time barristers out that way, don't they? I mean, tell this plaintiff's counsel to go buy a lottery ticket, but they're not getting a penny out of us." "You should always offer something," said Lizotte. "Give him costs, provided of course he discontinues today." "And if he refuses?" I asked. "Oh, that's simple. Then we crucify him. Never forget, the client wants general deterrence."

One of the junior partners, who had been flipping through the report, deadpanned: "Give the boy credit, he won't die a virgin." Another chimed in: "But no heirs, shame." "Is it though?" rhetorically asked a third, looking at his watch, and heading out. "Gym break," he announced. "Watch your backside," said the first and everybody chuckled, the file was closed, and each of the rising barristers returned to the next item on the agenda, the ill-fated plaintiff was entirely forgotten, and 299 other files and a dozen fires to put out before the afternoon was over.

My role was still minor, but my unique linguistic status placed me in a curiously privileged position. Whenever English was required, DD now had an in-house, overeducated solicitor who could put a spin on anything, act as intermediary or communicate by phone. It just so happened that the Quebec government at the time was run by Robert Bourassa, an on-the-make crafty Cassius of a politician who had married into the wealthy Simard family, but who, rumour had it, was gay and keeping his closet door firmly shut, despite Prime Minister Trudeau's name for him as the "mangeur de hot-dog."

And it also so happened that the Bourassa government had been handed a scalding-hot potato by the previous administration of Black Jack Parizeau, who had greedily overreached his sovereignist grasp by nationalizing asbestos, just when it appeared it was going to be the next AIDS epidemic, and maybe worse. I was mulling over all of that during the days when that dog-file of all dog-files threatened to topple the government, no small feat when it was an open secret that any Quebec government was corrupt by definition. But 12,000 cases worldwide, charting where builders, electricians and shipworkers were dropping like flies, put us into a whole different league of chicanery. Desjardins Ducharme barristers were no longer local pros — we were the last guardians before the barbarians burst through the gates.

CARRIÈRE

ONE DAY, CARRIÈRE entered my office, wearing her usual tweed skirt, curled hair to her shoulders. Bucolic and sophisticated somebody had written in the firm newsletter. Whatever that meant. A cutting-edge quality control administrator. Nothing wrong with her you could pin down. Nothing right either. She was holding a piece of paper at the corner between her thumb and forefinger.

"What's this?" she asked. Quiz time.

"I dunno. You tell me."

"It's a JPS."

"Silly me. Of course. It's a JPS."

"Job performance sheet."

She dangled it in the air in front of me.

"Fine, leave it with me."

"There's nothing to leave; you've already filled it out."

"Excellent."

"I can't use it."

"Don't use it then."

"If we use it, we'll have to fire Guylaine."

Guylaine was my secretary.

"Funny you should mention Guylaine. See her around in the last day or so? Tell her to drop by sometime to say hello."

"She's unable. You're too intimidating."

"Must be my towering aura of invincibility."

"You see?"

"Of course. She's invisible because I can't see things her way."

"It's all the dictation."

"Too many dictators in the world."

"I'm glad you understand," she said, smiling, tearing up the sheet, and then adding: "Here, this is for you. A TSR."

"TSR?"

"Time sheet re-calibrator."

"That's a TSRC."

"The left side of the form is detachable. Along the dotted line. You fill in the right-hand side and give it to me."

"How can I read the left-hand side if it hasn't been filled in."

"You don't. You fill in the TS. I fill in the TSR. And don't worry. No-one will know the contents of this. No-one. Your confidential name for your file will be Tarzan. When you want to see your file, just say: 'Where's Jane?' Got it?"

"Got it."

The next morning, I had a special TSR seminar in Conference Room B led by Gingras, the new HR consultant. Pointing to the flow chart.

"Here's your new lexicon. With acronyms. Each hour is divided into twelve parts. Units of .05. To help you time allocate, please keep your TC Time Codes taped to lower left side of your desk. Column I is worker's name. Column II, file name. Column III NBT. Non-billable Time. Column IV HNBT. Home non-billable time. Column V. HBT. Home Billable Time. MAD — Maximum allowable Downtime. Check sheet two. Performance gradient. MAD must not exceed 2.0 in week 1, 1.25 in week 2, enzoforth, enzoforth."

Coulombe, the Dove, senior tax lawyer, entered the room.

"Remember everyone, as far as I'm concerned, you're all cheap labour, heh heh."

Bilodeau chimed in.

"As far as I'm concerned, you're cheap labour, sir!"

"Not me, you blathering idiot.You."

"Not me, you blathering idiot."

Coulombe stared at Bilodeau. Then back at the rest of us.

"Now first question, what are you doing in the shower at home?"

"No shower at home, sir!"

"What do you think about, Bilodeau?"

"I think we should invade Poland, sir!"

I knew Bilodeau was taking private acting lessons with Louise Marleau, a beautiful and great Quebec actress and in-thick with the oulipo crowd. He came from a family of twelve kids, all in media, theatre, showbiz, and he truly didn't give a shit. One day during lunch, he'd mentioned that they were so poor his father read them out "In case of Fire" instructions at night instead of nursery rhymes.

"Tell me, Bilodeau, where do you see this firm going in the future?"

"Firm has a great future behind it, sir!"

Carrière was passing out PGs, Performance Gradients, where we were to predict our future with the firm.

"Sir," said Bilodeau enthusiastically, "turnover is low, especially in my Apple!"

Later I asked Bilodeau about these new systems.

"Where did Carrière come from, anyways? She came out of nowhere."

"She's part Japanese," he responded by way of explanation.

"What's that got to do with it?"

"Good question, Tarzan."

"Wait a minute. Tarzan's the secret password for my desk station."

"MacKinnon, where does Carrière get her acronyms?"

Bilodeau staring at me: Don't you get it?

"Are you even aware of VID? Voluntary Input Data? We can make suggestions, and Carrière likes my ideas."

"Your ideas."

"Here's the next one. YOBs."

"YOBs."

"Sure, I get it."

"It's like subcontracting to yourself. Your own business. The idea is you can bill as long as you're thinking about a problem."

"Even if you're not thinking about it."

"Look."

He threw a file on my desk. *Quilbor vs. Quebec Medical Association.* Quebec Superior Court. File No: 500-05-23324-777.

"It's an AIDS case. Class Action. A friend of patient zero. Another flight attendant with a dozen venereal diseases."

"So what. I'm working on a half dozen Quilbors."

"I bill five hours per day on Quilbor."

"You're Quilboring me."

"Quilbor was here."

"What do you do in the evening, come to think of it?"

"Studying to be an actor."

I looked at his timesheet.

"You got two hours here, "sitting on the bidet. Serious?"

"Once a week I do it."

"What's TT?"

"Turd Time."

"Turd time. So, NBTT is lemme guess, non-billable turd time."

That grin.

"What's X2?"

"You bill double because TTs are QRs. Quality reflections."

"How do they collect on Quilbor?"

"They don't."

"How's that work?"

"I refer the accounts to Collections. Then they figure out Quilbor can't be traced, so they call up Equifax. Equifax does their gig. No sign of Quilbor after six months, so it's a write-off. No questions asked."

PATIENT X

BÉNIN WALKED IN with his client at 10 a.m., which is to say Bénin walked in followed by two orderlies walking in his client at 10 a.m. on a stretcher and in a body cast. Not even the face was visible, just a hole with tubing emerging, and an IV bottle clanking on a mobile stand.

"How am I supposed to interview ... that?"

"Monsieur MacKinnon, you have asked for a discovery; we are here for the discovery."

"How do I know someone's even in there?"

Giselle our receptionist interrupted.

"I'm afraid you'll have to move out of the lobby area, gentlemen."

"All right, we'll move this down to Conference Room G, if it's available."

"I can give you ninety minutes."

"Send down a couple of articled students. The court steno as well when she arrives."

The two students arrived — Monique and Jean — and froze on entry. I pointed them to chairs.

"Just sit. I may need you as witnesses."

"Proceed counsel."

"How can I proceed if I can't identify him?"

"His identity is confidential. Patient X is sufficient. That's the name on the court record."

"There's nothing but that tubing sticking out of a hole."

"What's that noise?"

Bénin looked at his watch.

"He's evacuating."

The two orderlies approached, adjusted the tubing and exchanged a bottle.

"I'm not convinced someone's in there, Bénin. And I'll have you strung up by the balls by the law society, boyo."

"Oh, come off it, MacKinnon. They don't string anybody by anything anymore, you know that."

"You're still insisting your client is somewhere in there?"

An effervescent bubbling came through the tubing.

"He's in there. And you're getting him all worked up."

"Off the record. Stop typing, Julia."

"I'm curious. Did he once fuck thirty men during a new year's party in Bermuda?"

"Quit being such a prude."

"Answer the question: Yes or no?"

"That's none of your business."

"Then, what are we doing here?"

"Come off it. It's not your business to get answers and you know it."

I waved the two articled students out of the room and looked at Julia.

"This is a code red, Julia. Not a word to the other stenos, right?"

"What's my business, then?"

"It's your business to ask questions."

"And how the fuck do I justify that to the client, Bénin?"

"Look, it's an active file. It's billable, and your client has deep pockets."

"*He's* not active. How do I know he's not dead?"

More bubbles from the tubing.

"Nothing personal. Patient X is my ticket out of this bullshit."

"This isn't Patient X. It's a fucking mummy. Of your confection."

"I don't care. And neither should you."

"Me care? Who ever said I cared?"

"Good. Then just ask your questions and file them. Bill the medical association. End of story."

"End of story."

"It'll just follow its course. All cases do."

"This is an AIDS case. Do you get that? It's like the fucking bubonic plague has returned. And that has nothing to do with my client. It's god's business, not mine.

"General deterrence. Sure. Read my lips MacKinnon. Sweet fuck all to do with it. Ask yourself the right questions!"

"So, all right, what's the question?"

"Ask yourself what happens if you *don't* ask the questions."

"Even if you parade into our offices with a fucking mummy."

"*Especially* if I parade into your offices with a fucking mummy."

"What difference? He's not answering. If there's even somebody in there."

"If you don't ask the questions, I pack up and leave and this house of cards collapses, dude. Think about that, dude."

"Even if he doesn't answer."

"*Especially* if he doesn't answer. Can't you tell when somebody's trying to help you?"

"You should meet Bilodeau. You two would make a hell of a tandem."

"Bilodeau? I taught that little motherfucker everything he knows."

"What? Between his acting classes?"

"Acting classes? Is that what he told you? That shit is smarter than I thought. Tell him he's up to the plate on my next claim. For his own ass."

"For what?"

"Copyright, that's for what. I sold him a franchise in my system."

"First you get *that* out of here."

I walked up grabbed the stretcher and rolled it to the door.

"Out."

"You're making a big mistake."

"I'm filing for ex parte judgment. And a claim against you."

"For what?"

"Copyright."

"This has nothing to do with copyright."

"That's not your business."

"Not my fucking business? Whose business is it then?"

"You're still not asking yourself the right question."

Bénin smiled. Waved the two orderlies to keep moving.

"Get that thing out of here!"

"Feel like doing lunch next week? I'll pick you up at the Barristers' Lounge."

BILODEAU

BILODEAU'S COLLAR-BONES extended into his bony arms like an immense wingspan — he reminded you of one of those seagulls who feed on garbage and pluck small dogs from their owners because the eco-warriors won't let you shoot them — the kind who spend days hovering over your sandwich at the beach. He would have made a big gull, but he was on the small side for his elected species. For a brief time, our extraterrestrial legal trajectories crossed, and we both agreed from day one that something was dead wrong with any organization that would hire either one of us. During his job interview, he had asked whether he could film his first year "in captivity" and somehow still got the job. On the Johnny Doyle file Bilodeau let me know why. He had joined the law firm the way other people go to the zoo — to see some real-life predators on the prowl. Johnny Doyle was a golden boy we were mandated to investigate for securities fraud on the Toronto Exchange who was running his gig from Panama, all for the Canadian government. It was a mythical file, when Bourque, senior litigator and pit-bull extraordinaire had done something to cement his myth in the firm and beyond as a hall-of-famer. A corrupt government minister had come into an office tower in Panama, interrupting a discovery being conducted by Bourque, glad-handing Doyle, in short trying to screw everything up. Bourque invited him out on the balcony, "for a word," grabbed him by the suit lapel and held him over the railing.

"Fuck with my discoveries ever again and you go off the balcony head first! *C'est clair*?"

It was clear. Today's senior counsel Lizotte was in Conference Room G, 23rd floor, asking Bilodeau for the results of his research.

"After my research," Bilodeau responded in his cheerful staccato caw, "my conclusion is that if Doyle knew about the meeting but that the meeting was to explore whether the Russians had dirt on the government which they could use, rather than to conspire with them on a criminal enterprise to get dirt on her or to work together to spread that dirt, it doesn't seem like a criminal conspiracy. Even though it probably is. Similarly lying about whether he knew if the meeting or not is not obstruction of justice but may be another US crime. Either way he is a slime bag and is headed for big trouble."

Bilodeau slammed his file shut with a bang.

"What's your name?" Lizotte asked.

"Bilodeau, sir. Manu to those who care for me."

"That's the extent of your research, Bilodeau?"

"Yes, sir!"

"How long have you been stringing this type of bullshit, Bilodeau?"

"Most of my life, sir!"

"Are there any other juniors capable of drafting a proper legal opinion, Bilodeau?"

"Yes sir. Proulx."

"And where's Proulx, as we speak?"

"Proulx's dead, sir!"

"Dead? Proulx's dead?"

"Cocaine overdose. Last Friday."

"What about D'Amour?"

"She's on sick leave. Depression, sir. Prevailing winds pushing depression this way. Permission to be granted toilet leave, sir. Billable toilet turd on the horizon."

It was easier to keep Bilodeau on the payroll until the annual pay review. Or so he informed me when I wondered aloud in the staff cafeteria how he could still be on the payroll.

"That's not why they're keeping me on," he informed me after the meeting.

"You'll be lucky if you're not fired today, Bilodeau."

"Trying to get fired, sir!"

"So, what gives?"

"Question, counsel. Who is the highest billing lawyer in this firm?" he said, pointing at himself with a crooked grin.

"You?"

"I'm the highest billing lawyer in the firm. Billing 6000 hours per year."

"Not enough hours in the day, Manu."

"More than enough hours in the day. Recent studies show more than enough hours, just not detected. If you work fast enough there's somewhere around 37 hours per day. Last week, I billed 200 hours. Just rough calculations, sir!"

Bilodeau spoke in an amazing staccato allegro, as if he were a machine-gun shooting bullets made of wool.

"How's that work?"

"About 30 per day."

"Excuse my vernacular, but how the fuck do you plan on not being disbarred?"

"Actually do plan on being disbarred, sir!"

The next time I saw Bilodeau, he was living with a beautiful and neurotic Quebec actress and starring in a Quebec television mini-series on separatist Premier René Lévesque. He was also a star of an amazing Quebec cultural sport called the "National League of Improvisation," and I could see that, while the rest of us were learning the ropes of the legal profession, he was honing his talents.

The National League of Improvisation is played in an octagon, much like UFC fighting. Our office had never been an office for him. It was a ring, and his colleagues were sparring partners, though they didn't know it. He had a nice dog too — a golden retriever, and if you stared at that dog long enough, you'd swear it had the same smile as Bilodeau, as if he got his jokes and his crazy staccato puns. Just like Bilodeau, that dog was an anarchist from the word go.

MISO SOUP

IN 1988, PAUL Granda came to my office, and informed me I would be assigned to a major litigation file. "How big?" "You'll see," he said, smiling and continuing down the hallway. That afternoon, Benoit Pépin and I drove to Thetford Mines, the head offices for three asbestos companies owned by the Quebec government since Jacques Parizeau had nationalized the mineral in the eighties, part of the idea of making resources the engine of the province's independence. The first thing you sighted driving into Thetford Mines were the slag heaps of asbestos by-product. We dropped into a local disco for a drink. They were celebrating Hawaii Friday and serving Singapore Slings and Blue Hawaiis at half price.

The next morning, we drove down to head office. We were greeted by Alain, the counsel overseeing all the files as a sole practitioner, who looked overwhelmed. Two boxes were in front of the door, unopened. He shrugged.

"Already know what's in there. More writs. Looks to be over 400 this morning."

The remainder of the office was a shambolic mess of boxes, stacks of writs and half-empty Styrofoam coffee cups. Two days later, we had finished our calculation: 12,000 cases and counting. Only one or two had made it to trial.

"What's the prognosis?"

"Here's a Delaware judgment, one of the first ones to come."

"Holy, fucking Christ. Fifty million in punitives!"

"Civil juries, *mon ami*. And it gets worse. The World Trade Centre is filled with the stuff."

We returned home and filed our report. My office was at the end of a hallway on the twenty-third floor. Later that week, Pierre Bourque dropped by for a visit. The *capo di tutti di capis*, fresh from his latest kill in the courtroom.

"What's that?" he said, jerking his thumb in the general direction of the wall.

"Diplomas."

"Take 'em down."

"Why?"

"You leave with Maître Lizotte tomorrow."

Lizotte was another senior partner litigator, a tough bastard, a product of the Limoilou tenements in Quebec's lower town.

The next morning, we left on a five-city junket across the United States to look into the asbestos files and potential liabilities of the Quebec government, but more importantly to see whether astronomically expensive US counsel weren't just lining their pockets at the expense of a panicky government trying to cover up the scandal. We started in California, and to give credit to Lizotte, he was great at putting our local counsel on the back foot. It was great watching a silver-haired, smooth-talking San Francisco attorney squirming like a schoolboy within five minutes, and Lizotte crucifying him on his performance defending against the tsunami of plaintiffs in the California courtrooms. By the time he left, he told him to withdraw as solicitor of record within the month.

More of the same, through Chicago, New Jersey, Philadelphia and finally Columbia in South Carolina, but there, the attorneys were tough nuts to crack. At every chance we discussed the Quebec government's liability, already estimated in the billions, even as the first cases were being filed. Lizotte also was busy showing me he was boss, something totally unnecessary since he was a bigshot, and I was a nobody. But I was the anglo, and the tables had only recently turned. Admittedly, there was a lot on the line, but by the time we hit Philly, there was tension in the air. While walking towards a meeting in the downtown area, Lizotte turned to me.

"Let's get one thing straight. When I whistle, you jump."

"Sounds good. Let's try it."

"Try what?"

"Go ahead and whistle. Let's see if it works."

Lizotte, hard bastard, to his credit, burst into laughter. I wasn't going to jump for anybody and he knew it. Not after Drayton Valley.

I'd had the time to research a bit and was filling him in on all the pleural conditions of asbestos, mesothelioma and a string of other asbestos-caused cancers of the lung, oesophagus, ovaries, and testicles. It was a medical Armageddon and death, though nasty and brutish, was not short, but preceded by a gauntlet of conditions. And so we happened to be in mid-discussion on the prognostics for victims of mesothelioma as we entered the Japanese restaurant we had booked. The Japanese waiter approached, and Lizotte asked what was on special.

"We have a special this evening on Miso soup."

"Miso soup," he echoed, then mouthed the words again "miso soup," his eyes glistening. Lizotte made an attempt to stifle his mounting giggle, then it burst out, and it continued and continued until the tears rolled down his cheeks. Miso soup.

Lawyer exodus shutters Desjardins

Jim Middlemiss, National Post, Aug 18, 2007

"An era will end for the 100 lawyer law firm Desjardins Ducharme LLP in September. The once-esteemed law firm will close after more than 50 years in business"

CALANDO

ONE DAY I walked into Calando's bookstore on Van Horne near Champagneur and, since I'd developed the ultimate work-around i.e. quitting the law firm where I worked, I'd opened up my schedule quite a bit. A short, round-shouldered man wearing a heavy cashmere sweater, with thick black hair à la Gustave Mahler tended the counter, drinking black coffee and smiling as if beckoning me to speak.

"I am looking for a book by someone named Michel," I decided to ask.

"This is your lucky day, *mon ami*. All my books are by someone name Michel."

"This book is by Romain Gary," I said, pointing at the book he was reading.

"All my books are by Michel, and every Michel comes from France, excluding the ones who don't."

"Romain Gary's name is not Michel."

"Do you believe, sir, that a man can climb inside a book?"

"I once ate a book."

"Bit off more than you could chew?"

"E-dible at a time."

"I sell Michels by the cheese shop."

"Who sells the seashells?"

"Sechelt."

Pierre primarily sold authors named Michel from France. Michel Fournier, Romain Gary, whose name was not Michel, and Blaise Cendrars, whose name wasn't Michel either. He sold Michel Tremblay, who was from Montreal, but didn't stock him, and his store was perched on a connector road halfway between an empty stretch of Park Avenue in the Greek district that didn't look like boulevard St-Michel.

"If I were not here, then there would be nothing on this paved connector. I am like a kiosque on the road to Compostela."

Since I was planning ways to avoid doing the type of work I'd been doing, and only a few casual passers-by would drop in, and then move on after perusing unfamiliar names, that left Calando free to talk about Cendrars.

"There is a quality shared by all Cendrarsiens."

"I am not a Cendrarsien ..."

"They deny being Cendrarsien."

"Cendrarsiens are a sect."

"... while being careful to say that there is a sect of Cendrarsiens who are conspiring to steal Cendrars' heritage."

"... out to steal Cendrars' heritage."

"Ah, Cendrars, there's not too many who know him in these parts in the way you do. What is your interest?"

"I just want to take a Gance at him."

"You look Abel enough, just give it a try."

"I don't give a Modigliani."

"His work is very Léger."

"I hear he was very big on eels."

"A leading expert. Even founded the school of Sir-Eelism."

"I have heard of Sir Eel, and his elevation to the Academy."

"Yes, his thinking went very much against the current."

"Indeed, his thinking was considered to be cupreolic."

"Ah, one of the Leuvenists, I take it."

"No more than they. Would it be advancing the schedule to offer you a glass of wine?"

"I wouldn't Breton it."

"Why is it, do you think, people don't understand you and I?"

"I painted a picture once, and a man called me Pig-Asso."

"He was trying to fit a square peg into a round hole."

"When everyone knows you cannot divide by zero. And if you disbelieve that, I'll prove to you that two equals one."

I knew Cendrars' books, and some critical work of his poetry, but Calando schooled me in the art of derivative leuvenism, a practice I had left off since lurking in De Werelt, the café in Leuven where the Vlaamse absurdists reside. Calando talked to me day after day of the kaleidoscopic talents of the vagabond poet — his conceptions with Honegger, Satie and Stravinsky, his adventures in cinema with Abel Gance and Fernand Léger, his work in advertising and typography with the graphic artist Cassandre. And his work as a war reporter and later as a Mémoirist. Calando, like Christy later on, had a jangled trail of anecdotes about Cendrars, and it seemed to me that he came far more alive through these oral tales than through even the works I had read.

After my catastrophic junkets to Hong Kong, and then, becoming persona non grata on the Main due to my romantic misadventures, I had no choice but to leave town. I had heard through the vine that Calando had suffered a breakdown, that he had gone under, but that he was somewhere in Montreal. His son had been forced at knifepoint to empty his bank account at an ATM.

When *Leper Tango* was published in 2012, I called him up and he met me at the Blue Met festival. He bore an uncanny resemblance to the French actor Christian Clavier, thick-haired, short, an elfish smile. I admired him, because he appeared supremely indifferent to the world's indifference, whereas I always took these things personally.

"What news?"

"A Jamaican of the Rasta persuasion, and an unhealthy attraction for crack mistook my son for one of his patients, while making a cash withdrawal at an ATM machine."

"Why wasn't he concentrating on the cash withdrawal?"

"Oh, he was, but my son was having an appendix attack, despite feeling no pain, except for the cutting instrument deployed by Dr. Rasta."

"Has your son developed an aversion for ATMs since?"

"No, but he won't read anything digital anymore."

A year later, I contacted him again.

"Ah, I've been attacked again. This time by a very skilled fighter — cancer. It leaves you with two choices. To watch the multi-headed Hydra eat up your body, or to hand over your fate to surgeons with large scythes who want to cut you up and fry you. Not much of a choice, David. And, even worse, long periods without *la dive bouteille*. That is truly unfair. I am resigned to watching my body fragment and dissemble, but to deprive me of Bacchus is a cruel destiny indeed.

PARIS NOCTURNE

IN DECEMBER, WE found ourselves in Paris, staying in the 5th just across the street from the Sorbonne nearby rue Cujas and one of Blaise Cendrars' old watering holes, that has since disappeared as if into a Parisian sinkhole specially designed for immortal poets. I contacted Caracalla at Editions Denoël, and he agreed graciously to receive me, notwithstanding the fact that I had sorely tested his refinement and indulgence. From the outset, I had proved to be a lousy investment for Denoël and even a liability. In 2004, just as I'd been discovered by Denoël and they were preparing a campaign to market me as the new Henry Miller, I informed them I wasn't available for TV interviews and was leaving for a long-term sojourn in the Seychelles islands, Indian Ocean. They were polite, but obviously you cannot spare resources for someone who refuses to play the PR game. There are times I could weep at my naïveté.

Over morning coffee, I expressed some regret to Hannah, not for the first time, over not taking fuller advantage of that opportunity. But it would have been the end of our Indian Ocean saga before it had even begun. Even then, in the shadow of Cluny, at the heart of the 5th, I somehow failed to grasp just how unbelievably lucky I'd been in life. Other men seized upon material wealth. I was burrowing downwards, without any clear idea of where that would lead me. There are worse fates.

"Anyways, it's over."

"What's over?"

"Paris."

"David, you're in Paris. Look out the window. The Sorbonne's across the street."

"Indeed, that is the Sorbonne. You are correct. But what use is the Sorbonne if I'm not dead drunk in front of it, punching out a priest?"

"You're just attached to something that has no reality."

"François Villon?"

"No, not really. I'm talking about the opinion of others."

"I remember that Blankstein once said I was the only business owner he'd ever heard of who had an unlisted phone number."

She laughed.

"You're not really gunning for fame."

"I believe my goal is self-spoliation. It's an organic thing. My next title will be 'Bad Cabbage.' Or how about 'Taint misbehavin'?"

"I think you're trying to bring self-abnegation to a new level. Bringing you in the public eye solely to achieve ridicule."

"Existential. I'm aspiring to a state of existential rot."

"Actual social ruination. And it only seems to come into play when you deal with people from your own country."

"They see me as rotten tuna. Or bad cabbage. Or both."

"It's not a bit true. It's radically true. Everyone you know in Europe respects you. You are held in esteem. You have done more for me than anyone else. And look who I am. And, when we see your old friends or especially your family in Vancouver, you're another person."

"In Europe, I begin to take on human form. It's almost a pleasant experience."

"It's strange. You hobble around like a broken man. How is this possible? Why would you voluntarily bring yourself so low?"

Hannah had a very bad habit of remaining serious, just when I was busy dismantling the remains of David MacKinnon. I think that I learned more during our reliquary pilgrimages than during the time I actually lived in Paris. My former life in Paris did not really correspond to the nostalgia I felt for it. If it amounted to anything, it was a frantic escape from something I couldn't define — a tearing away at the hinges of my life because I could not bear the status quo. That rebellion would usually personify itself, and be focussed on one person I felt was doing me irreparable injury, my father. Yet, my father, like his father before him, was caught in the same prison, one that had silenced him, and made him unable to express his love for me, despite feeling it deeply.

In my writing, and in my life, the Catholic Church appeared, but oddly enough, despite the violence and perversion of the Christian Brothers of Ireland, despite Jim McCann's rape of Schmidt's sister, despite friends having their eardrums punctured by blows, I didn't feel hatred towards that, only that I wanted nothing to do with that organisation. It was only the indigenous who taught me the source of my angst, and then the realisation that the fate of our family was terrible indeed.

I had read about the Highland Clearances, and particularly details of the ill-treatment of certain branches of the MacKinnon clan. You could sense the shame of those reporting these incidents, which only escaped the public eye because the long-suffering Scots suffered in silence, their humility relegating them to historical obscurity. But until I learned the truth—of what happened to Grandpa—I was on the dark side of the moon, in my own mare vaporum.

At every opportunity I would disappear from Montreal, flying on dirt cheap discount flights—a hundred and ten bucks to Paris—and then take up quarters in the *Hôtel des Alliés*. From there I would set out into the night on a redundant trajectory. Aye, but there's the rub! For it was in the repetition that you discover the secrets of the Parisian nocturne. Indeed, my choices in life always began with the process of elimination—a negative reasoning that would flush out all but what was necessary to hold my attention and carry me through the evening.

My trajectory began on the r*ue de l'Arbalète* at the junction of *rue Ulm*, where a triangular building housed the local police precinct. The door to the station was always ajar, and inside, you could see one or two *police nationale* time-servers, the underpaid low-level officers shipped in from the provinces—languidly gazing at the "Sports hippiques" section, announcing upcoming horse-races down at the local track. For me, this particular station had a significance, like something out of *Alice Through the Looking Glass*—the first gatekeeper standing by my entry into the labyrinthine Parisian night.

I suppose it was the bland monotony of that station—its grey, immutable stasis. Oddly, it was close by, only metres from a plaque commemorating a former laboratory of Marie Curie, the discoverer with her husband Pierre of radium. As if that *zone de passage interdit* was itself radiated. I was never in a rush at this stage. I knew what was coming and that I was being swallowed irrevocably by the night itself. My destinations would remain the same as on earlier excursions—there was very little invention coming from my side. But the actors would vary.

At this precise location, I stood back to a graphitised wall, looking across the street at the CROUS, where only 15 years earlier, I scrounged up a resto-U ticket worth fewer than three francs. Each step I took erected the Paris I was looking for — the passageway into the world of my imagination. At these early moments of the evening, I could be seized by a terrible, mind-bending, almost epileptic ecstasy, contemplating something that in reality was banal, the end of a non-descript street that could just as easily have been part of a neighbourhood in one of the suburban projects.

I was not yet at the gate. Another step or two and I was through and there it was — the first outpost of decadence marking my nightly excursion. The *Café Egyptien*. The hookahs at the entrance announced not so much deadly intent as an invitation to enter the secular world of ancient Egypt. Only a few denizens and me alone with the bartender, who poured me a 33 Meteor with exquisite delicacy. It was the sixth straight night of my latest spiral, and he had become a confidante over that short span of time.

"What is it that you are looking for?"

"I'm not looking for anything. Something is looking for me."

"Like Giacometti."

It really didn't matter what words came out of this man's mouth. His presence was as ephemeral as ancient Egypt.

"I would like to confess something to you."

"You have the wrong cult. I cannot help you."

"No, I don't believe so. I was in your land in 1976. During Ramadan. Something happened."

"The something looking for you?"

"You've heard of psy-ops," I said in a confidential tone.

"Of course," he replied, interested.

"This was Key-ops."

"Key-ops?"

"Cheops Pyramid. The Great Pyramid."

I sucked deep on my cigarette. I was on the road to perdition. I knew it. Anything, just to taste from the tree of knowledge.

"I was inside, by the tomb and felt the presence of something. It came from the beyond. I am convinced of it."

"So, you felt it. It is possible."

"Later, I was outside and when our guide had his back turned, I took a stone from the South face and hid it. I spoliated the tomb."

"Where did you hide it?"

"In my pocket."

"The rock disappeared, but you were still there."

"You understand then!"

"Of course. And the rock only a stone's throw away. Where is the rock now?"

"I have no idea."

"Then you are truly cursed."

Those words were prophetic, and it was the Parisian night — in fact that very night, when I took a step that was very near fatal, and ruined me for the next decade."

Rue Mouffetard is quite banal really, but for the fact that it has survived as a memento of days gone by when Paris was a collection of infinitely varied neighbourhoods. It seems even to me romantic and absurd that I would wander into the Café le Descartes on rue Cardinal LeMoine close by Place de la Contrescarpe in the hope that a few beer-swilling denizens would solve my existential conundra. But that is exactly what I was doing.

The fact is I said little during my visits there. I never sat, ordered *démi-pressions* and soaked up the banal conversations of Parisians living out their daily lives. After a pint or two, I'd exit onto rue Clovis, named after the first King of the Franks, the Merovingien 5th century ruler, and then up the street past the old church of St-Etienne du Mont and the graves of Pascal and Racine.

Sometimes I would stop in, again, not giving myself to rational, historical reflection, but rather sinking into an atavistic pit of my own invention, not unlike a trance. I did not feel privileged to be there. It was stronger. I felt I was communing with the spirits of Paris of prior times, as if my arrival heralded their temporary resurrection from their graves. This thinking, aided and abetted by drink, walking, and the endless stream of les Parisiennes, whose dialect served as a refuge, was leading me to exactly the place I desired, and that would bring me as close as a man can come to ruin and still survive. She would be waiting for me in the Café de Flore. I was six hours away from utter perdition, strolling down the rue Descartes towards the river, free as a man can be and about to be chained and fettered for the next five years of my life.

麥天麟

BOND

DURING 1986, I prepared a brief for my taskmasters at the firm, examining the nascent form of the European Union and its potential for the firm and for opportunities in Quebec and Canada. On my own, I had travelled to France, ostensibly to hand in the final version of my history thesis, but with a plan of my own—to conquer the city of Paris. I had sent two hundred letters to law firms in Paris. I was surprised by how little contact there was between the country that had founded Canada and the colony—probably in no small part due to distance, to conquest, but also the residual effect of *l'abandon* felt by the Québécois, the pain and resentment of a family member at being left to its own devices when the English bully took over the playground in 1759.

However, now things looked to be evolving. And, I had met with Jean Thieffry, the Belgian lawyer who had successfully argued before the European court under the *liberté d'établissement* or mobility rights clause entitling him to practice in Paris. No one suspected how this creation of a mobility right would be the red herring supremo, unleashing a medusa head of migration from Warsaw to the sub-Sahara, and bringing Europe to the brink of extinction. I had also convinced two blue-chip medium-sized firms in the 16th arrondissement that I was worth the gamble. I had only to return to Montreal and *boucler le boucle*, by presenting the plan to my employers.

I was stunned upon my return to learn that no one shared my enthusiasm. I presented it to Louis Payette, prince-in-waiting of the securities department. But, Louis, like the other senior partners succeeding the founders, was a wolf in a bow-tie, and my scheme for world conquest based on the Paris-Montreal-New York-Vancouver axis, didn't fit his, let alone the audacity of the plan, simplicity itself. He needed an "English-speaker" who could work on securities prospectuses, because the Mergers and Acquisitions department was on overheat. Chainsaw Al was at his peak in America, reverse takeovers and asset sales were turning an entire continent into Storage Wars. If I wanted international, I could work on the Free Trade Agreement. But I wanted more than being a paper shuffler. I decided to call my father and tried to explain the situation.

"Well, why would you turn your back on this prestigious law firm?"

"I'm not turning my back on them. I'm offering them an opportunity."

But, as those words came out of my mouth, I realized that I was being nailed on all fronts. I'd made the first mistake of negotiation and should have acted first and talked later. I ran up to a conference room, and dialled Paris. Thieffry et Associés.

"Maître Thieffry is not available. This is his son."

"This is David MacKinnon."

"I know who you are."

"I've called to accept your offer."

"Surely, you're joking. That offer was made five weeks ago."

"But it was to start in September."

"Good day, Mr. MacKinnon."

All the offers had lapsed. I'd made the whole play as a complete amateur. No mentor, no supporters. It was one of the risks of going solo. But I swore I wouldn't miss my next chance for greatness. And within days, I would get my wish. My ticket to the fast lane came in the person of Charlie Lee, aka Joseph Lee, aka James Lee aka Lee Fook Lam.

* * *

James Lee was his fourth name, but I didn't know that yet. He had begged off for a few hours upon our arrival in Vancouver, and was coming up to the door for dinner at my parents' home in New Westminster. He was all smiles and had three large bags with him. Arriving in the living room, he began opening everything. A 10,000-dollar Rolex for my father. A fur coat for my mother.

"I'm sorry, we cannot."

"Of course, I understand," James (or Joseph, or Romeo or plain old Lee Fook Lam) said, smiling and politely repacking the presents.

The next day we left for Hong Kong. In those days, a twelve-and-a-half-hour flight, and anybody flying never forgot a single landing at old Kai-Tek airport, first razing the tops of the first skyscrapers, from the South China Sea, then seeing that large Marlboro Man cowboy on the massive billboard visible outside the plane, starboard side, and finally the asymmetric screeching to a halt on the runway, just prior to sliding off the end and straight into the ocean nearby the Star Terminal.

My apartment looked out over Jaffe Road, Hong Kong Bay and the mountains separating Kowloon from China. Our office was not far, in Guardian House on Oi Kwan Road. I now operated under a Chinese name, but the weight of my family history was upon me as never before, both as a sword and as a shield.

Our first difference arose within a day, when I informed Lee Fook Lam that he was not my partner, that it couldn't work that way with lawyers. I'm pretty sure that he thought I was the worst piece of work he'd ever run into. But, then again, maybe not. I think, in retrospect, that he was running five lawyers simultaneously, like horses, to see which one panned out. I was the nag, a loser proposition.

One day, after an immigration conference, Lee Fook Lam explained how the Chinese approached Canadian immigration business. There was a talk being given by someone, and behind him, I could see four Caucasians representing four branches of Canada: a law firm, an accounting firm, a real estate firm and someone from a Pacific Rim promotion branch of a public service.

"Do you know what he is saying?"

"No."

"He is telling everyone that he is a Canada immigration genius, and that these men are his employees. That he owns a "piece of them" and if they follow him, they'll get their piece of Canada. And that Mandarin power is finally back."

"Do those men have any idea he is saying this?"

"Does it matter? MacKinnon, listen to me. When you don't have the treasure, you must use a trick."

"And what about when you do have the treasure?"

"Ah, when you do have the treasure, you must defend it with all your life."

During our Friday night trips to Macau, Lee Fook Lam would tell me stories of his youth. I met his colleagues, friends who had swum across the shark-infested South China Sea to escape the Cultural Revolution, only to live as slaves in Hong Kong.

Another time, when we had just spoken to someone who it turned out was a smuggler, and in response to my expressed doubts, dismissed them, saying: “A businessman has no enemies, MacKinnon.” Lee Fook Lam taught me more about China than I would have learned from a hundred books. But the one thing that stayed with me is that we have the treasure — Canada — and the Chinese are doing everything in their power to take it from us using a trick.

During one of those Friday nights, Lee Fook Lam mentioned once that James Lee was his fourth name.

“I was in a Catholic school when I was young, so they gave me the name Joseph. Then I was looking for romance, so I changed my English name to Romeo.”

“Interesting. But why James?”

Lee Fook Lam looked at me, saying nothing, just making sure our eyes were fixed on each other. And then he broke into the slyest of smiles.

“Bond.”

WANCHAI

IT WAS NOT the carnal violence of Hong Kong that brought me down — although a random incident that was near-fatal set the stage for the other factors — but the peculiar workings of my own mind that led to my breakdown post-China. Lama island stands out — the easy humour of Boase, Cohen and Clark, and the Irishman Sheehan, bantering away in Cantonese, the twenty-course meal, the carnivorous fare killed on your plate, and the limitless flow of beer and cognac, long before wine and single-malt became emblematic of the ultra-rich. It was odd; I experienced the danger when alone, and the pleasures in crowds — an attempted kidnapping in front of my eyes in the Commercial district, nearly being killed for pleasure by an off-duty special services cop in a Wanchai strip club, and the sure knowledge that Lee Fook Lam was having me followed during my own private meanderings from the Jaffe Road apartment.

But, mathematically speaking, the equations were wrong for a Canadian from a judicial family. The law is heavy, ponderous slow, that is what gives it its power, creaking everything to a halt for a better look. But Hong Kong was mercurial, chemical rather than organic, and the stakes whether you were a Friday night punter at the Happy Valley Race track or the Kingsway Casino or a slave swimming across the waves of the South China Sea to freedom, were life and death.

But the inner fibre was rotten to the core. The Buddhist temples were kitsch and reeked of death rather than worship. The floating restaurants were a cacophony of joy and raucous conduct, but across town, Lee Fook Lam showed me firsthand the heroin addicts dying by the thousands in squalorous tenements, and the cages penning in Vietnamese boat people under the freeway. HK 89 had death march written all over it — Tiananmen, the death of democracy, the bloody carcasses of sea life in the market, open and pulsating as if to advertise the cruelty of its denizens, the brazen luxury of the saunas, the open bribery of diplomats, and the jack-of-all-trades waging trade as expatriation agents for the astronauts, those who wished to plant their family abroad while wallowing in the sensorial chaos of the island. It all stunk, and that led me to the consoling arms of Carmen Ip, which in turn led to other problems.

There was a day that remains, in the Excelsior Hotel, when the subject came up, like any other, about vertical integration of immigrants. The intent was clear, and I knew enough of the modus operandi of my HK colleagues, that the key was creating a line of dependency which resulted in people being held in fealty long after their arrival in Canada. I had no doubt that I had been cast into a moral desert and asked to choose between riches and possible death, and certainly the knowledge that I had betrayed my country, family and truly tarnished the ensign, or the option, an inglorious return and once again, perceived failure. But the problem remained, what to do with this knowledge, if anything?

Upon my return to Montreal via a short trip to Tokyo, I went up country to the Portneuf region. After several days in a log cabin, watching the fire burn after hours of cross-country skiing on virginal trails in thirty below weather, I found myself staring at the pristine beauty of that snow, and a thought crossed my mind — "nothing will ever be the same" — and the superimposition of that thought on the contemplation of this image of inimitable beauty acted like an immense screw torqueing out of the celestial realms and driving two hitherto joined parts of the mind into separation. I was aware of tears coming down and freezing onto my cheeks, but could not move, and of the presence of François peering at me and seeing immediately that something was terribly wrong.

"Ça va, mec? Allez, brasse-toi!"

Each of the words emerging seemed to have entered the hibernal air, a breath of the lexicon that humans normally use, I recall thinking, and a panic beginning to take hold of me, a sense of asphyxiation.

Later in the day, I found myself in blankets, swaddled, and François handing me a hot brandy.

"Hostis, mon mec, ils t'ont cassé là-bas."

He was right. I was broken, broken by the world that I had so longed to discover. For a year, I floated in a dream, and only thank the gods now that my profession as translator removed me from the purview of my fellow man. But, if a man wants to fight back, the last thing he needs are witnesses. And, over the next year, I travelled through the day robotically, and in the night, I left down our rear stairwell and joined the nocturnal world of Montreal, punishing myself, and being drawn, independently of my will, into proximity of evil, the ambiguous grey force of *hery*, that would lead me away from everything and everyone I love and towards the discovery that both heaven and hell do exist, and are but mirrors of each other. And I was about to go through the looking glass.

CRIME & PUNISHMENT

DEATH OF THE PENIS

IN 1999, KENNEDY, a former rugby man, Irishman via South Africa and other southern hemisphere ports of call and history professor, invited me to speak on the topic at a conference on the theme of North-South, to be held at the University of Avignon. Kennedy personally picked me up at the train station and drove me back to his place at La Roque Alric, a village of about fifty people perched between les Dentelles du Montmirail and the vineyards of Baume de Venise just down the road.

Kennedy was talking about the area. He'd arrived from South Africa after his marriage went sour, and had found a teaching position, then discovered the old farmhouse/residence in La Roque, with a dreamlike view of the chalky façade of Les Dentelles de Montmirail and under the shadow of mythical Mont Ventoux to the east, of Tour de France cycling fame and a walk away from the mythical villages of Gigondas and Vacqueyras.

"When I found this place, I realized that God did exist."

During that first visit, Sean's son Erin showed up, a spindly sixteen-year-old redhead whose thoughts were a mystery.

Since Erin didn't talk much, I decided to take him along on a hike up Les Dentelles de Montmirail. The sheer face and tooth-like shape of their peaks were formed by horizontal strata of Jurassic limestone that folded and forced into a nearly upright position and subsequently eroded into sharp-edged ridges and spikes. I decided to go for the highest peak, St. Amand, a reasonable hike as it was 700 metres. Within a couple of hours, we were at the peak, and sat down and unpacked our lunch. Mont Ventoux off in the distance and vineyards below.

"Visiting your dad, are you?"

"Yeah."

"You like walking?"

"Sure."

"I'm going to walk to Compostela as soon as I can. It's an old pilgrimage trail, and I've promised myself that I'd walk it — from the Pyrenees to the west of Spain. 800 kilometres. Here's some Jambon de Pays. Tear off some of this baguette."

"Why?"

"Spiritual pilgrimage."

"Sure."

"You don't buy that."

Erin didn't say anything.

"What I meant was that walking this pilgrimage route is a good way to step back and get a take on my life."

"Other people bugger up their lives, and they don't go on pilgrimages."

"I never said I buggered up my life."

He shrugged his shoulders.

"Look, I only just met your dad, right, and seems like you haven't seen him in a while. But I see something in your father I recognize. He'll go to any extreme to realize a dream. So, you want a boring father, you're in the wrong place. But, here — this is the place for fathers who aren't boring."

"So, you're a dad."

"Yeah."

"Where are your kids?"

"Thatta way," I said pointing due west from our perch. "A few hundred kilometres, as the crow flies."

"Do you see them?"

"Not from here."

"No, *see* them. Visit them."

"If I saw them, somebody, and maybe more than just somebody, would end up in the bottom of a river."

Livingstone, another historian in for the conference, had also shown up to stay at the house in La Roque Alric and so I accompanied Kennedy into town to pick him up. Livingstone was euphoric, coming out of the train station, grinning from ear-to-ear. He shook Kennedy's hand fiercely, and boomed out:

"If you can't fly then run, if you can't run then walk, if you can't walk then crawl, but whatever you do you have to keep fucking moving forward!"

The entire ride back, he was talking, madly, joyously, as if he'd escaped from prison. Later, after dinner, we learned why. Livingstone was in the latter part of a wind-up of his marriage, and his wife, also a public figure, had decided to even things up in a dramatic way. Going public with the story of her new life as a lesbian, she had succeeded in posing for a triumphant photo-op with her new significant other on the cover of *Saturday Night*, a national weekly, followed by a juicy article accusing Livingstone of a litany of crimes and misdemeanours in the marital home which she later admitted to be confabulated.

So, despite being recently introduced, Kennedy, Livingstone and I had plenty to share experientially and the conversation flowed seamlessly into the evening, under the chalky spectre of the *Dentelles de Montmirail*. All the shit, the mess, the torn canvasses of our earlier domestic lives seemed more than worth the price, because it had led to this. It was better than rebirth. Better than god. It was Provence.

Around midnight, the others retired, but Livingstone and I were in overdrive, and still popping bottles of Gigondas and drinking it like juice.

"I'm just curious about something. In part because I don't know you. Have you drawn any inferences of a general nature as a result of your experience with this psychopath?"

"Actually, none. Outside of ticking a few boxes on my mental PCL checklist when I meet people like her."

"Tell me something. I'm curious about this she-devil of yours, forgive me the term, but I'm pretty big on runes, curses and the like. I'm sure men are curious for other, uhm, baser reasons, but consider my questions as those of an academic if you like."

"Sure, what do you want to know?"

"I don't know. Give me a day in the life."

"Ok, I had this large loft in the old part of Montreal. She'd wake up late and come up to my desk, wearing her usual gear — baby doll and pumps, and she'd be saying things that I only realized later were spells and curses."

"Then what?"

"Then, she'd crawl under my desk and err, you know, perform an act of moral outrage."

"Interesting. Go on."

"She'd remain there sometimes for hours. I recall dictating a 99-page emphyteutic lease and she never let up throughout."

"Hmm. I'm interested in hearing whether you recall the experience in any non-sexual way."

"I recall thinking at the time that my soul was being

sucked out. No, wait, I know what it was ... like being embalmed. That's exactly it."

"Your blood being removed and replaced by formaldehyde. Metaphorically speaking."

"No. Existentially speaking. Like being embalmed while you're still alive."

"What about eating, conversation, the rest of what a human needs to live?"

"We did all that, but it was in service of whatever her bigger plan was. She also liked to spend a lot of time in this black book of hers, plotting revenge on people from her past."

"That's fucking crazy. How long did that go on?"

"For several years. But it taught me a lot."

"Not sure about that. Law of diminishing returns etc. You must have been more than a bit crazy in the end?"

"How could I not be? She was like a goblin. Someone making an announcement from the invisible world. That we're a death culture."

"And you say that you lost family, friends, your business, all because of this person."

"Well, big deal, look what happened to you."

"What? You mean my ex-wife posing with her new girlfriend on the cover of a national weekly magazine?"

"Yea, that."

"Sometimes people get desperate."

"Sure, but that, just to sell copy? I didn't realize the publishing industry was getting that desperate."

"Worse than desperate. She might even have been pushed into it, I'm thinking."

We were in a zone of euphoric redemption, honesty and forgiveness, driven by Kennedy's seemingly endless supply of Gigondas, one of the world's finest soul lubricants.

"Clifford, you know what? The more I think about it,

the more I come to the conclusion that I'm the one responsible for what happened. I wanted to dig a trench between me and my past."

"Come on. I don't buy it. Let me ask you something. Do you know a lot of women?"

"Sure. I know a few."

"Close friends, sisters, colleagues for the most part?"

"All of the above."

"Have you confided in them about the inner workings of your ex-wife? Her modus operandi?"

"Broadly speaking, yes. I was flayed publicly, so to speak. You had to be there. My entire life was reduced to roadkill. So, I had to make amends."

"Steps four and five? An honest look at yourself?"

"Who said anything about honesty? I was just delivering up apologies to the fucking rabble. Waiting for my luck to turn, so to speak."

"How did the women react to your, uhh, explanations."

"Come to think of it, I suppose they didn't."

"And, what do you conclude from all that?"

"I haven't given it a lot of thought."

"Well, put it this way. Would you trust them to argue your case in front of a third party?"

"Christ, never!"

"And yet you remain on good terms."

"I already lived with someone who tried to erase my past, so on a point of principle, I had to preserve mine. So, you're expecting what here, Clifford, a statement on the species? Qua species? I mean you have to set the bar low if you want any kind of social relations, don't you think?"

"I understand setting the bar low. You're like a fucking onion, mate. Take a decade to peel away your layers."

"Well, I still like them, qua species. I like their, err, forms. A little more cautious on their charming little quirks."

"That tendency to grab your arm and say, 'just stay the night'."

"Not really. Yeah, I suppose you've a point. I'm aware of the price tag."

"Tell me, why wouldn't a man like you just turn gay? As a practical option."

"Funny you'd put it that way. I have a friend I suspect turned gay because he said it was a calling card for the San Francisco art scene."

"As a career move."

"Absolutely."

"Do you even realize how homophobic that sounds?"

"It's tougher than you think to make it in the art world. Some consider that a small price to pay."

"That's not self-promotion; it's self-abasement."

"It's just the timing always struck me as suspect."

"I don't know. Sodomy as a career move. Sounds speculative in the extreme. Where's the evidence?"

"What's evidence got to do with it? Evidence is a thing of the past. It's all about what you feel, *innit*?"

"I'm intrigued. And, since I'll never hear this again, go on."

"Well, just out of curiosity, what's the state of fellatio these days in North America? Hetero version."

"You're asking the wrong person…I don't think there have been any studies. It's like I dunno, deaths of the homeless. Certain stats don't make it to analytics. I'm assuming fellatio is one of them."

"Well, when I look at the issue of fellatio, only the gays seem to still be practicing it, I mean as a part of their sexual culture."

"Okay, I'm going with that, I'm with you."

"Well, yeah. Exactly. Unless you have evidence of some alt-fellationist cell somewhere out there in the digital exosphere."

"Empirically speaking, you may have a point. There's almost no doubt that it's fallen into disuse."

"You're assuming its prior existence."

"Chronologically, that's a fit with the rise of the gay movement. Wait a second. Didn't you say earlier you were taught by the Christian brothers?"

"Your point being..."

"You sure one of the bros didn't do you as a kid?"

"Are you kidding? My father was a criminal assizes judge. He'd have locked them away for life."

"You're a survivor."

"Not in the way you think. The Christian brothers knew better than to fuck with my friends. Now, the Cree, they call themselves survivors, but they got nailed, literally. Some of them had pins driven through their tongues by the priests for speaking Cree. I have that from source. But, back to your point. I'm a utilitarian on all matters, including sexual, and I believe in a certain form of morality. My form. So, I'm not absolved of my responsibilities just because a few women have excoriated me, cuckolded me, raked me over the coals, stabbed me or emptied my bank accounts. I have a residual duty. Particularly knowing that other options are available."

"I'm interested in duty. Tell me about duty."

"Well, the way I see it, I have a phallic duty and should not be deterred from that duty by something as derivative as individual female personality."

"A phallic duty."

"Have you ever considered how many vaginas there are in the western world—untended vaginas, lying fallow because their emphyteutic lessors are neglecting to till the field? Or even worse, sub-letting them to squatters or similarly irresponsible guardians ignoring the sacred trust with which they have been vested? Or hoarding a jewel in the crown of the common weal?"

"What are you saying here? That this is a property issue? Something to do with riparian rights?"

"I'm not saying anything."

"C'mon don't kill this idea. Can't you see I'm running with you on this one?"

"You sure you want to hear it?"

"Hear what for chrissakes? Are you saying consent is a non-issue?"

"I'm not saying anything. I'm singing *Fields of Gold* and staring at the most beautiful range of chalky mountains I've ever set my eyes on. Isn't that enough? I'm not in the business of generalizing; it's the wine talking. You're the historian; you draw the lessons. I'm damaged goods."

"How many times do I have to say this? Run the fucking idea past me."

"All right, since you're begging for it, and nothing but the night to hear our words. Let's just say the issue of radical title is open to debate. Epistemologically speaking."

"Let me understand you. You're saying women don't own their vaginas?"

"They enjoy beneficial ownership. Usus and Fructus. Pretty well since time immemorial."

"And no Abusus? Christ, so basically, you're arguing the vagina enjoys a position comparable to that of aboriginal title, is that your position? The vagina is a rabbit running free until the settlers arrive? Tell me I'm not hearing this."

"Not exactly. Let's put the proposition *a contrario*. Do you really believe you have free and clear title to your own dick?"

"I can abuse it at my leisure, if that's what you mean."

"But the use of it has never triggered any obligations?"

"Well, maybe a statutory lien or two depending on umm...past use?"

"See?"

"There's something perversely appealing in your views, but it seems to me that your thought processes are corrupted. Sometimes this means from a scientific standpoint that something just hasn't been quantified. Or maybe you have some kind of trauma, or then again, some gift of prophecy because part of your brain has been shut down for whatever reason. It's not impossible. Lemmee see...hum-de-dum...okay, let's try out a test query. Where do you see the penis in, say, give or take fifty years? Mummified or glorified?"

"Extinct. Going the way of the bison and the dodo bird. It's already stigmatized, considered pretty Nimby."

"Sorry, you're losing me."

"People are starting to look at penises the way they look at garbage dumps or drug rehab centres. Or even worse — as storage depots for weapons of mass destruction. So, it's not that big of a leap from "Not in my backyard" to public sterilization. Like I say, give it a few decades, maybe even less. Penis pogroms. You heard it here first."

Livingstone laughed, then resumed his earnest tone.

"There's a difference between your plight and mine. This might surprise you, but the first thing I felt when I saw her on the cover of Saturday Night was pity. It was beneath her to do it and it didn't really demean me in a fundamental way. Basically, it was self-harm. A public act of seppuku."

"Right, I get that."

"But when I hear about this succubus of yours, I see a harbinger of something more general. An ill-omen."

"I've often felt that since. I have strange dreams now—visitations."

"It's rarely discussed in my circles, but do you believe in evil?"

"Affirmative. Now I do."

"What do you make of it? Was it just her?"

"No, I don't see it that way at all. It's something that is here now. It wasn't here for a while. But I'm getting the feeling that something broader, something bigger is on the horizon. She was part of that. She could feed off it, because it was there, in the air."

How could you dislike Livingstone? A man whose wife chose the front cover of a national magazine to announce she was a dyke. And he was scarred, but as the French say, he'd saved the essential.

"I'm going to tell you something, Clifford. I'm walking to Santiago de la Compostela pretty soon. I have enough spare change to last about three weeks, so anybody climbs in the sack with me, it's caveat emptor on all fronts. I've got nothing left to pilfer."

"Yeah, baby, you got the secret. Now crack me some more of Kennedy's plonk! You know the old cliché—about divorce being so expensive because it's worth it? It's true, brother, we've cut our chains. Let's never ever forget what it took to get us here!"

At the end, 7 a.m., we climbed the rock and sat at the top, staring at Mont Ventoux, wordless, inarticulate in a state of gratitude. I refused to sleep inside the farmhouse, because I wanted to be ready for walking to Compostela, and dragged my sleeping bag into the garden and fell into dreamless sleep, awoken by the dawn sun and the sight of les Dentelles de Montmirail.

Whether at Le Tambour, my haunt in the 2nd arrondissement in Paris, or at the top of La Roque Alric contemplating Les Dentelles de Montmirail, or from my seventh floor flat in the old textiles district perched between rue St. Denis and rue Montorgueil, my cronies and I understood an unspoken truth. We were co-conspirators, enjoying the fruits of France, the most marvellous country in the world. Our days stretched out without thought to the future, and our evenings were filled with high humour, Vacqueyras, Côtes-du-Rhône and Gigondas, and we adhered to a common code, which was more the absence of a code — a reckless, organic disregard for the rules that governed the great masses of humanity.

Eighteen months later, events would drive a cleft into the tectonic plate of our hedonistic unity and divide us forever. Where there was once joy, now there was muted silence, rage, the gnashing of teeth. The seeds of future purges were planted. The conspiracy of hedonism had descended into an aura of suspicion and retreats into armed camps, as it were. There were many causes for this. September 11, on my forty-seventh birthday, nineteen men, fifteen of them from the Saudi tribes, a creation of the Balfour declaration, would divide the world for the foreseeable future into two new clans: true believers and kuffirs. The Montagues and Capulets of the new millennium.

Then the spreading of the Internet would be like a bursting star, and we the fragments, no longer able to hold the centre. Hardened doctrines, the bastard children of Marxism — from feminism to extreme ecology and on the other end of the spectrum, a resurgence of hordes of predators, who saw the world as nothing but spoil. For reasons unexplained, the heirs of Che and Sartre would abandon the working classes, and join in on this new race to acquire, as if material wealth could protect against what was to come. Then, they would yield to the old demons, purging, and then the children of these makeshift revolutions would turn it to ends unanticipated.

All of those things would impact on our lives. And for me and Hannah, who I met on that fateful weekend, the expression of these forces would be distilled to their very essence, like a perfume of Grasse, but this one as malign as the venom of a pit cobra, as a strange sequence of events would bring us within a hair of losing everything—livelihood, health, friends, even the history of who we were and what we stood for. But I will not allow a cawing bird to interrupt my tale when others demand my full attention.

HASTA LUEGO, MAQROLL[1]

I HAVE MY own litmus test for writers. I ask whether my literary heroes — plain-speaking men such as Henry Miller, Charles Bukowski, Blaise Cendrars or Harry Crews — would drink with them. It's unlikely that Blaise Cendrars — who had lost his writing hand in World War I, counted serial killers and gangsters among his acquaintances, couldn't stomach Picasso ("the son of a curator"), André Breton (a "liar" who barely knew Apollinaire) or Rilke (whom he punched out in the Closerie des Lilas for his pacifism) — would welcome say, Alice Munro, with an open arm, or for that matter, Ondaatje, Umberto Eco, John Irving or Salman Rushdie. Henry Miller wouldn't be fooled by fake tough guys like Nick Tosches.

On the other hand, I'd bet that vagabond poet Jim Christy would find a place at Cendrars' or Bukowski's table. For what it's worth, Christy, and his pal the excellent poet Len Gasparini could match Cendrars yarn for yarn and drink for drink at the same tempo, having followed the same delirious trajectories that Cendrars was capable of and Christy would probably get Cendrars laughing in that nasal pre-television twang that belied the rough exterior of

1. Everything in this story has been extracted from my obsolete memory banks, other than the quotes. If Jim Christy has a different version, let his prevail.

the vagabond poet with some of his own humourous tales of woe and wildness.

Jim Christy first contacted me out of the digital netherworld on a cold January Friday the 13th through my writer's site, in early 2012. The subject line was "Blaise Cendrars":

"I figure anyone who writes as well as you do and likes Blaise and the rest of those scoundrels can't be all bad. [I also did a short book on Bukowski (ECW Press)]."

He mentioned that we had the same publisher, and that he'd written about thirty or forty books. While searching for his work on the net, I fell onto a video of a reading of a poem called "Forever Maria," a 2008 performance in Melbourne, Australia. The video was a fuzzy-toned sepia production that was filmed about ten rows back from the stage. Christy stood on a stage, dressed in a peach-orange leisure suit, straight out of Miami, and was rasping a poem while a four-piece band led by a clarinetist screeched out a torpid New Orleans jazz number — it was hard to tell whether the band was back-up or there'd been a double-booking that day for rehearsal space.

People in the audience were shuffling in front of the cameraman blocking the view of Christy. Christy however was oblivious to it all — he seemed to feed off the casual disorder of the reading to tell his poetic tale of Maria, a woman who was kicking the poet out of her apartment and her life. The tone of the reading seemed to imply that it wasn't the first time the performer had been kicked out of an apartment, and that quite possibly one of those "I quit; you're fired" conversations had just taken place. I was witnessing that rarest of rare events — an artist actually enjoying himself onstage. An almost extinct species, to be treasured alongside the Java rhinoceros and the cross-river gorilla.

Christy was self-deprecating to the point of carelessness, but at the same time he looked like somebody who could throw a little deprecation your way if he felt like it. His delivery was flat and his voice raspy, and immediately you got the sense that Jim Christy had never really picked up the habit of taking orders from anybody.

Four days later another Christy missive landed in my inbox, informing me he was scheduled to speak at the Fiery Tongues festival in Amsterdam, where I reside, and not to send him anything "as I'm going to India in ten days."

I did a little more research on him and found out he was a south Philly poet living on the Sunshine Coast in British Columbia. But when I wrote him back, he informed me that he had since relocated to rural Ontario and would be out of touch since he was leaving for India for a month. As a PS, he mentioned he had written a book on Bukowski, and was writing a column called "Scalawags" for a "glossy Canadian rag."

"I got two items off to you in the mail a couple of days ago. Unfortunately, neither of them was the Bukowski book. Someone has made off with them which is ironic because at the beginning of the book, I mention how frequently his stuff is stolen. So, I sent you a CD of poetry and music, and a book of poems. I note that the thieves (posing as friends) did not take any of the translations of Bukowski."

Christy was sixty-eight years old at the time, running about ten gigs at once, including his private investigation agency called "Extreme Research."

"I sent a query a few days ago to the head of a circus research centre in Virginia; I'm on the track of a cult of people from decades past who searched out very unusual phenomena, both human and animal."

On January 27, I learned that his real name was Christinzio, and noticed that the initials of his assumed name were the same as those of Jesus Christ. Since I'd referred to

Rashaan Roland Kirk in my previous missive, Christy informed me that he happened to have a great story about the Mississippi musician "which involves him, me, my new girl friend and her mother (this was in 1971). Will tell you when we meet."

Sometime in February, a message turned up in my Inbox from Pondicherry, India, where "twenty dramas were going on simultaneously":

> Swimming elephants, pygmies, naked people: the usual stuff! No, listen, this place is truly unique but ruined somewhat by the groups of young "hip" tourists who all look exactly alike whether from Germany or Israel. Dressing like slobs they are totally unaware that they are insulting the locals who, although dirt poor, try to maintain the respectable appearance. I sincerely hate this smug self-righteous middle class "hippie" bullshit.

Another email arrived the next day, this time on Bukowski:

> I saw a copy of *Women* at a store here. Might get it and reread. In the Vancouver section he gets involved with a woman who I got involved with a few years later., though *I hadn't known of the connection.* She told me once that he didn't drink anymore than she or I did. And stuck to white wine. Expensive and German. Said he was very, very funny. The guy could write ten bad poems then floor you with one that came out of the blue.

By February 8, he was in Bangladesh:

> And again, went into the bookstore I was in a few days ago when I saw the copy of *Women*. I was thinking how

> I hardly even see a copy of Cendrars in a used bookstore in most parts of the world, and NEVER in Canada, and what do I do but turn around and there is a copy of *To the End of the World*. And then I eat in a hotel that could be out of Celine's Africa or someplace by the great Alvaro Mutis, after which I come here and there's a letter from a guy in south of France who is the authority on Blaise buddy Albert t'Serstevens. The two of you are the only ones I have any talk with about B.C. nobody else gives a flying you know what."

On February 10, he was scribbling from a Bangladesh dentist's office, letting me know that after returning home to Canada, he'd be leaving town again, "taking off again for Guyana a few days later" and asking for one of my books to "read when I go off into the jungle."

By the thirteenth, he was on the topic of writer's voices and who was and wasn't good at reading:

> Last night finished *To the End of the World*. I don't think anyone has ever written that well. It's really too much. There is a woman in India who has done a book about a certain temple and all that goes on there. Levels and levels. Reminds me of *To the End*. I can see why so many people can't begin to read him. He's like dealing with both Klitschko brothers at the same time and then Charlie Parker and Mary Magdalene pop up here and there to change the pace. I'd read it before but didn't appreciate it.

Our correspondence over the next month or so involved his upcoming visit to Amsterdam. He was coming to town for the Fiery Tongues festival, via some of the old guard — a Brooklyn gangster poet named Eddie Woods and a member of the old Dutch provo movement named Hans Plonck, who's keeping things alive for a hardcore group of radicals who were cronies of the Beat poets and have somehow managed to survive to the twenty-first century:

> Listen, I don't expect ANYTHING in regards my visit. If we get together at your place and it gets late, I can stay in a local hostelry of some kind. Is there one? Don't know and won't know when I read, until I get there. Last time I read twice and bombed once: trying to head off a migraine with booze, this before I read at ten AM! Last time I got photographed for the society pages with some punk rock singer turned poet. Some good people; met the richest man in Netherlands—some department store dude. Also, a crazy Jewish woman lives in a cave in Italy, etc.
>
> You will find me a respectable house guest—if it comes to that. I mean, my table manners are passable and I don't tell risqué jokes or get obnoxious when drunk. Gad, I sound dull.

I hadn't had a visitor in about six months, but as luck had it, the morning Christy was due to arrive, there was a group of stick-in-the mud anthropologists in my backyard droning on about Merleau-Ponty and Bourdieu. Christy showed up four hours late at my home—2:30 p.m. for a mid-morning meeting. He looked jet-lagged, and was skinnier than in his photos, as if he didn't care enough about eating to get around to it, but you could see the man still had plenty of resilience. I was reminded of the early-twentieth century gentleman super-tramp, W.H. Davies.

"Shit man, don't they have road maps in this city?"

"They do, but nobody uses them."

"I took the right bus, but the wrong direction. And you know that park you told me about, the one with the church? There's four parts to that park, David, and there's a church at the far corner of each. Just in case you're interested ..."

"They should rename that park," I said lamely. Christy ignored me.

"I had to duck into a pub to get proper directions."

"Wine or beer," I offered.

"Gimme both," he said, grinning, showing a full set of gold teeth, "after that Kafkaesque jaunt. Holy shit, man," he said, now glancing outside. "What's with all the important people in your backyard? You sure I'm not bringing down property values?"

I introduced Christy to Josh, a handsome Kenyan poster-boy for the new Africa who had that "president-in-waiting" look.

"Kenya, you say?" Christy said. "Do you know the king of Swaziland?"

"You know King Mswati?"

"Know him? Last time he walked by me, he even winked."

"And where might that have been?" the Kenyan asked, his smile wary.

"Lemme see. Must have been the airport. Pretty hard to get closer than that. I think he's got something like forty-nine wives, doesn't he?"

Christy laughed, at himself I thought, but still checking out the Kenyan man-with-a-plan's reaction, his golden front teeth in full view, reminding me that one of his introductory missives had been from the waiting room of a Bay of Bengal dentist. I figured from his sharp look that whether he'd tossed back one or two was irrelevant. This was a real pro, à la Bukowski. Christy casually surveyed the coterie of four black Africans, a couple of Malagasy and an anthropologist named Dr. Delaney, from the University of Pittsburgh.

"Doctor, doctor, anybody not a doctor around here? You from Pittsburgh?" he asked as he was introduced to Delaney. "Down in South Philly, we hated people from Pittsburgh. The enemy!" Then he laughed, while waving me due north towards the fridge. "Anything available, David, pour it into a glass, I'm ready!" Enjoying himself, and not quite ready to let "the enemy" off the hook.

Then he smiled warmly, all charm.

"Don't take me too seriously. I wasn't born there. I was born in Richmond, Virginia, but don't get me wrong," he said, smiling. "I'm no southern gentleman."

The Kenyan said: "Well, you've told us where you're not from. Where are you from?"

"I was raised among hoodlums in Philadelphia — South Philadelphia, if that conveys anything to you. My mother's people — the Clantons — were gunned down by the Earps at that corral. My father's people were all petty criminals and mob-related figures."

Two of them begged off and went for a walk. Christy didn't notice, as he was explaining the musical form of finger-snapping, created by blacks hanging out by the sewers of south Philly.

My wife had noticed that I was dipping into the libations, and the combination with some antibiotics I was taking was producing unforeseen effects. She thumbed me a quick "both of you get out of here," signal so we stepped out into the street, and headed west for some ribs and Argentinian rosé at the Abina, my local watering hole. By this time, it was late afternoon, and we were on to Kerouac.

"Hey man, I hope you're not in shit with your wife," he said as he refilled my glass upon arrival.

"You were a hit. They're just not used to people with actual opinions."

Over a plate of ribs and another flask of rosé, we talked about Cendrars, Rimbaud, Catallus, the levitating saints St. Theresa of Avila and Joseph de Cupertino, boxing, working in circuses. Sometimes Christy would mention strange titles I'd never heard of, like *The Bird that swallowed its cage* by somebody named Curzio Malaparte. He dwelled on Kerouac a lot, saw him as one of the great writers still, and instead of talking about the "beats," he emphasized Kerouac's deep religious fervour.

He didn't have much use for Hemingway.

"Hemingway makes and has always made me sick. And the rest of that bunch too. The big American three of that era, Hemingway, Fitzgerald, Faulkner, I think were inferior to Dos Passos. And Wolfe. Even Steinbeck. Certainly, to Miller.

"Tell you, I live in Canada, and both the country and Guernica and Ekstasis Editions and a few other people have been good to me, but listen, don't go anywhere near the Canadian literary scene. It's pretty nasty, the nastiest being the would-be bohemian elite. It's the Can lit types, man. Nasty and timid, those are their qualities. Start fights and then run out to the parking lot while others settle it.

"It's not just the writers either. Tell you what, I was in Australia a while back, doing some film work and I asked the director, how is it possible that Australia, with a similar demographic base and history, made so many good films and that everything out of Canada was shit. He answered: 'The Canadians are good at looking like film directors. We Aussies just make the films, mate.'

"I wrote this article once on the workshopification of Canadian culture. There's all these people making more than you and me ever will, and they're selling bogus goods. Anyways, I started getting threatening letters, man. One guy said I'm gonna come and take you out, man. I wrote him back with instructions how to get to my farm. Said I'd be waiting for him. He never showed up.

"Well, there's nothing wrong with it. But that's the whole point. Nothing wrong with it, technically speaking, and nothing right about it. You can't tell the difference between these people. I've always had a sneaking suspicion that every book in Can Lit is the same book."

The man hated hippies, hipsters, Can-Lit and Hemingway. So, what's not to like about that?

"Fuck 'em if they can't take a joke. Prophet in your own land and all that. Go figure, I'm leaving for Norway after this. I wrote this C & W song, and this guy put it to music in Oslo, and it's on the charts, baby ... in Norway."

"No shit."

"I might have told you I have one 'on the charts' well it's a song about a dead woman but the fact that she's dead is not revealed until after the second chorus. Well, the guy has removed the lines wherein the crazy fact is revealed and replaced the lines with one from another song — to me it makes no sense but maybe it makes sense to them. To me it is number twelve by mistake.

"Funny, your name being MacKinnon. I just lost out in an outdoor sculpture commission worth ten grand to a guy named MacKinnon."

"Sorry to hear it."

"Don't worry about it. I won't hold it against you. You any relation to that Judge MacKinnon?"

"Sure. He's my father."

"No shit. Was he on the Eddie Haymour case?"

"That was him."

"Every single thing the government said about him was true. A complete psychopath!"

"Everybody seems to have an opinion on that case."

"Look, I didn't just have an opinion on the case! I wrote an article for *Canadian Business*."

"You're an Eddie Haymour expert."

"Listen, buddy, I didn't just write about him. I moved in with him. Even though his wife tried to warn me off."

"Why would you move in with Eddie Haymour?"

"I was at Castle Haymour 'managing' his joint—which meant mollifying customers who complained about the beer and wine. This might sound trivial, but Eddie would turn off the beer-filled fridge at night to save electricity, and he wouldn't put the white wine in the fridge to save electricity, and then he got me to wash dishes to save electricity. Are you getting the picture? Then it was some landscaping and hustling customers."

"How does that save electricity?"

Christy ignored me. He was somewhere else, washing dishes for Mad Dog Eddie Haymour.

"Three months of pure hell."

"My old man wouldn't have changed his mind. He was no fool, and on the evidence, he thought Eddie deserved a million bucks for his troubles."

Christy shook his head.

"Lemme tell you. Eddie's wife used to say to me: 'The thing about Eddie is that he's always three steps ahead of you.' Ah, to hell with Haymour. I didn't come all the way to Amsterdam to talk about that psychopath. You remember that note you wrote me about Cendrars?"

"Sort of."

"There was a phrase in it—about what Cendrars pointed at. Yeah, that's the thing. Or the things. He pointed at so much. Opened up the world. Threw open his windows, I immediately responded to that when I read it. Modern literature, left its goddam laughter at the door. I think Blaise was the best I've ever read for capturing the spirit or possibilities of vagabondage. Or, if you'll pardon the expression, of Life. Have you ever read Malaparte?" he suddenly asked. "I've been meaning to ask you that."

"Never heard of him."

"I tell you I've just been taken on as an actor in a mega-German gold rush western to be filmed in British Columbia? I'd like to get it in order to ride a horse in the movies. Did that once in Mexico, in a film called La *Batailla Desconocida*. I don't think I mentioned it in my 'jobs' thing but I was in a lot of movies. Big deal. I had little interest in all that."

He'd sent a photo of one of the takes in the film, and there he was dressed up in cowboy gear and knocking back whisky. He wasn't too happy about the take:

"The photo I sent makes me look really old. On the other hand, I am old." He laughed. "I prefer not to dwell on the 'really' part. I'm sixty-six; I'm guessing you are not far passed fifty-five.

"I'm getting too old to write. I'll never write a novel again. I'm more in the brick and mortar and stone stage, doing landscaping, and sculpting. It came late in life, but I immediately had a feeling it was in my blood. Incorporate all that now in sculptures I do outdoors.

"As for my stories, they are mostly based on mis-adventures and ludicrous experiences. I have managed in my time to fuck EVERYTHING up. Especially my writing life and my love life.

"I always look for Maqroll bars wherever I go. Not too many of them these days. My second biggest literary kick was when I was leaving Mutis' house and he gave me un abrazo and said: 'Hasta Luego, Maqroll.' And the first, Charles Bronson read my *Flesh and Blood*, and told our mutual friend to tell me he liked it a lot. Okay, I should probably reverse the order.

"I'm one of those guys who has buggered up a few relationships, had the cops involved etc., and then finally found someone worthwhile."

I don't know what happened. It must have been the antibiotics, or just the inebriating quality of Christy's speech, because we'd only gone through about three bottles of rosé and suddenly, I couldn't see straight. I don't recall the end of the day, but Christy got me home okay, so I probably owe him something there too.

I was in the north of British Columbia sometime in 2014, and Christy's partner sent me a note saying he'd had a heart attack, but survived, after being clinically dead for a minute or so. I managed to track him down in Belleville hospital.

"Yeah, lucky, turns out I died, but it all happened in the hospital, while I was talking to the doctor. I asked him after what we were talking about just before I died. He said: 'Vietnamese food.' Which reminds me, I'm getting hungry!"

We've only seen each other once since that day in the Abina, and since then, he's died once and come back to life, got divorced, and last week married a Tzigane. Jim Christy is seventy and he's outshone Cendrars in one area — he is still on the road ...

AUTO-DA-FE

A PLAGUE OF LOCUSTS

YOU DON'T APPLY to be a scapegoat. It's a calling. A religious appointment, kind of like Céline going to war, or Dostoyevsky finding himself being brought out to the countryside to be hung on the Tsar's orders. The goat's at the centre of proceedings but he doesn't have any say in the matter. There's no relation to guilt, no crime to answer for, no prelude. And when this fate came our way, why would it be any different? The fact that the trials we endured were inflicted by people we had thought to be lifetime friends was of no avail. Maybe that is even of its essence.

After all, doesn't the goat know his master? Isn't he petted, cajoled, fed, fatted, then coaxed out of his stall, held up before the madding crowd swaying in exalted bloodthirsty madness, seeking carnal redemption, and now, eyes bugging with fear, until the scythe descends upon him, or until he is simply burned alive, as the mob reaches the pitch of frenzy?

No one knew in 1999 what was coming, but in retrospect, and perhaps even then, I sensed something had to be coming. I'd been sitting with Tony on *rue Montorgueil.* We were discussing Tony Blair's decision to kill hundreds of thousands of heads of cattle purely because one of them had been diagnosed with Mad Cow's disease, a condition that could not be transmitted to men. And I was asking Tony: "How long do you think this will continue?"

"This being?"

"The madness of cows. The madness of politicians."

"It will continue until something happens. A convulsion."

"What would you be thinking if you were an African? Just curious."

"That Europe has one hell of a lot of flesh to spare."

"Boomerang baby, coming to your neighbourhood and mine."

Something had to happen. It took another thirty months. Then a festering wound clawed out of the core of NYC. I recall flying over the Suez Canal, so clear even at 25,000 feet, thinking *that blue isthmus, and the shit it has caused.* And then ... and then within days of our return from Madagascar under harrowing circumstances, it happened. On my birthday, more precisely, that I was celebrating in Paris at 11:30 a.m. Paris time by listening to France Informations Radio on the terrace of *La Palette, rue de Seine*. The commentator was saying that World War III had broken out and that 50,000 New Yorkers were dead. Haemish had been wandering in the quarter, lost, disoriented, seized with vertigo, and he hadn't even heard the news. He would lose himself in Paris, in Chinatown and finally in Amsterdam where I would find him. Then he'd find himself and everyone else would lose their way.

Yeats had seen the circling falcon in his uneasy dreams. We, of poorer imaginations, would see the reality of the second coming—of a man, also the son of a carpenter, who would declare that the law of Jesus was now obsolete and would choose my birthday to send his message to the world, or more precisely the World Trade Centre Twin Towers.

Love thy neighbour had run its course. Extinct. Game over. Now it was "Hate thy neighbour."

Like the plague, the purge came to us in waves. Hannah, who had lived as a slave in Betsileo land, spoke to me of *hery*, an ill-wind, that occasionally visited malign energies upon the Betsileo. More often than not, it was an offence to *fomba gasy*, tradition, that triggered *hery*, but once unleashed, *hery* was indiscriminate as to its victims, preferring the malevolent joy of sweeping up both good and less good in its path, the better to leave a memory of what it had done.

In our case, it was Sid who signalled the descent into the Hades. And, after the strangeness of his downfall, and the retrospective inevitability of it, what I recalled, after the violence, and the wretched fate he endured, more than anything was a story his wife Cory told me after he left the planet. When they had fled the city together in his old olive-green Dodge pickup and were crossing Alexis bridge into the lands west of Williams Lake along the Gold Rush trail. And Sid saying: "Now, nobody knows where we are."

But, even the recesses of Tsilhqot'in country could not resist *hery* and later when I went up to Williams Lake to see what kind of place could bring down a man like that, I saw, breathed and smelled *hery* everywhere. There was no difference between those venal cowboys of Williams Lake eating their hamburgers, and the figures of the Betsileo, who had captured my wife and oppressed her, and made her the lowest of the low, only to resurrect her and turn her into a bride-elect of the great Rakotavao, who one day I would cross in that desiccated village on the RN7 heading down to Tulear and the mines.

RAW BENCH PRESS

IN 2006, I was invited to a dinner party in Mile-End, Montreal, and found myself at the wrong end of a discussion on Islam. My memory of Quebec in 2006 was flawed, and a decade and a half out of date. I had left in the wake of the 1995 referendum on independence. No need for diversity box-ticking in those days, because it went against the very grain of what they were trying to achieve—a nation for French Québécois, and a social democracy to boot.

I had heard that *Charlie Hebdo* editor Philippe Val was in town, speaking at the Blue Met literary festival, and was looking forward to seeing this modern-day Rabelais, a self-created media man and anarcho-leftist speak about the defiance of the Islamists by the *Charlie Hebdo* cartoonists, as merry a band of renegades as you could imagine, and nobody immune from their mischievous pens, not even the feared Salafists, who had been responsible for 150,000 deaths in Algeria during the nineties and were now stalking higher profile prey in the Hexagon. Feeding on suffering, these ideological vultures were ready to spread the message in points north and west in ways that had as yet excited no interest in the West. Not even after the game-changing 1995 bombings in the Paris Metro. It was seen as an Algerian problem. Now it was a French problem, but the French had seen problems before. End of story.

The *Charlie Hebdo* offices had already been attacked once, but still nobody knew about it beyond the Seine. We were still seven years away from the carnage of their offices, where twelve human beings, ironically exponents of the anarcho-left of France, would be gunned down by two men claiming to speak in the name of Islam.

While the anarcho-leftists like the merry troubadours of *Charlie Hebdo* were doing a credible job, the mainstream left was busy abandoning their jurisdiction, which ironically laid the basis for the return of the extreme left. When Tony Blair gutted Labour of its moral/historical link with the trade unions and Hillary Clinton began giving speeches for 150 grand a pop, the rise of the extreme left in America and Great Britain became inevitable. Trotskyites with a millennial twist, they transformed internationalism into second homes in Provence, art retreats and a full-on embrace of quality control, outsourcing and contempt for their traditional jurisdiction.

The working man, hitherto the moral spine of the left and its connection with the real world, was to become a racist deplorable in the deflective lexicon of the liberal left. Kennedy, who I was visiting on my way to hear Philippe Val, had played the Irish nationalist card well. And, I was about to ignore Grandma's warning to stay out of politics and learn why she'd issued it.

"But, colonialism, Sean, is very much in the past, and don't you think it's time we looked a bit closer at Africa's black leaders' role in poverty?"

"That's fucking rubbish, MacKinnon, propaganda of the colonial powers."

"... endemic corruption, nepotism, assassination of a home-grown, charismatic Third World elite. I hate to disagree, Sean, but ordinary Africans, at least those old enough to remember, are hearkening from Kenya to South Africa for the good old days of colonialism when at least the white farmers produced crops and the roads were paved and you could get a fair trial."

"You better not repeat those words this evening, lad. You're liable to get your head bit off by the company."

"Of course, I won't. Don't get me wrong. The one thing that I'd like to see preserved is infrastructure."

"I'll grant you this," he said, handing me the first beer of the day, "the lines of argument are changing. Something strange happened only yesterday in my history seminar. An American student, a Black Lives Matter activist, interrupted my intro on Malagasy slavery practices. Cut me off fucking cold in mid-phrase, started ragging: I'd no right to talk about slavery ..."

"Because you're white."

"Can you believe it? I know half the gunrunners in the provisional of Belfast and she serves me up that."

"Of course, I believe it. I'm probably the only person you know who reads Marx anymore, and I'm not from your side of the divide, politically speaking."

"What do you make of it?"

"Well, it's basically job creation, isn't it? Gender studies. Hundred years war. DNA proof of the first indigenous peoples. We've all basically become useless as tradesmen, sorry, err ... tradespeople, so we make up shit. Keeps the subsidy-mill grinding."

"What about getting laid?"

"What about it?"

"Forget it. Withdraw the question."

"I'd better go. I don't want to miss this Philippe Val conference."

In fact, I had to get a call off to British Columbia. I had received a call that morning from my older brother, informing me that Sid Wick, a former rugby mate and now headmaster at a high school in Tsilhqot'in country in the BC interior, had been charged with sexual assault or something that looked like sexual assault because the papers were implying that, without coming right out and saying it. The nurse who fielded my call at Kamloops General Hospital put me through to his room.

"Hello. How did you track me down?"

"What's up?"

"It appears I'm now an undesirable. I think I was a hero principal up until twenty hours ago. Perhaps you can remind me, memory's a bit shot today. Word is I've been acting out."

"Sorry, Sid, sure you don't feel too good, but what the hell is going on?"

"Damned if I know. The local Detective Sergeant, Brisson by name, doesn't really like me. He's going to follow this to the bitter end."

"And you?"

"Me? I'm waiting until I have a chance to do what I have in mind."

It didn't sound good, not by a longshot. There wasn't a lot of information but it sounded grim, and I'd be filled in with the particulars of a scenario that I would see played out again in other hidden dramas of other friends slain at a later time — a lazy, media-hungry lawyer, a kangaroo court comprised of former colleagues, neighbours who no longer acknowledged him on the street, an ex-husband with revenge on his mind, and a blood feud with a detective-sergeant.

Less than a year later, I'd be in Mananjary, a shithole

town on the east coast of Madagascar, reading that Sid Wick had shot himself and was three days from death. Sid, who could still raw bench 500 pounds at the age of fifty, would take his last trek down to the log cabin he'd built alone with manual tools. As I walked in to hear Philippe Val debate on the right to mock Salafists, I had forgotten my visit, as I recalled Sid's tattoo on his right bicep: *Death before Dishonour.*

MANANJARY

I RECEIVED THE news in Mananjary, a malaria-infested hell hole at the end of RN 12, running due South from Irondro on the East Coast of Madagascar. Mananjary is a hard day's drive from Fianarantsoa along a stretch of road which still hasn't received infrastructure manna from the European Union, and lies in a state of disrepair from the Ratsiraka era. Mananjary is the Mekong Delta, Malagasy version, swamps and everglades, run by criminals and immune to nothing but change. Everybody was in varying degrees of ill health, but we were sticking it out.

Hannah's long dormant malaria had been reactivated somewhere in the highlands, as if her body were recalling the old days. Niall was sick and emaciated, and there's not much a four-year-old can vomit up before there's nothing left of him. When we tucked the children under their mosquito nets at nightfall, we feared the heat-marinated stench of the garbage dump outside the south window, or the burnt zebu being cooked by the staff mightn't cause one or both of them to retch into their bed sheets and drown in the worst of all places. We had arrived in the city at nightfall. Once dusk fell, there was no way to tell if there were a few hundred or a hundred thousand souls in the city. Only the odd generator-powered streetlamp, leaving you with the wind and a chiaroscuro of moving silhouettes.

The Hotel Vanille's proprieteress was a tall, dark-haired Basque woman who showed the wear-and-tear of her years living in the outpost, but still put her smile, svelte contours and generous bosom to good effect during her ongoing dealings from the round table in front of the bar/reception desk. Her supplicants, suppliers, whores and the rest filed in one by one, with Scotch whisky, lingerie, profits, foodstuffs, and a ream of products that you couldn't find anywhere else within 400 kilometres, unless you were barricaded into one of the NGOs. Her staff were all young whores — gatekeepers to a sure death, but a pleasant one until disease broke down the immune systems of whoever penetrated the inner enclaves of their dubious honour. An Antaimoro enclave, settled by river dwelling bastard descendants of Arab navigators, unblemished by the taint of compassion and retaining nothing of Islam but obscurantist medical and magical formulas to create their own hierarchies and techniques for paper making.

The day after arrival, I spent some time unloading sacks of manioc from the roof of Sister Maria's Land Rover Deserter under a pounding rain, and then decided to go for a walk to evacuate some of my thoughts, and to find a garage to replace a blown gasket. On the main road, across from the police commissariat, I spotted a large barn with a sign: Cybercafé — and decided to check whether I could log on to my email.

The cyber café was a barn with four computers, and one employee, no less warm, and nearly as dusty as the main road outside. I looked outside and spotted Hannah, standing with the children and Maria who was heatedly bargaining with a fishmonger woman, pointing at a broken set of scales, peppering the woman with Betsileo terms of friendly banter, while the fishmonger barked in an incomprehensible dialect. Women and men appeared out of nowhere in the unlikeliest of places when Maria was there. She had planted the seeds of her legend by going it alone with Hannah in the extreme Southern Highlands, and the power of her presence had saved us many times from Kalashnikov-toting adolescents manning ad hoc roadblocks back in the days of Ratsiraka.

Further down the road, the train station with a colonial era sign — Fianarantsoa Côte Est. From there, right to road's end nearby the Hotel Vanille, there was a constant parade of traffic — *pousse-pousse*, zebu carts, and heads carrying every form of produce — litchis, coffee, cloves, *bichiques* and *civiques* from the rivers — and goods from hay to bicycle parts. Feral dogs, poultry, and zebus zig-zagged down the road, scattering in every direction only when approaching traffic came within yards of them. Every sentient being undernourished, every hand extended, and dust, dust in every direction, clouding and choking everything in its wake. I turned back again to the screen of an old Hewlett Packard, trying to fathom the words displayed on an email message sent from a man I hadn't seen or heard from in 25 years:

> *I don't know if you are aware of this or not, but I have some horrible news — I was notified last night by Sid's ex wife that she received news that Sid shot himself on Wed night and is on life support. The family has rushed up to Hundred Mile House to be at his side and the situation is very dire — she really has no more information than that — she assumes he is not going to make it based on the reports given. Shocked and incredulous.*

Jackson had first contacted me a few months earlier, which was about ten months too late for Sid. He had a list of questions he was burning to ask. He had held committee meetings at the school with former rugby comrades to discuss his fix. Everyone, of course, wanted to help, but first of all, they needed an explanation. Sid had his skeletons, he presumed I knew about all that now, but why was he avoiding him? He'd tried to make contact, but apparently the phone number had changed.

Jackson was easy to recall. Maybe he looked different, maybe he was fat or bald or puffed up with a position on one of the school boards, but he'd still spend an hour brushing his fu Manchu, and he'd still stop at all the amber lights. Brett was a team man, loyal to the collective. A born prop, toiling in obscurity, and unlike me, prepared to "go over the top" so others could live a better tomorrow. It was hard to know how a man like that would turn out after he'd been laundered and bleached by thirty thousand committee meetings with school board types. I couldn't know; I'd pulled out of what was called society early on, long before anyone could snare me into a role as a compliant citizen. There'd be no ceremonies for me.

As for Sid, I was sure that wherever he was, in the fields of Aaru, or in the hall of two truths, or in the eight-gated hells, he'd be gnashing his teeth at the fates for allowing Brett Jackson to drench his final hours with Christian pity, while he lay plugged to the life support machine, every drop of choking tears acting like alkaline on him, turning his last chances to go out like a samurai to pathos, and distorting his message forever. It was his first excruciating punishment for his sins on earth, and he hadn't even left the planet.

HOTEL LA VANILLE

MANANJARY, DURING THE day, was a mobile grid of humans moving through the filth and dust like elemental particles —*pousse-pousse* drivers, military men driving chain gangs of miscreants, languishing women sprawled lazily over their banana stalls, vendors of useless *bric-a-brac*. The beach offered relief from people, and a chance to mull over things. Sister Maria, the Maltese nun, stood ankle-deep in the shoreline water with Zoé and Niall, laughing. Watching her, you could wind the clock back sixty years, and see a little Maltese girl playing in the turquoise waves of another sea.

Behind us, a series of colonial government buildings, lapsed into complete disrepair during the Ratsiraka era. Sid's spirit seemed broad, limitless in the limbo of pre-death —and dual somehow. He would be wandering, I mulled, out on a hilly plain of the Hades, re-enacting what he had been doing while on the planet—riding a horse of the Apocalypse, maybe meeting his natural father who slit his own throat while he was yet an embryo. As for Sid's dark secrets, who doesn't have a dark past? Who doesn't have a dark present?

Hannah passed me a large slice of papaya and some bread.

"Tomorrow, on the road, there are some villages I want to stop off at. Six of my students worked up there, in a project."

"You think it's reactivated?"

"What, the project?"

"No, your malaria."

She shrugged.

"It's possible. The bites are big."

"That's a sign?"

"Some people think so."

We were both pretty zonked on the Malarone, and THB beers in my case, and long driving.

"What's on your mind?"

"Sid is on life support."

She stared out the window, saying nothing.

"Jackson is there, already finding excuses."

"What do you think about it?"

"What do I think about it? Nothing."

"I understand. It's too early to think."

"He offed himself. Nothing I think or say makes any difference. He's powder now, in some urn. It's over."

"What is that supposed to mean?"

"Means nothing."

"I know what *that* means. You're just feeling so much; it's too much for you, isn't it? I can understand that."

"Actually, I'm not feeling too much, I'm feeling very little, to tell you the truth. Another wasted night at the Opera."

"You've just tried to save someone again, David. Where has it led? What has it given you?"

"Why is it that I am so attracted to people who have changed their names? Remember, I told you — I'm taking a boat across the South China Sea with James Lee, and he tells me his real name is Lee Fook Lam. What about James, I ask. Oh, that's my fourth name. I'm not even sure what Sid's real name is."

"That's it?"

"No, that's not it. I'm glad he's gone. Don't get me wrong. It's not just him. It's the whole lot of them, top to bottom. Bunch of losers. Fuck-ups. Bunch of Canadians. That's what they are. Dead or alive, bunch of fucking Canadians. That should be his epitaph. Loved by Canadians, killed by Canadians, a Canadian. I am Canadian."

"How did he die?"

"That's the whole point. He's not even dead yet. He's on life support."

"That's awful, just awful."

Niall hadn't said a word for a while; he was white as a sheet.

"You okay there, Niall?"

"Is Sid the cowboy dead, papa?"

"No, darling," Hannah said.

"Tell him. Yea, he's dead Niall. Dead as a doornail."

"Was that necessary?"

"What, Niall and Zoé are ready to come here and risk their lives, but they're not ready to hear about the concept of death?"

Hannah grimaced.

"That was really uncalled for."

"Did you give him Gravol this morning?"

"Of course I did."

"He doesn't look good."

I looked at her, really looked at her. We were both in the business of getting at the truth — me as a writer, her as an anthropologist. But what was the truth? There was no truth anymore. Sid had been playing at being above it all. He'd been tasered, drugged, dragged off the job, torn away from his family.

"Your guts are in a knot, David. Really, in a knot."

"Oh, they're in a knot all right. Right fucking knot, they

are. Getting sick of losing people, and nobody talking about it."

"You're just going to have to postpone some of your own feelings; you're going to imperil things for us."

Back in the yard of the Vanille, a sixty-year-old Greek contractor sat at a table with two Malagasy men, in front of large plates of seafood and half a dozen bottles of wine. He was putting on a real show, shouting into his cell phone, giving orders, then returning half drunk to his plate and pushing his shrimp into his face with his hands. The owner sat at her table, glancing occasionally in the Greek's direction.

"We've been waiting two years for that man to do something. You know the work on the roads has been allotted to several contractors — cutting up the pie. The SOGEA people are doing the other end, and every week, they are laying new asphalt, erecting bridges. This man, he has laid twenty kilometres of road in over two years. With 1500 workers at his disposal. It is quite an achievement. Are all Greeks such lazy bastards?"

She smiled mischievously.

"Niall, eat some bread. I'll get you some ice cream."

"I can't mama, I'm sick."

"David, you know, happiness doesn't come by that often. We had better try to hang on to ours."

"I'm glad to hear you say that. That helps."

* * *

The flow of contraband traffic went on uninterrupted — whores, fish mongers, luxury goods, diamonds, cartons of cigarettes, Johnny Walker Black, from early morning til late at night. Her staff worked from 7 to 22, and they weren't doing dishes the whole time, judging from the traffic going up and down the stairs.

The trail of supplicants continued right into the night. Madame received the ongoing flow of traffic — the fish mongers and the beggars had left, giving way to other forms of cargo, waved in enigmatically by a man standing at the unhinged gate, but none of them daring to move inside without a signal. The owner was married to a liver-lipped, pudgy bastard who spent his days sprawled on a couch watching Indian soap operas on television with their children.

During the evening, the Greek contractor was back at his table with his two Malagasy partners, playing it cool, murmuring as they poured out the wine. The Greek was very upset about something. He didn't raise his voice, but the way he pointed his finger at one of his cronies left no doubt as to his sentiment.

"Something I don't like about him."

Hannah kept her eyes on me.

"Nor do I, but it's not the place."

"I still don't like him."

"Why don't you come upstairs? Your mind's on other things."

"I'll just sit here and have a couple of beers."

"Have it your own way, but don't walk out of here, David."

"You know me, Mister Cautious."

"David, everyone is watching. Don't forget that. Even when you're alone."

"I'm not bothering anyone."

There was no light whatsoever for two hundred metres once you got outside the yard. Blackness of the night. The owner was visible inside at her round table, just on the other side of the open window onto the terrace where I sat, doing her figures, noting things down. She smiled at me. I poured out another glass of THB, nodded towards the Greek.

"Where's your husband?"

"Oh, he disappears around this time of the evening."

"Disappears?"

"He likes to prowl along the lower edges of the river, see what he can dredge up."

"And, when he's not prowling?"

She shrugged, rolled her eyes."

"Television."

"I hear there's a lot of disease at the lower end of the river."

"Would you care for another drink?"

"Why not?"

She stood up and moved towards a cooler, slid open a glass door and removed a large bottle of beer.

"Where do you come from?"

"I can't remember anymore."

"Maybe your wife can tell you."

"I'll ask her tomorrow."

She shook her hair, bent over, letting me catch a glimpse of her breasts, watching me watching her.

"A friend shot himself yesterday."

"I'm sure he had his reasons."

"Sure, everybody has their reasons."

"Come with me; I will show you something."

The next day, we hit the road amidst a flurry of waving whores and madame and the staff, and her TV addict husband, who had spent three weeks in Norway. They all had suddenly decided we were of them. We backed out with another load of burlap sacks filled with manioc and fish on the roof, and a pounding rain, and famine-stricken women and their near dead children, and Sid Wick somewhere in the mind's eye as he lay plugged to a life support machine twenty thousand miles away, somewhere between Dog Creek or Horsefly, and awaited release from the burdens the gods had laid at his feet. Leaving us to pick up the pieces.

MAU-MAUING IN MONTREAL

Charlie Hebdo *est le plus grand hebdo anti-raciste de ce pays.*
—Dominique Sopo, SOS Racisme, France

PHILIPPE VAL, SALAFIST-BASHER, was even more impressive in person, with his Gallic hawk-face allowing the slightest curl of his contemptuous lip in the direction not only of the Salafists, but of their apologists and appeasers. I mean how do you resist that? I rushed up to introduce myself at the break, and met with a cool and elegant brush-off, but it made no difference. In 2007, there was him, there was Christopher Hitchens and there was Oriana Fallaci. The world was a lonely place for independent voices in 2007.

Val was impressive, brilliant, and incisive in his analysis of the cynical use of threats and the role of the left in appeasing and even supporting Islamists in France. By the time I left, I felt exalted. My faith in our ability to resist this strain of totalitarian thought renewed. And, exhausted, but ready for an evening of what had been promised as intellectual, I returned to the scene of the afternoon's conversation, where our common experience in Madagascar turned us toward talk of the savage sapphire mines north of Tulear, which we had navigated during our year of living dangerously in the extreme southern highlands of Madagascar.

"Well, I can tell you, personally speaking, the only thing I've seen, mine-wise, is sapphire. I know because I've seen them and nearly got shot filming one of those Sri Lankan bastards driving Malagasy slave-crews. He whipped, kicked and cursed them as they crawled down those holes in the ground, standing on nothing more than a pail tied onto the end of a rope, then lowered down by a pulley into shafts with vertical walls barely holding back the soil with planks. It reminded me of the oil patch, actually, just hotter."

The dinner guests — *diversité oblige* — included a Franco-Québécoise woman, a Canadian journalist in exile, a Muslim writer and the three of us. So, eventually, the talk at the table turned again to BDS, the campaign to divest the world of anything Israeli until the "apartheid regime" collapsed, something I'd not followed closely in the news and which appeared to be yet another tendril of the thousand-and-one new activisms born of this infernal new digital connectedness.

"What is that about? Similar to the South African campaigns, then?"

Nods all around.

"Well, what's the goal, the desired outcome?"

"That's simple. The dismantling of the state of Israel."

"Really? To be replaced by Hamas, presumably."

"That's a matter for the Palestinians to determine, not us."

"So, we're here to determine only that the Palestinians deserve to win, and then it's up to the Palestinians to determine the terms of the peace. Unless, of course, the Jews have already been driven into the Red Sea."

"Who said anything about that?"

"Isn't that a bit radical, only six decades after the holocaust?"

"Sure, it's radical, if you're treating the Palestinians as outsiders in their own land," Sean said.

"Still. I mean, driving the Jews into the Red Sea ..."

One of Emma's friends, an ex-pat journalist living in Berkeley interjected.

"I think you're conflating anti-Semitism with anti-Zionism."

"Oh, I'm a conflater from the word go."

"So, change of topic, how was your conference with Philippe Val?"

"Illuminating."

"I've heard he's a bit of an arrogant cunt."

"What's not to like about that? At least he's a cunt with balls. Transgender and all that."

"Don't worry about MacKinnon. He's nostalgic for the colony."

Kennedy was goading me; he could see I would take the bait.

"I come from a fucking colony, mate."

"I don't know," the Québécoise said. "I'm all for the free speech part. But it strikes me as intellectual bullying."

"You're serious."

"Of course, I'm serious. Most Muslims have no idea why they're doing what they're doing."

"What about the Christians? *Charlie Hebdo* has been taking the piss out of them for three decades. Why should Islam be given special protection? Besides, it's not even Islam. We're getting the extreme varieties — Salafists, Wahhabis, Deobandis."

"So, the fact that one billion people are deeply offended or not is irrelevant?"

"The whole point is to offend. Have any of you actually seen them?"

"I'm not going to dignify that with a response," Kennedy said.

"It's harmless satire. More Robert Crumb than Mohammed, I would have thought."

"You're operating in an echo chamber," Kennedy said. "You don't even know how fucking wrong it is what you're saying."

"But, Sean, what are we doing kow-towing to the religious? Your Marxist lexicon is outdated, don't you see? We're all kuffirs for the Salafists, heathen. So, as far as the Salafists are concerned, no disrespect to present company intended, there's no difference between a Napoli peasant and a Scottish highlander or an Indian novelist, don't you see?"

"Why is it so necessary to be mocking some poor Muslims for? Couldn't they just leave them be?" Emma said.

"Cabu and Wolinski are brilliant. They also happened to be on the barricades in May 68. They've been fighting against fascism from the word go."

"They didn't get droned for doing it."

"If they'd chopped a few heads off, they might have."

"Every Muslim's a terrorist of course, right?"

It was down to the Berkeley journalist and me. Take no prisoners. No-one else was saying much, but Kennedy loving the fireworks.

"Of course. Every man's a latent rapist. Every Muslim's a latent terrorist. Give it time. Every man'll be a latent woman and vice-versa. Of course, the one exception to all this is Ireland, right Sean, where nobody's a terrorist. They're just freedom fighters. Oh, and of course, women. Women, luckily have no evil latent within them."

"What the fok do you know about Ireland?" chimed in Kennedy.

"Very little. That's neither here nor there. But the thing that turns my stomach — whether it's the IRA, or AIM or Al

Quaeda — it's these cheerleaders on the sidelines, little twits from decent families who have to do the radical chic thing. Present company excepted of course."

"How many Muslims do you know anyways, David?" Emma asked.

"Oh, I don't even know myself. I haven't even signed up for the diversity register yet. Call me old-fashioned, but I get a bit squeamish when I hear people in my neck of the woods talking about eradicating the Jews. Just not *woke* enough, I guess. But, seriously, let's look at what these preachers of the religion of peace are doing to fellow Muslims. Salafists, in the 1990s, spring to mind. The ones behind the 1995 Paris bombings."

"Well, you can thank the French colonial regime for that."

"150,000 Algerian innocents — all presumably Muslim — we're slaughtered by the Armed Islamic Group. Did Rudyard Kipling order the massacres?"

Nobody looked ready to dignify my profanities.

"C'mon Emma, concede the point. *Charlie Hebdo*'s just a few boys with pencils. Taking the piss. No-one's forcing people to read their poor rag."

"We seem unable to leave the poor Muslims alone," the Québécoise said, suddenly, out of nowhere. "We're obsessed with them. I'm so fucking fed up with it all."

She said it with no little emotion.

"Well, Cabu and Wolinsky are great cartoonists. Gentle souls. Too bad you don't know them better."

"French racists."

"Correction. Anarchists and Oulipo clowns."

"What is there to actually like about *Charlie Hebdo*?"

"C'mon. Do we have to shout at each other?"

"You're the one raising your voice."

"That's because my goddam glass is empty!"

Of course, that had nothing to do with it.

"Look. You don't have to *like* them. The whole idea of the enlightenment is to be able to listen to the point of view of your enemy."

"Oh, Jesus F. Christ, I'm not letting that one pass. Enlightenment to the rescue again," Kennedy said. "Typical fucking Gallic arrogance to call their thinking the enlightenment."

"Well, what do you call Voltaire, Rousseau and Diderot?"

"I call them three arrogant French bastards, that's what I call them."

"The issue here is about freedom of speech, isn't it? I thought this issue was settled in 1961."

"What by the Bay of Pigs invasion?" Kennedy said.

"No, by the Tropic of Cancer obscenity trial in the U.S."

"Oh, so Henry Miller justifies the attack on Islam."

"I better go now. I just want to first present my excuses. You've succeeded in changing my mind."

"I don't believe it," Kennedy said.

"I'm serious. Dead serious. I've just been looking at this from the wrong end. We are guilty all of us. It doesn't matter what for, we are guilty, and as kuffirs we must die along with the Jews. The Jew-apes must be driven into the Red Sea. The Christian monkeys must perish. Then the Scots must be stuffed into their bogs, inchallah and their bagpipes punctured. It's been too long since we had a crucifixion. Time to get the ball rolling. I don't mind going first either. This freedom shit is for the birds. Wait a moment! I think, inchallah, that I am drunk, even drunker than the rest of you. Pay no attention to me. I am covering my true emotions. Not to mention jet lag. So, I'm kicking myself out of your house and onto the righteous path."

"Where are you going?" Emma asked.

"I'm leaving for the Gaza strip. To throw rocks at Jewish Zionist pigs."

I stumbled out the door, walked along Duluth avenue up to Mount Royal, and a path leading upwards. After a time, I found a bench, fell down onto it, turned onto my back, and stared into the Montreal night sky.

"Sid, my friend," I said to the night sky, "I'm on a bench, and you're rotting in a hospital. We're both fucked, but weren't it always so?"

* * *

While lying on the mattress in a sparse room the next morning, I started crooning a stupid self-constructed melody: "*How many Muslims do you know?* A Muslim we will know, A Muslim we will know. Hi ol' the darryo a Muslim we will know."

Wait a minute! I recalled. I know a ton of Muslims! Where do I start? With Karim Errouaki, who recruited me as part of his board of directors of a consortium to rebuild Beirut with the Aga Khan? Or Moustafa who forced his poor wife into a hajib after ISIS took over Iraq in 2012? Or Zeenat Virani, Ismaeli escapee of the brutal dictator Amin, a fellow Muslim, welcomed into my father's firm and our family? Or my daughter's friends Inji or Samia? Or Samia, the Parisian solicitor? Or Mohammed, my football playing pal, during my days on the Main? Or El Hadi, who paraded up and down the rue de la Victoire in his jalaba, and when he attempted to decapitate poor Ghassim in the TV room, came first to see me to tell the story? Do I fill out an official register, or is my name now to be placed on a twenty-first-century Otto List, as an undesirable because I backed a few harmless and innocent cartoonists.

Then I thought fuck the intelligentsia and their pogroms, every last one of them. The truths I'd discovered were on the streets of Montreal from the Italian north to the vacant back alleys of the old port, not sponging Portuguese Dai Alto. Philippe Val didn't have it so good. Seven years later, on January 7, 2015, twelve beautiful and utterly innocent members of Paris' most irreverent artists lay dead in the offices of *Charlie Hebdo, rue Nicholas Appert*, Paris 11th arrondissement, massacred by Salafist thugs, and marking the number eleven as a numerological benchmark for future atrocities to be committed later in the year.

Many of those dead were personal friends of my editor at Editions Denoël, Jean-Paul Caracalla, my publisher Olivier Rubinstein and my friendly nemesis, the mischievous and infinitely charming Miriam Cendrars. They at least had the consolation of the past, but the future looked bleak in the early days of the second decade of the new millennium. The thing is the only reason I probably survived is because nobody would read, let alone buy my books. In a perverse way, my life had worked out, being just beneath the radar, two degrees of separation from celebrity, and no risk of that improving in the long haul.

For some reason, after the *Charlie Hebdo* massacre, I Googled Karim Errouaki. Coincidentally, the first link that appeared was a tribute he had written to Bernard Maris, one of the victims gunned down in the *Charlie Hebdo* massacre. Maris was brilliant, the son of Spanish Republicans, a Sciences Po' product, friend and fan of Houellebecq, author of the scintillating "Anti-Manuel de l'Economie." Karim wondered aloud how it was possible that Islamists could murder someone who so regularly denounced Western power. But what struck me most about Karim's words was his appeal to tolerance on all sides.

He was a sweet guy, Karim. Shit, then somebody else —Khalid, who tried to seduce me outside the Maison du Mexique in 78! I'd forgotten him. And El Hadi, trying to murder Ghassim. No, those people weren't Muslims. They were Maghrebians. El Hadi the former machine-gunner, Mohammed the Engineer in Alexandria, Ingi, Moustafa, Zeenat Virani, and coincidentally, a Mohammed, Private Investigator, who would save my entire family outside Bremen Germany during a crash that nearly took all our lives, shortly after witnessing four others lose theirs during a treacherous rainstorm on our return from Sweden.

FRED THE RED

ON SEPTEMBER 11, while I sat outside La Palette having just heard in the initial France Info bulletin that up to 50,000 people were dead in Manhattan, my friend Fred Naylor was already packing his bags for New York, having organized a mission to dig out whatever remains he and others could find of his fallen comrades, held an honour guard, with the cloud of asbestos dust at ground zero not yet fully settled. Fred spent ten days honouring those brave men and women of the NYC Fire Department. Only I knew — although Fred surely suspected it — that he would pay for that heroic ten-day junket with his life.

I wasn't surprised. I'd seen Fred after a major dock fire at the mouth of the Fraser River in New Westminster. 110 firemen and he was the only one of them crazy enough to fight the fire from under the docks, burning his eyebrows off in the process. After a couple of beers in his New Westminster home, the conversation turned back to 9/11.

"For a few years, I was more on the live and let live philosophy. Now, I think we should just nuke 'em."

"Hope you're getting checked up. There's a lot of shit in those buildings."

"Yeah, I suppose," he said, shrugging.

What I left out of our discussion was my stint at Desjardins Ducharme, when we were retained to defend the Quebec government's assets in the United States because asbestos litigation against three Quebec companies nationalized by Jacques Parizeau was spinning out of control. After three days of work on site, my colleague and I had uncovered 12,000 pending cases naming the Quebec government's three nationalized asbestos corporations as defendants, and the liability was off the radar screen. The first case alone that went to trial, in Delaware, had resulted in a $50 million award in punitives. This was tectonic liability, unprecedented.

I became somewhat of an expert on asbestos, and travelled throughout the United States, dealing with the tens of thousands of deaths caused by contact with the deadly mineral. One of the plaintiffs we had to deal with was the World Trade Center Twin Towers. Anyone remotely connected with the WTC knew and was extremely concerned about the massive amounts of asbestos contained within, and the unprecedented public health hazard that might be created if any accident, fire or the like threatened the structure.

The key to this type of case, which involves hazardous products, is the duty to warn. The duty to warn is commensurate with the current state of scientific knowledge about that hazardous substance. Unlike tobacco, for a long time, scientists and even asbestos companies themselves have been unequivocal in recognizing the extreme health hazard which any exposure to this product triggers. That hazard is common knowledge, going far beyond the industry, in part due to the vast scale of litigation and settlements arising out of the very matters I was working on. Tens of thousands of ruined lives, the leukaemia, the mesothelioma, asbestosis, the poor prognosis, the limited treatment options.

Fred was surely aware of the dangers, but for him it went with the turf. But what he didn't prepare for was the danger within his own department. Fred was a fanatic for precision. Trained in the army, and as an aircraft maintenance engineer, he could single-handedly dismantle and reassemble a Spartan Heavy Rescue vehicle. You see, that's the whole problem, a builder and a hero spends a lifetime putting things together, but when your back's turned, a single stroke and everything can be turned on you.

Fred made the crucial mistake, one that would cost him his career, of criticizing Captain Greg Simpkins, working out of the Queensborough Fire Hall, over an issue that was trivial in the extreme, but ballooned after Naylor tried to enforce some procedural requirements on the recalcitrant Captain, a man short on upgrading but long on union experience as a shop steward. Shortly after that he was driving across the Queensborough Bridge, witnessing letters covering the entire wall of the fire department saying: "Fred Naylor is an asshole." Fred, unfortunately, did not have as many friends as Simpkins.

On December 17, 2009, Fire Chief Tim Armstrong issued a department-wide memo. The memo mysteriously leaked to the media. This is what it said:

> All staff should be aware that the Department and the City have been investigating a complaint brought forward by the Union. This is in regards to harassment in the workplace and the City's policy on harassment. After careful investigation, Management has taken this matter very seriously and is acting on this in the following manner.
>
> In response to the findings of this investigation, as of December 17 1800 hours, Deputy Chief Fred Naylor

> will be under unpaid suspension for a period of one month.
>
> This unfortunate situation could have easily been avoided with proper communication and mutual respect. That being said, it is my position that I will have zero tolerance of any form of **Harassment, Insubordination** or **Inappropriate Behaviour** in a workplace.

What MacManus didn't mention alongside her defamatory insert was a poisonous union/management battle going back to 2005, when Greg Simpkins was secretary of Firefighters Union local 256, and in the very thick of accusations against management's perceived authoritarian style, contenting herself with rubber-stamping the slur and sending it to press.

When things went the way those things go — a conspiracy between Wayne Wright, an ad man mayor, a fire chief who had half of his knowledge, a city accountant, a shop steward abusing his office, Fred knew he was on his way out. But what hurt the most was finding out that his photo had been removed from the department, and with it the day he had gone under the docks when no one else had, the day he'd flown to ground zero and sucked in the asbestos that eventually killed him, and all those other days when he'd fought for what he believed in.

After Fred died, I came across an old article by Theresa MacManus, explaining ex post facto why she'd published that intra-departmental memo to the public that portrayed Freddy as something that he wasn't. It read in part like an excuse and in part like a confession. And, then I fell across another article of hers, naming the high earners at the City of New Westminster. Dated June 13, 2012:

City administrator Paul Daminato was the city's top earner at $201,166.
Fire Chief Tim Armstrong, second-highest staffer at $165,524.
Joan Burgess, Director of Human Resources: $138,153
Greg Simpkins, fire captain, who retired in 2011: $103,318.

Strangely, it included every single one of Fred's tormentors.

Before Freddy died, there had been some fireman's gig and all the old guard had shown up — Carl, Jim Cornell and of course Freddy. Some of the old guard were lacrosse players, like Parnell, and he was making what he thought was a funny speech about being drunk while fighting a fire and his pants catching on fire, and all the lacrosse-playing firemen were falling in the aisles, but Freddy and Carl and Cornell were stone-faced, old bastards who believed the only thing about a fireman that counted was *were you willing to go in first*. At one point, the three of them were taking a leak at the stand-up urinals in the washroom, and who comes in but Armstrong, with this fake hale fellow well met bs look on his face, pumping Fred's hand and saying something about bygones being bygones between brothers, and big Carl just shook his dick a last time, zipped up his coveralls, turned around and stepped on Tim's toe, so hard he couldn't move any further, but Timmy was too, well, too scared to move.

"Heh, heh, you always were a joker, Carl."

Carl just kept pressing harder on his foot, not saying a word.

"Hey, that's enough now that's starting to hurt, Carl."

But Carl kept pressing until Tim had to just wrench his foot out with a real effort, and then just exited the can red-faced.

Fred said mournfully: "You didn't have to do that, but thanks anyways."

"Don't mention it. It wasn't just for you. That son-of-a-bitch never went in first in his entire career."

Freddy wouldn't want the rest of the story told — the endless and futile attempts to save his life. He only emerged from his house in those last two years when he could find his way to swallowing a beer and a cup of coffee. During my last visit to see him, he only wanted to bring me out on his boat at Point Roberts, Washington. It was a great ride. Niall was ten years old, and Freddy gave him the wheel of the boat. It was a spectacular day. Mount Baker, the old volcano, Washington's Mount Fuji overlooking our ride. Not a word about what lay behind or what lay ahead. A couple of months, Freddy wrote to say goodbye. Nothing had worked. Even in death, he was the one who "went in first," to see whether everything was safe on the other side for the rest of us.

On September 11, 2018, the *Guardian* posted an article titled: **September 11: nearly 10,000 people affected by 'cesspool of cancer':**

> "Tens of thousands of people who lived or worked in the neighbourhood at the time found themselves breathing in air thick with toxic fumes and particles from the pulverized, burning skyscrapers. Many have since become sick, many have died and new cases are still occurring all the time that are linked back to the poisons that were in the air around the wreckage."
>
> "Michael Guedes, a retired NYPD sergeant who rushed to Ground Zero, and in the following months worked at Fresh Kills landfill on Staten Island digging through the debris and remains that had been taken there, said future health consequences had been the

> last thing on his mind. "You really don't think about it. You just want to get the job done," he said last week.
>
> Guedes, 65, was diagnosed with breast cancer three years ago after his girlfriend found a lump on his chest. He went through surgery, chemotherapy and radiation, and remains on medication."[1]

And then it struck me that Tim Armstrong had been with Fred at Ground Zero. Suddenly, I couldn't help feeling for the guy. He was rewarded for the worst thing he'd ever done, and now he was faced with mortal peril because of the best thing he'd ever done. I was starting to understand that I knew pretty well nothing about the time-frames of the Creator.

---

1. https://www.theguardian.com/us-news/2018/sep/10/911-attack-ground-zero-manhattan-cancer.

APRÈS NOUS LE DÉLUGE

IT WAS CHUCHI who introduced me to the *Hôtel des Alliés.* Chuchi who has suffered forever, since she saw her own friends go missing in the Argentina of the seventies. Chuchi who survived during her early years in Paris by becoming the mistress of Claude, a businessman from Normandie, who loved Chuchi, or so he tearfully explained during his final speech when he informed her that he had no choice but to return to his wife. Then she became entranced by Jean who also drifted into the ether, because he couldn't take her temper and was bored with his Andes fixations, leaving Chuchi to fend for herself, handing out advertising brochures on the scruffier end of rue St-Honoré nearby Chatelet station. The 5th arrondissement family hotel became my pied-à-terre in 1987, when I finally returned to Paris for a series of work interviews with law firms after a nine-year absence.

The Hôtel des Alliés offered a *petit déjeuner* served in your room at the time of your choice, for 5 francs. Baguette, croissant, café au lait, jus d'orange. The price for a single was thirty-eight euros in the early 1990s, and for another six euros, you had a front-facing room. It was run by a Catholic couple from Auvergne, *monsieur et madame* J-P Albessard.

And now, a decade later, as I descended the Avenue de

Port Royal, towards *rue Berthollet*, I recalled the last time I had spoken with the owner of the Hotel des Alliés, Madame Albessard. She had stared wide-eyed at me, as she recounted that she had received a phone call from a certain woman. That the woman was actively looking for me, that the authorities had been notified, that she was most surprised after all my years frequenting the hotel that I had never mentioned the fact that I had an entire life behind me in the South of France.

"I had no idea that you had taken measures to assure your *déscendance*, monsieur MacKinnon," she had said,but at the time, I was too frantic to worry about dignity, when only escape was on my mind. But now, I felt it keenly as I returned to the scene of my abasement, to recall that humiliating time when I was a man fleeing from his own obsessions. And, the sight of a crucifix hanging from her silver neck-chain did nothing to diminish my feeling of acute embarrassment. Another American, she must have thought, running from the Old World the moment the idea of duty was introduced.

"Well, it's good to see you again. You look well,"she said warmly, adding: "*Ça fait quand même du temps que vous veniez nous voir.*"

"*Quinze ans.*"

"*Je vous trouve bien là*. You went through some hard times if I am not mistaken. But, now, you look better ..."

She paused, took her pen, and lodged it in a pencase.

"There is only one man who has been coming here longer than you. He is from Buenos Aires. He was so happy here. He told us he was an Argentinean cowboy, so people always referred to him as John Wayne. But, last year, one of those awful television investigation crews called to see if he were a guest here. They had come all the way from Argentina with a 32-year-old woman who claimed she was his daughter, and wanted to meet him. Initially, he laughed, and would only say: '*Cette affaire ne me concerne pas.*'

"But he quickly became agitated, and with each passing day, you could see he was getting more and more worn down by his conundrum. After four days, I believe, he walked into the lobby. He began to speak, but I couldn't make out what he was saying. It was gibberish. Then, he collapsed in convulsions. It was very upsetting. He survived the incident, but it was so very sad to see this person collapse in this way. There is something not correct in the way this woman acted. *Eh bien, tant pis*!

"There were other memorable guests, of course. And, they made it interesting. But, the only difficult ones were the children that came to receive cobalt treatment up at the Curie institute. The parents always wanted to talk. People don't usually talk to a hotel manager. Is the room available or not, is there a shower, etcetera, and nothing more. But always these parents felt compelled to talk. So, I listened."

When I returned again to the Hôtel des Alliés the following year, the hotel had been sold to a group of business graduates from Paris, and had been renamed the Hotel Seven, inspired by the fictional secret agent James Bond, in order to cater to the fantasies of the new ultra-rich Asian clientele. The hotel brochure described luxurious stays in the Agent Secret Suite, the Lovez-Vous Suite, or the Designer Suite, or the Cabaret suite, and as part of the package, evening entertainment at the famed Crazy Horse cabaret in the Faubourg Montmartre. Gone was the room where I charted my midnight departures on foot for Chartres, or number eighteen, where I prepared my interviews with Jean Thieffry or Martinet Bataillon or J.F. Rambaud in the 16th arrondissement. I continued reading the brochure.

"The cozy wooden-decked inner courtyard features comfortable rattan sofas and armchairs ideal to enjoy a morning coffee, a pre-dinner drink or a nightcap at the end of your long Parisian day."

Coincidentally, I happened upon Madame Albessard in the Tunisian grocery on *rue Berthollet.* She invited me in for an *apéro.* They had chosen to move across the street from the hotel on *rue Berthollet.* Inside, her husband, Jean-Pierre Albessard, was busy arranging a vast historical reconstruction on a large table, comprised of miniature figurines from everyday life in what appeared to be the middle ages, probably a depiction of the famed Les Halles market that had been razed to the ground by the Pompidou government in 1969. The display contained an impressive scene — butchers, bakers, ox-carts, cheesemakers, butter makers — a bustle of the day-to-day life of Paris in times gone by. During our visit, madame Albessard, as if my presence evoked him, picked up the thread again about the Argentinean, who in her memory, seemed indelibly linked with me for some reason.

"And then the Argentinean, *imaginez-vous,* monsieur MacKinnon, who one day collapsed in my arms, suffering a heart attack. That was a memorable day, but you also gave us some memories, and some surprises too, monsieur MacKinnon," she said.

"Coincidentally, it was an Argentinean friend who introduced me to your hotel."

"Vraiment? C'est quand même curieux, la vie, vous ne trouvez pas, monsieur MacKinnon?"

"Indeed, life is curious, and there is surely meaning in these coincidences."

"Oh, of course there is," she rejoined, "but a meaning that can be discerned without necessarily being understood."

Behind her faultless courtesy, and her gentle caressing

of the crucifix while talking, I thought I detected the trace of a glint of amusement, and even some gratitude, that I had added in my erratic way to the tales that had survived even after the *Hôtel des Alliés* had become the 007 and was put to the service of a new breed of tourist, who drove Lamborghinis and drank their Bordeaux using straws.

MacKINNON'S CAVE

THE FIRST TIME I travelled to MacKinnon's Cave, just west of Gribun on the Isle of Mull at Balmeanach Farm, Hannah was three months pregnant with Zoé, Niall two years old and it was raining hard enough to make the trek hazardous. The cave had first drawn my interest when reading Boswell's *Tour of the Hebrides*, that spoke of their visits to both the Cave and Staffa in 1773. They had entered with only a candle and measured its dimensions with a walking stick.

We had no directions except for a page out of the Boswell Journal. After continuing along a tarred lane running adjacent to the sole farm in the vicinity, we climbed up an uneven track left of a fence, where I was sure that I spotted a cleft in the hills about 800 metres further up to the left.

"Let's do it."

After another half hour, and several dips and rises leading towards the opening, a highland steer appeared, and then a second, and after we saw more clearly, there appeared to be thirty of them, all heads turned towards us at a distance of about one hundred metres..

"They don't look too friendly. Do you know anything about highland steers?"

"Not a thing."

Not for the first time, I realized I had dragged my family

into the line of fire. The bull at the front of the v-formation facing us was chewing on his cud and doing the same thing as me. Deciding how he was going to spend the next five minutes of his day.

"You turn around, slowly and walk back, I'll retreat while keeping my eyes on him."

A couple of years later, I returned with Thomas and Robert. Our visit coincided with the worst rainstorms in the history of the Hebrides, and some roads were not passable. On the second day, we decided to take a crack.

This time we arrived at the same fence corner and turned right, and walked through heavy bog, but managed to find a trail. We'd heard you could see Staffa, where there was another MacKinnon's Cave, the place where the last Abbott of Iona, John MacKinnon, repaired to repent for his occasional trysts with his lover Mathilda, in the last decade of the fifteenth century. None of that was visible. We walked through an old, iron gate, and then continuing along the dipping edge of the hill to the left.

Over the next dip, we could see a high waterfall, and down below, five-metre waves crashing against the coast. But the low section of the cliff fell straight down onto the rocks. We couldn't see the path, supposedly traversing throw boulders closer to the waterfall, and the heavy rains were now turning into a storm.

"What now?" Thomas asked. Thomas is a direct descendant of Edward the Confessor. In principle, we are mortal enemies, but not even approaching the ancestral lands has heated up the ancestral blood. There's something still there — Thomas is unfailingly polite, but he cannot entirely mask his sense that the England he stands for is the best thing the world has ever seen. And, to a certain extent, I agree.

"I'm not going to stop you, MacKinnon, but you'll be crazy to go."

"Let's go back to the pub."

That blood has driven me to extremes in my life, but there's not a thing on those islands that awakened some atavistic urge to return. There's a limit to a man's suffering.

A couple of days later, we were on Staffa Island, inside the cave where Mendelsohn had composed his psalm to the Hebrides. In the cave once over, John MacKinnon would sneak away. Just as we did, but in the opposite direction. We spent the next days drinking Talisker Single Malt, eating haggis, tramping up the hills to Bonnie Prince Charlie's Cave on the southern coast of Isle of Skye, where he had hidden after the failed rebellion in 1745, and another John MacKinnon would arrange his escape to France, and pay for it by spending a year in the Tower of London. I visited the ruins of MacKinnon tombs and of the clan chief's house on Skye, the same chief that Johnson himself had praised as having a library and erudition equal to England's greatest scholars.

There is a story about John MacKinnon's release from the Tower of London, when the judge asked: "What would you say to the Pretender if you saw him today, having spent a year in the Tower?"

"I'd say the same thing you are to me and grant him his freedom in perpetuity."

"That's a nice story, now how do you feel about that, David?" Thomas asked.

"I'd say what my son would say to me. That he was an old fool and a typical MacKinnon, dying for a cause that perhaps wasn't his own. We've made a virtue of being brave and then being forgotten."

I've thought about our motto since: Audentas Fortuna

Juvat. And, I suppose that you could say that hasn't been the case that for all their audacity—from Culloden, to Bannockburn to the great wars, the MacKinnons have shown unusual fortitude and bravery in great causes. I'm no less atavistic than the next. Show me the road to battle and I'll reach for my halbard and broadsword, no problem. The problem for a MacKinnon doesn't lie there in the least. It's peacetime that irks us, and irritates, and makes us reach for the whisky.

There's something in those long, lazy days that brings out the worst in me, and drives me to want to stir up shite wherever I can. Anybody who knows me doubts my sincerity in leading a troupe of Aboriginals to Rome to take on the Pope. I know my own heart fairly well, and I suppose that being from my blood-line, I never entertained the illusion that our cause would improve the lot of the indigenous downtrodden. That's not what drives a MacKinnon in the least. We like to lead from the front once we are certain, in our heart of hearts, that the cause is a hopeless one, and so confirm that we shall join the fray when only a madman would consider such a thing. When defeat is certain, and escape no longer an option, there's bound to be a MacKinnon somewhere in the neighbourhood.

O CEBREIRO

CHARLES PÉGUY WALKED to Chartres around the time of the First World War because his son was sick. I discovered the walk to Chartres through reading Péguy's poem "Présentation de la Beauce à Notre Dame de Chartres". But what I liked most about it was that the three-day pilgrimage generally began for me with a couple of days of wanton ribaldry in the Latin Quarter and ended by stumbling through Rambouillet forest, onwards across the Beauce Plain, finally arriving in mediaeval Chartres. Chartres was built by Charlemagne, and contains some of the most mystical symbols of the Christian and pagan world, particularly two which have remained symbols for me throughout my life. Our lady of the underworld evokes almost a voodoo aspect, and the labyrinth of Theseus on the floor, exhibits yet another of Christianity's forms of genius — the ability to incorporate local beliefs from voodoo to pantheism to mythology.

These obscure and totemic icons exercise an irrational attraction to pilgrims such as myself, as the reasons pilgrims go on pilgrimages are not primarily rational, but rather an obeisance to intuition. Once on the road, another logic moves into the ascendancy, the logic of the Camino.

My first departure for Chartres was preceded, as the others, started with a night on the town, starting at the counter in La Palette on the rue de Seine, and ended in a brawl with a journalist who later became a close friend, at least until that also ended badly. In the early morning, three of us left, severely hungover, along the rue Berthollet, turning onto avenue du Port Royal, and along boulevard Montparnasse and past La Rotonde, Le Select, Le Dôme, as the garbage trucks were cleaning up from the night previous. I was in wretched condition, my two childhood friends who I had lured over from Canada, were propping me up as only I knew the path to Chartres. A few hours of walking and we found ourselves in the midst of the Meudon forest, Céline territory, and by the end of the morning, we had arrived in Versailles, and the previous night almost forgotten, although it took me until the afternoon to feel my heart rate finally slow to an acceptable level..

The walk, probably little more than one hundred km in total, takes you along paths trod by Racine and Pascal, through the paths of towns transformed by migrants, and into the depths of the Rambouillet forest. The latter part is on the Beauce plain, a slightly undulating plateau, where the cathedral of Chartres is visible from a distance, rising up on the horizon, disappearing, then reappearing, like a mirage.If I experienced any epiphanies upon arrival, they could easily be explained by my blood-alcohol levels at the time I dragged my unrepentant carcass onto the floor, where I had a close-up view of the labyrinth of Chartres carved into the floor.

A couple of years later, I left again for Chartres, this time alone, and then, in 2002, I set out on a longer pilgrimage, this time to Santiago de la Compostela, an 800 km walk from the Pyrenees to the west coast of Galicia. I recall dining in Bayonne, and then taking a long steep train up to St. Jean-Pied-de-Port, our point of departure. Then having a *poulet basque* and a half litre of red, prior to signing off for the evening. Then wandering down the narrow streets and spotting an office of the pilgrimage, and the pilgrim's shell outside the door. Then, the next morning, stepping through the gate with a pack far too heavy, and hitting a steep incline upwards, more than 2,000 metres climbing that first day. But this time I was ready, healthy, clean, and so I had the vantage point from which I could watch unprepared pilgrims stumble their way along, or stopping at the edge of the Camino to tend to their sores, blisters and callouses. The Camino Frances makes no allowances for amateurs, and yet the pilgrims include more yahoos, illuminati and freaks than I have ever seen moving towards one destination in my life.

For Santiago, none of the prep should be spiritual, all of it physical. There was no shortage of freaks on that road to Santiago—Jesus freaks, German scouting troops, Shirley MacLaine disciples, rugby coaches, healers. And Germans everywhere with their maps, their ironed shorts, their perfectly made sandwiches. Half a century gone since the war, and some of them still trying organize Europe. And the rest of them trying to prove they weren't like the others—they also cropped up on the camino—one crazy megalomaniac with a fixation on a fictional film character called Fitzcarraldo, and Costa Rican banana plantation to perform the mediaeval rites.

Somewhere around Astorga, I first began crossing a black-haired German woman, middle-aged, who generally would be smoking and drinking water, and yet mysteriously would arrive before me at the next destination along that road. Whether it was the Pico Mountains, the desert outside Burgos or the Galician hill country outside O Cebreiro, she always managed to beat me to destination.

On the morning of my arrival, after 800 km of walking, I met a man, also with a Germanic accent, who took up a conversation with me.

"So, you are American," he said.

"No. Canadian."

"Same thing," he said, settling the matter for all time.

"How about you?"

"Indeed, how about me?"

"Where are you from?"

"I am from Vienna."

"Ah, a German."

"No. Austrian," he said.

"Same thing."

I continued my walk alone, the last twenty kilometres or so, arriving in the main street of a singularly unimpressive, kitsch, overblown baroque city, Santiago de la Compostela. Coming down the main street, I noticed the ubiquitous German woman, sitting in front of two empty bottles of Vino Verde, clearly intoxicated and smoking.

"I've booked the most expensive hotel in the city, and I don't even have enough to pay for this wine!"

"Do you mind if I ask you something?"

"Go ahead," she said, slurring.

"How do you manage to always arrive before me?"

"Oh, you fool, you don't think I walk, do you? I have taxied every day from St. Jean-Pied-de-Port. And, now I have no money left!"

I begged off and returned the next morning by train to San Sebastien.

Years later, a fellow pilgrim, Michel Maret, a Parisian, called me to recount a story.

"My friends are asking: 'We understand pilgrimages. But, why is that friend of yours bringing all those aboriginals to Rome? It makes no sense.'"

"I told them: '*C'est pour emmerder le pape.*'"

"*Ah, d'accord.*"

ELECTRIC KOOL-AID ABORIGINAL ACID TEST

For a brief scintillating moment ...

...WE REACHED FOR the stars and they seemed within our grasp. We were hours away from Rome, and it seemed that after 500 years the opacity that had blinded humanity would be seen for what it was: a cover-up of greed planned, confected, perpetrated on innocents worldwide. And that our common cause would bind together men who had been driven apart by that terrible force — self-interest. For a moment, our rag-tag band of luminaries, Wounded Knee refugees, indigenous popes, tribal court judges and Apache warriors arrived in Vatican City. For an unrecorded — aye, but there's the rub, for it was recorded and I've got the recording! — eleven disciples and two aging warriors of the great nations — Haudenosaunee and Cree — walked into St. Peter's Square. The Pope's security spotted them coming from a long distance.

Himko Kaps Kap, direct descendant of the warrior who fought alongside Chief Joseph at the Battle of Bear Paw, was magnificent in his warrior attire and eagle feathers. Grand Chief Willie Littlechild, he of the Truth and Reconciliation commission, of the Treaty Six Nations spanning Alberta and Saskatchewan and the north, where their lands reach as far as those of the Inuit, the founder of the Indigenous Games, stood proud, his hand shaking from the passage of time, but his resolve iron-hard.

Dr. Kenneth Deer, he of the Mohawk federation, with the full blessing of the world's oldest democracy, the Haudenosaunee, those of the Two Wampum Belt, stood proud, and signalled us back in Florence that they had arrived. The Haudenosaunee had been burning tobacco and praying for us for five days. Steven Newcomb, Lenape, the people who had sold Manhattan for 24 dollars to a Dutchman, but a man with a mind sharper than the edges of a tomahawk, was there, as was Chairman JoDe Goudy of the Yakama nation.

The architect of the mobilisation of Canada's 641 First Nations, Former Chief Keith Matthew of Simpcw nation stood proud, as did Grandmother Belinda Ayze, Navajo. The heirs of Wounded Knee, Loretta Afraid of Bear Cook and Barbara Drybones, mandated by Beatrice Long Visitor Holy Dance, one of the original Indigenous Grandmothers, just prior to her death, stood by. Michael Hill, of the Apache arrived armed with the recent *Apache*-Ndé-Nneé Working Group Shadow *Report* on the history of Church discrimination against their peoples. Herson Huinca Piutrin, Mapuche, entered next. When the security patrol insisted that only four of the delegation could be received in the special audience with the Pope, they stood their ground. It was all or none. And the Pope's security guard relented.

We remained behind, 300 kilometres to the north, up on a Tuscan hilltop, outside Florence, amidst vineyards, under the pale blues and oranges of the Tuscan sky, and huddled, left with our broken, shattered selves. It was the necessary price, but at that moment, it seemed heavy that our children would have to share the burden with us.

"They have arrived," I announced, watching Hannah pack suitcases for the return to Amsterdam. She had put her credibility on the line in service of my folly. She had given, the children had given and I had received. And paid them back with madness. This glorious, knife-edge madness that had us on the verge of losing everything — security, health and the sympathy of our own peoples. It truly was madness, and me the architect of it all.

"Good," she stated softly, then fell silent again, returning to folding shirts.

"Let this now, all of this end. It is time to go home."

We had taken on the language of our friends, short phrases, invocations of the Creator, as if our delusion had placed us somewhere on the Trail of Tears.

"What about the Pontifical Council? Shouldn't you ensure they arrive there safely?"

"Oh, we'll hear about that soon enough."

"True."

"Belinda wants to see you. She has a gift. A Navajo shawl."

"It will have to wait. I may not make it. Just get us home."

Little did we know that the centre would hold only long enough for even this historic encounter, and outside the Pontificio Consiglio della Giustizia e della Pace in the Palazzio San Calisto, Città del Vaticano, in the intense triumph of the moment, two of the chiefs would be at each other's throats in a spontaneous revival of a blood feud or a difference of opinion on the travel itinerary or the intense realization of what had just transpired. But that also was part of that day, May 4, 2016, exactly 523 years to the day after the enactment of *Inter Caetera*, the Papal Bull that served as the blueprint for the conquest of the Americas by Christian kings. Each of the indigenous leaders, upon meeting Pope Francis, spoke identical words: "You must revoke the Papal Bulls".

We left our mountain retreat, our Range Rover descending through a rocky, steep lane crossing a vineyard, and an olive tree orchard. I gripped the wheel hard, rejoined the road passing by Bagno a Ripoli, six kilometres south of

Florence, where only a day previous, treachery and glory were being planned concurrently in the makeshift sweat lodge constructed by Enio. I continued driving past the Grand Hotel Mediterraneo on the bank of the river Arno, close to the Ponte San Niccolò on the Lungarno il Tempio, leaving a Navajo woman waiting with her handwoven gift as we raced for the airport and escape. I took a wrong turn, U-turned against furious *autistas*, and entering a roundabout at speed.

"Look out!"

I jaked and swerved hard left as a local bus entered the hexagonal crossing, cutting us off and missing us by centimetres, fraying our nerves further. That I recall, vivid as a fresco of Fra Filippo Lippi, unhinged as it were from Spoleto Cathedral and anchoring itself in the mind's eye, just as we had been unhinged from our day-to-day lives for reasons unclear to either of us. The rest is a blank, including our return home to Amsterdam and safety. Even during that insane sprint, Hannah knew and I knew this was the necessary result. That someone had to be sacrificed along the road to Rome, and there were no other candidates to play the role. We arrived at Toscana Aeroporti Firenza forty minutes ahead of flight-time.

There would be no recognition and there would be no celebration. What had occurred may even have happened in spite of us. We were spectators at our own production, and yet we took no pleasure in the spectacle. It was only a year later that we realized that something truly special had occurred. Something unique. A truth long denied had been bared in all its raw essence. The wounds had been exposed, and those wounds had exposed another crucifixion, one carried out in the name of God by unprincipled men who had denied the very title of "human" to those they prepared to spoliate, all the better to *reduce their persons to perpetual slavery* and those men had reserved for themselves the title of "chosen" or "elect" or "reborn in the Corpus Christi."

Such was the magnitude of their crime, of their blasphemy. Such were the words of the edict, and such was the result, and until those words were acknowledged and retracted, the sin would remain, a shroud hiding not the image of the son of god, but the stain of unbridled greed, and how far man is prepared to stoop in order to elevate his imperfect self at the expense of his fellow man.

THE BIGGEST LAND GRAB EVER

"... — **TO INVADE, SEARCH** out, capture, vanquish, and subdue all Saracens and pagans whatsoever, and other enemies of Christ wheresoever placed, and the kingdoms, dukedoms, principalities, dominions, possessions, and all movable and immovable goods whatsoever held and possessed by them and to reduce their persons to perpetual slavery, and to apply and appropriate to himself and his successors the kingdoms, dukedoms, counties, principalities, dominions, possessions, and goods, and to convert them to his and their use and profit."

Romanus Pontifex, Papal Bull issued by Pope Nicolas V on Jan, 8 1455, authorizing King Alfonso of Portugal to conquer Africa and beyond, and to engage in the slave trade

"...to seeke out, discouer, and finde whatsoever isles, countreys, regions or prouinces of the heathen and infidels whatsoeuer they be, and in what part of the world soeuer they be, which before this time haue bene vnknowen to all Christians... And'that the aforesayd Iohn and his sonnes, or their heires and assignee may subdue, occupy and possesse all such townes, cities, castles and isles of them found."

Excerpt from Letters Patent issued by King Henry VII to the Explorer John Cabot and his sons for the discovery of new and unknown lands, Feb 3, 1496.

"Although we do not mean to engage in the defence of those principles which Europeans have applied to Indian title, they may, we think, find some excuse, if not justification, in the character and habits of the people whose rights have been wrested from them."

Chief Justice Marshall of the US Supreme Court in *Johnson v. M'Intosh* (1823)

Only two years after we undertook this impossible mission, we stood on the cusp of changing the world, and electricity was in the air from Ottawa to Santiago to Jerusalem, from the Cape of Good Horn to the lands of the Sami peoples in the Arctic Circle. On March 31, Bishop Crosby of the Canadian Conference of Catholic Bishops had personally sent me, in my capacity as President of the Long March to Rome, a letter explaining the position of the Catholic Church on the issue of the Papal Bulls of Discovery.

Unknown to me, the CCCB had conducted a year-long study on the impact of the Papal Bulls of Discovery. Only two weeks earlier, Cardinal Turkson, President of the Pontifical Council for Justice and Peace, had written to the Right Honourable Bob Rae, ex-Premier of Ontario, confirming that the "Indigenous Question" and the "role of Church documents" was very much in discussion in Canada, implying that indeed, the problem had to be addressed and that he would be discussing it with the "competent authorities."

We had the backing of an unprecedented number of indigenous leaders worldwide, including the major thinkers on the issue of Discovery from the indigenous world, the pre-eminent Haudenosaunee confederacy, the Thirteen Indigenous Grandmothers who had travelled to Rome a decade earlier and been shut out of its gates unceremoniously. At the peak of our momentum, the Canadian government had unofficially made an overture to join in our cause, and we had declined, for historical reasons and out of the belief that destiny was in our control.

The Bishops' report was impressive, unprecedented, but a factor no-one, including myself, had taken into account was that I had begun entering into my own indigenous Heart of Darkness. That journey was unforeseen, and took me to places unanticipated. There are many taboos within the indigenous world and one of them was that it was forbidden for those outside the tribes to lay claim to a similar experience. And yet there was nothing to be done about it. My family, not just my people, my direct family were sent out on a Trail of Tears to rival the worst of the fate of the Cherokee.

I would discover only weeks before that my grandfather was subject to being strapped for speaking his native tongue, Gaelic, in the confines of the dank, cold Maryvale, Nova Scotia schoohouse sometime during the closing decade of the 19th century, until that barbaric tongue was extirpated from his system. A bitter reminder of the aftermath of Culloden, when our mode of dress, our music, our mores were prohibited, pending the moment of our total expulsion from the highlands. But I would subsequently discover that my own clan had just as many taboos as the most aboriginal of my new acquaintances. Our past haunted us, and our remedy was the law of silence.

I expressed on one occasion to Himko Kaps Kap that the fate of the indigenous — spoliation of land, cultural genocide and forced exile — would resonate with any MacKinnon. He had laughed. "What, you guys gonna take even that from us?"

After reading the landmark case *Johnson v. M'Intosh*, I became convinced that Chief Justice Marshall was a genius. Oddly, the decision that has been held up to the world right to the present day as proof of the white man's title was riddled with the interrogatives of a Chief Justice finding great difficulty in countenancing the gravity of the crime. He knew also within the darkest recesses of his privilege that one of the world's wrongs had been committed, and yet never been properly examined. Something that left the stain of an original sin on the soul of the recently liberated American people. A tea tax was an unspeakable affront to their dignity, and yet denying property to the original inhabitants of the land of their recent arrival was already being airbrushed from the history books, and the Crusade — for "Discovery" bore all the marks of a Crusade save the name — that had justified the crime was already being reinvented as a European discovery.

The entire enterprise of "discovery" had a whiff of Genghis Khan and it had something of the madness of Lady Macbeth, and the elegantly-phrased judgment of Chief Justice Marshall could not remove the stain of conquest. His reasons were strange, shrouded in allusions and inverted syllogisms. I became convinced that he was sending a message to the future. Chief Justice Marshall's turn of phrase came out of nowhere, and had had a similar effect upon me — like a crack of lightning. "*Spain did not rest her title solely on the grant of the Pope.*"

Now, 800 days after reading that phrase, it felt as if we were advancing towards Rome, and despite not having physically left our homes, there was the sense that we were in a mountain pass, ready to ambush the Vatican. The backing of the leaders of the great indigenous nations was there — the most famous warrior nations. The Haudenosaunee confederacy. The Maya. The Mapuche. The air, from Tuscany to the New World and throughout the digital exosphere was electric with expectation.

I had tested the substantive value of our argument by publishing it on-line, and sending it to the leading experts in the indigenous world on the topic of Discovery. Not a single one of them refuted the core argument presented. There was an unbroken chain beginning with the first blueprints for slavery — *Dum Diversas* in 1452 and *Romanus Pontifex* in 1455. And then, the fatal document drawn up by the Borgias in 1493 — *Inter Caetera*. The enabling statute for the letters patent legitimizing the crime.

The thought that the Long March to Rome would not succeed never occurred to me. It all depended on how you looked at it. If we walked to Rome, and laid down a marker, it was a success. Until two months prior to arrival, I hadn't even considered the security issue — that ISIS was still knocking on the door of Europe, making the streets of Vatican City an armed fortress. Nor had I sufficiently considered that the success of the mission would trigger a panic within the ranks of a government taking an ad hoc and chaotic approach to getting resources to market after opening up the Pandora's Box of indigenous rights via the 1982 Canadian Charter of Rights and Freedoms, the biggest piece of legislative hubris devised in the history of the country. Section 35 of the Charter, by guaranteeing existing Aboriginal and treaty rights, set into motion an express train to nowhere, hurtling Canada onto a path to becoming the new Africa — as the 5th column of aboriginal rights eroded the very institutions that had allowed the country to hitherto thrive and be the envy of the world. I was quixotic to the point of self-delusion, but the graybeards working the levers of government from the shadows had me beat to hell on the issue of hubris.

THE PAPAL ENVOY

THE ISSUE OF the Papal Bulls of Discovery was neither one of conquest nor even exclusively one of racism — the one-size-fits-all argument of intellectuals and activists who had hitched their wagon to the cause of the indigenous. It was something else — a corporate strategy, very post-modernist and global in its conception — based on the notion of a "manufactured inequality."

One of the things that had struck me was the extent to which political boundaries had confused the issue, and in more than one way. The relations of indigenous peoples are transnational. Whereas we might see the 49th parallel as the "longest undefended border," the Haudenosaunee, Ojibway and some of the Plains tribes view it as a sword plunged directly into the aboriginal heart. Keith Matthew, ex-chief of the Simpcw nation, had relations running right down to California.

"When we sign our letters 'All my relations,' we mean it literally," he had once informed me, then went on to explain his remark. "They really are our relations, David. We have left children behind during our migrations as far south as California."

Keith was, by his own admission, both First Nations and Canadian. The Canadian First Nations, to my eye, were locked into the truth and reconciliation process, a creation of the federal government emulating the South African proceedings. This is somewhat ironic, as Canada's *Indian Act* was, according to some sources, an inspiration for South Africa's apartheid legislation, including the practice of requiring passes to leave reserves, although that possibly should be classified with similar "urban aboriginal legends" such as Terra Nullius, unchallenged, yet unproven by those making hay out of the bi-millennial tragedy. Part of the Canadian spin on that process — a key part — was the Assembly of First Nations or AFN, headed by Perry Bellegarde. But among the pros out in the field, AFN was "All for Nothing," a cash cow constructed on the cronyistic reconciliation road show devised by men who alter destinies with straight rulers from distant rooms. The elephant in the bureaucratic living room was resources, and the Assembly of First Nations served as a turnstile processing complaints, a chamber full of pomp, and implying that although the law had changed, the reality remained the same. But, Keith nevertheless — a businessman and politician of great acumen — had a plan, one that he shared with me in late 2014.

"Could you give me a draft resolution for the upcoming AFN meeting in Winnipeg? If they're behind us, it gives us instant credibility. I'll see what I can do. Everybody knows me since I worked on Phil Fontaine's campaign to become National Chief."

That was no problem, and I drafted a resolution accordingly.

To understand just what we accomplished with the Long March to Rome, you have to go to 1984, when Tupac Enrique Acosta, writing on behalf of the Traditional Natives Alliance of the Western Hemisphere, wrote the following letter to Pope John Paul II:

> We as members of the Traditional Native Nations of the Western Hemisphere feel that the time has come for your office to re-evaluate the principles and effects generated by the Vatican decision of Pope Alexander VI to grant domain over our lands and peoples. In effect, this decision proclaimed that our way of life, thinking, and existence as nations was meaningless in the eyes of Christian civilization. We were to be "discovered," used and discarded.
>
> We now ask that you examine in your own conscience the fallacy of this decision. We humbly ask, how can someone give away what does not belong to them? A re-examination of this historical event and public comment by your office on this matter is clearly in order. A revocation of this doctrine would be a milestone for the peaceful attainment of our universal human rights.
>
> We do not ask this in anger or vengeance, but in the Spirit of Truth, trusting in our common faith to the Universal Creator.
>
> For Traditional Xicano Nation, Tupac Enrique Acosta

The statement of the argument was framed in straightforward, eloquent, irrefutable juris de jure logic. The response of the Church was eventually issued by the Catholic diocese of Phoenix, Arizona and met this eloquence with an equal dose of haughtiness, indifference and contempt:

> Dear Mr. Enrique,
>
> Your letter to His Holiness Pope John Paul II was referred by the Vatican Secretary of State to our Bishop, Thomas J. O'Brian. He has asked me to respond on his behalf.

> We all appreciate the fact that the Europeans came to America and conquered the native Americans and took the land for their own. This has been the history of the human race — even though it may not be just or fair. If we tried to reverse the process all the English who are descendants of the Normans from France would have to go home. The Goths and the Visigoths who conquered Italy would have to go back to Norway, Sweden and Northern Germany.
>
> There is no way to reverse the course of history, but the Church is really concerned that Native Americans preserve their culture — have adequate jobs and preserve the Faith that was introduced to the Native Americans by Spaniards, French, Italians, etc.
>
> With best wishes, I am
> Sincerely yours,
> Rev. James E. McFadden
> Chancellor

This short note contained a perfect summary of how the Church addressed this bi-millennial problem: delegating the response to a subaltern, dismissing the issue as ancient history, and delivering the message in a tone of barely concealed condescension.

This is what we set out to change. Firstly and primarily to achieve one thing that had never been achieved in 523 years of oppression since the settler nations had "discovered" North America. In short order, the position of the Long March to Rome would be set out in our position paper that made a clear demonstration of the illegality of the "discovery" of the Americas pursuant to Letters Patent drafted by Henry VII's royal commission in1496 and issued to the

Cabots. The entire claim to the Americas depends upon the validity of these Letters Patent.

However, none of this would be anything more than academic discussion, had it not been for the shrewd back-channel mind and experience of Simpcw former chief Keith Matthew. While in Paris in December, I received a note from Keith.

"I'll have news for you soon."

We received the news just prior to Christmas. A resolution in favour of the movement had just passed by consensus:

SPECIAL CHIEFS ASSEMBLY
December 9, 10 & 11, 2014, WINNIPEG, MB **Resolution no. 46/2014**

TITLE:	**Support for Rescinding the Papal Bulls of Discovery**
SUBJECT:	Reconciliation
MOVED BY:	Chief Shane Gottfriedson, Kamloops Indian Band, BC
SECONDED BY:	Bernd Christmas, Proxy, Indian Island First Nation, NB
DECISION	Carried by Consensus

WHEREAS:

A. First Nations people and their descendants have suffered the effects of colonization by successive governments since before Canada was established based on a false doctrine of discovery – a doctrine which must be rescinded in order for healing and understanding between First Nations and Canada to truly begin.

THEREFORE BE IT RESOLVED that the Chiefs-in-Assembly:

1. Resolve to endorse, to support and to encourage the participation of its peoples in the Long March to Rome, a pilgrimage of Indigenous peoples worldwide to present a petition to Pope Francis I, seeking revocation of the two papal bulls Romanus Pontifex (1455) and Inter Caetera (1493), otherwise known as the Papal Bulls of Discovery, for the following reasons:
    a. They were the "blueprint" for conquest of the New World.
    b. They provided moral justification for the enslavement and conquest of Indigenous peoples worldwide.
    c. They are an ongoing violation of contemporary international human rights law.
    d. Other communities currently struggling to save their lands are threatened by modern-day ideologies of inequality anchored in the Papal Bulls of Discovery.

Certified copy of a resolution adopted on the 11th day of December 2014 in Winnipeg, Manitoba

PERRY BELLEGARDE, NATIONAL CHIEF

46 – 2014
Page 1 of 1

This was, to coin a favourite term in the milieu, leverage. Then, in the summer, I was invited as a delegate to the EMRIP, the Expert Mechanism for the Rights of Indigenous Peoples, and the doorway to a world stage to set down our plans to force the Vatican to revoke the Papal Bulls of Discovery. By July, Hannah and I had finished drafting the position paper: "Chains of Title: How the Vatican shackled post-revolutionary America" showing the problematic nature of America's legal claim to lands — the myth that native Americans were a sub-caste of humanity.

Keith and I met in Geneva, and there was a feeling between us — that we had both come out of nowhere, a couple of mavericks coming in to shake things up, to get a simple truth across. While Hannah prepared the presentation to one of the side conferences, Keith and I decided to check out the main conference hall at the UN. A large hemi-cycle, filled with delegates, each droning five-minute speeches. After ten minutes, we were both running for the exits.

"That was dreary," I said as we sat down in the cafeteria, laughing like conspirators at our escape.

"Even worse than the AFN. At least there, people complain."

"I don't care about any of this. We had to see it, but these are third parties. We need to go to the heart of the matter, and get a conversation between you and the Vatican. I doubt I'll even attend."

"Sounds good."

People were filing out, and for a reason that escapes me to this day, I decided to step inside the amphitheatre. There was only one delegate remaining, a St. Lucia delegate who ironically was the sole person openly complaining about the Doctrine of Discovery. In the seats, one other observer remained, and a card in front of him said "HOLY SEE." At first,

I was intimidated. Here we were at the very beginning of this adventure, and the representative of the Vatican was sitting six rows away and no-one else in sight. I decided to approach the St. Lucia man, and said I admired his speech.

"Well, it had to be said. No-one seems to be paying attention to the cause of all this."

"Tell you what," I replied, doubling up my courage. "I'm going to do something about it and talk to the Vatican. The envoy is right there."

"What a grand idea. Good luck!"

I walked up to the man and introduced myself, feeling no little relief that he didn't turf me out then and there. His name was Vincente Buonuomo, Vincent the good man, he said, smiling. I explained the nature of our enterprise, and that we would be coming to Rome the following year.

"Write to Archbishop Tomasi. He is the Papal Envoy, and he can assist you. But you must contact the Pontifical Council of Justice and Peace. Cardinal Turkson."

THE MOCCASIN TELEGRAPH

WITHIN THE INDIGENOUS world, there is an alternative network known as the Moccasin Telegraph—but that grid also exists in the NGO world, and sometimes overlaps. And one of the caminos that got me to the Vatican commenced with Sasha, a converted Rhodesian rock star, and in his own way an extraordinary man. Truth be told, I thought he had guts. He also had networks galore, ranging from the African tribes to Bono to tribal court justices to members of the Gore family and billionaire philanthropists I'd never heard of. But, one man would exercise a decisive impact upon the Long March to Rome—Bishop Riah, the Palestinian Israeli Anglican bishop who would clear the way to Rome from faraway Nazareth, birthplace of the Messiah.

I am still making my own discoveries of certain truths that only became evident long after the Long March to Rome. There is a currently popular book dividing the world between "somewheres" and "anywheres." Really what the adman who wrote the book is borrowing is the division between settlers and migrants. The perception of the world of migrants is fluid, delicate, violent, evolving, moving within a fulcrum of turbo-charged energy. Settlers are historical, rooted, constantly re-interpreting the past to fit the present.

Sacha is a fluid migrant. The central paradox of the indigenous lies in their concept of land. Land for the indigenous mind is immanent, ever-changing, delicate, prism and oracle, the entry to the innermost secrets of the gods.

Musically speaking, migrants are the "release" and settlers are the "tension" of our world, and when they remain balanced, one serves as the counterpoint for the other. I understand the conflict, being a vagabond born into a world where justice reigned as the supreme value. The oak panelling, the ritual of the courtroom, the red oak of the judge's bench, the hand-carved back walls, the witness stands, jury boxes, barristers' tables, lecterns all underline the gravitas of justice. Inspiring respect, even awe for the millennial genius of the Common law. But when lawyers have become turgid, sententious, pontifical and alas, greedy fools, when they renege on their duties towards the less privileged, the law becomes fossilized and abandons natural justice for the perks of privilege. Canada, my country also reflected this contrapuntal dilemma. The "natural governing party" had enjoyed the trappings of a political form of virtue-signalling, but beneath that, the graybeards knew that the ticket for success of the country depended upon stability, the precondition for a raw-resource based economy.

However, that was not the way things worked in this fluid, ill-contoured and constantly evolving world that I had just entered. After reading "Chains of Title," Himko Kaps Kap introduced me to a judge in the midst of the turbulent modern Indian wars of the Columbia River basin—Judge Ted Strong of the Yakama Tribal Court in Idaho. And it was Judge Strong who introduced me to Sacha, and in turn to the great Ariki, the indigenous Pope. The Yakama are another warrior nation who live in the Columbia River basis.

They rode with the Cayuse, and they hunted buffalo together. They fought alongside Sitting Bull. Himko Kaps Kap drove out to the Tribal Court of Judge Ted Strong and waited for him to emerge from his chambers, and then laid out our plan. Exposed the bare-faced treachery of the Borgias and how, upon the return of Columbus from America, Pope Alexander VI, wrongful usurper of the title of Vicar of Christ, proclaimed a Papal Bull, *Inter Caetera*, that would form the legal basis for the conquest and spoliation of the Americas. Judge Strong listened to Himko Kaps Kap, and then responded:

"This not just an idea. This is a world-changing idea."

Himko Kaps Kap later related this to me. Judge Strong had only one legal question: What is your view on laches — the doctrine that a case must be brought within a reasonable delay — an objection I thought rebutted by the fact that the offence was ongoing, and of the nature of a crime against humanity. Furthermore, the doctrine had been built into US law and had been applied as recently as 2005 in a trilogy of New York cases involving Oneida nation.

One of the greatest threats to the entire Long March to Rome was the strength of its theoretical underpinnings. The only defence offered up by the Vatican was "ancient history" and the sole defence of the US Courts was the flimsiest of notions that by purely stating that indigenous peoples were sub-humans, you could steal their land and confine them to enclaves. But, our wish to limit the scope of the mission to exposing the "manufactured inequality" that had led to the genocidal suffering of the indigenous was naïve in the extreme. Juris de jure evidence of this global treachery was unsustainable as a basis for reconciliation. Every sliver of truth merely whetted the appetite of the heirs of this ecclesiastical knavery, and with each passing day, the Moccasin telegraph reverberated with a plethora of voices seeking restoration of everything that had been pillaged, and nowhere more so than in the land of freedom. What the American tribes wanted was nothing less than melting down the gold of the Vatican.

THE SEVEN HILLS OF ROME

ON THE EAST of the river Tiber, within the walls of the present-day city of Rome, are the seven hills of Rome: Avenine, Caelian, Capitoline, Esquiline, Palatine, Quinnal and Viminal. Our plan was to have seven illustrious indigenous nations descend upon Rome simultaneously: the Maori, the Haudenosaunee, the Trails of Tears Nations, the Maya and Aztecs, the nations of south and central America and the tribes of Africa. We had no money, but we had the vision. There were some who had already succeeded in being received — from the Maya, Cree and Haudenosaunee — but there were no guarantees.

The attack would be on four fronts: a direct approach through the Papal Nuncio of Geneva, a hybrid Canadian front driven by the First Nations resolution at the Special Chiefs Assembly, a grassroots expression of legitimacy by seeking an NAIA statement representing all the tribes of the USA, a sacred element by a maximum number of hereditary chiefs, and a popular movement expressed through a worldwide petition. If any one of the above resulted in an invitation, we'd go with that, but remain faithful to the idea of a single avenue being the final road into Rome, but that anyone who made it there had a fiduciary duty towards the indigenous people of the world.

There were also networks that spanned NGOs, and in Europe particularly, associations which devoted their full time towards assisting indigenous initiatives. In addition to this, we entered into contact with the Sisters of Loretto, and other Catholic and Christian groups working towards revocation of the Papal Bulls.

In the end, the road to Rome would be opened by an incredible and unprecedented synergy — avenues opened up simultaneously but without knowledge of parallel efforts — from the Maya to the Quakers to the political backchannels, European indigenous organisations and historians. No-one held the key to Rome.

When our success became assured, those with vested interests from various quarters attempted, largely without success, to hitch their wagons to our cause. But the drawbridge came down through the efforts of a man who sat on the cusp of the world's oldest fratricidal war, born of the internecine feud between the Palestinians and the Jews. The man who was the quintessence of the contradiction and who, through his purity, saw the necessity of a solution and held several of the tendrils threading our way to Rome. That man was Bishop Riah Abu-El Essal, the Israeli Palestinian Anglican Bishop of Jerusalem. Others would lay claim to the mantle, others would work for the Long March to Rome in furtherance of their own aims. Bishop Riah was the only man who comprehended the full nature of the evil, and the need to address it at source.

Emeritus Judge Ted Strong of the Yakama court had put me in touch with Bishop Riah, and I had spoken to him briefly on Zoom. Bishop Riah wrote back to me by email the day following our conversation:

Dear David,

Greetings from Nazareth, and thank you for the information about the Papal Bulls of Discovery. Sorry for the delay in acknowledging receipt of your email. The reason is simply this: I made a little research and found out that others are on the same track, namely the Loretto Community. They too have called upon Pope Francis to rescind the Bulls of 1452 and 1493. Now that I am better informed, I join with you and all involved in the LONG MARCH TO ROME. Perhaps it may be wise to join hand with the Lorreto community. As promised, I will ask for a meeting with the Apostolic Delegate in Jerusalem, discuss the matter with him and the desire to have an audience with His Holiness Pope Francis, and wait to hear from him how best to proceed. It will not be a matter of days, but certainly not months. I will keep you updated.

Until then every good wish,

+Bishop Riah

On January 16th, shortly after our meeting, I fell across this item in the international news:

> UNITED NATIONS DECLARES THE HOLY SEE LEGALLY RESPONSIBLE AND ACCOUNTABLE TO INDIGENOUS PEOPLES FOR EFFECTS AND LEGACY OF RACIST COLONIAL BULLS AND DOCTRINES 14 January 2016 As the result of a comprehensive shadow report and presentations by members of the Apache-Nde-Nnee Working Group submitted to the United Nations (UN) Committee on the Convention on the Elimination of all forms of Racial Discrimination (CERD) for the Committee's review of the Holy See,

> the UN CERD Committee has recognized that the Doctrine of Discovery, the Holy See's *Inter Caetera* and related Papal Bulls are within the legal scope of racial discrimination under International Law and therefore require redress.

I mention this in passing, because I personally considered this study as the result of another approach. At the time, I considered it to be somewhat significant in that it illustrated that our efforts coincided with those of others worldwide. When I shared it with Bishop Riah, he responded enthusiastically:

> Dear David,
>
> Good morning. What better news than what you have kindly shared with me. The way to His Holiness Pope Francis must be wide open now.
>
> Kindly email me your phone number as I need to consult with you on how best to proceed.
>
> Kindest regards,
>
> +Bishop Riah

Our correspondence continued and on Jan 18th I received the following missive:

> His Excellency Archbishop Giuseppe Lazzarotto
>
> Apostolic Nuncio & Delegate
>
> Mount of Olives, Box 19199
>
> Jerusalem 91191
>
> Your Excellency,
>
> Re: Audience with His Holiness Pope Francis
>
> Salaam and grace from our Lord Jesus Christ, and greetings from Nazareth.

I turn again to Your Excellency, kindly, seeking your guidance and your support in the following matter.

The International Tribunal For Natural Justice, formally instituted and publicly announced on the 800th anniversary of Magna Carta at Westminster Hall in London on June 15, 2015, entrusted me with one of its divisions, namely, the "Truth & Reconciliation Commission."

As Chair of the Commission I write on behalf of the "Long March To Rome," a group I strongly support, as well as on behalf of the indigenous leaders in our Global Village, kindly requesting an audience with His Holiness Pope Francis, at which time a petition, seeking the revocation of the two papal bulls Romanus *Pontifex* (1455) and *Inter Caetera* (1493), otherwise known as the Papal Bulls of Discovery, will be presented for His favourable consideration and further action.

I will be happy, in fact honoured to personally present and discuss with you a copy of the petition. However, should you wish that I email it to your personal address I will gladly do so.

I wait to hearing from you, with my thanks in advance, and every good wish,

In Christ,

+Bishop Riah Abo El-Assal

On March 3, this arrived:

Dear David,

Thank you for the update. In response please note:

a- Between now and early May most of those within the Church will be busy with the Easter activities. I doubt whether I will be able to have another meeting with the Apostolic Delegate soon.

b- The idea was to have ten to twelve Heads to meet with the Commission at the Vatican, and/or have an audience with the Pope. Now we seem to have double if not more. Had this been left to me I would welcome all who are able to join, not only from the Heads and dignitaries, but also from the common people.

c- I wonder whether the Apostolic Delegate will succeed in setting up the meeting in early May. My previous experience: a request for such a meeting is made and then wait for the Vatican to propose dates etc.

I never lose hope. The age of miracles is not over.

Kindest regards and every good wish for Easter.

+Bishop Riah

In March, Bishop Riah forwarded a copy of the Apostolic Delegate's message:

Dear Bishop Riah,

This comes as a reply to your message of 4 March last, concerning the request on behalf of the aboriginal leaders.

As I pointed out in our conversation in Nazareth, the two Vatican documents to which they refer cannot, properly speaking, be "revoked." On the other hand, it should be clear to everyone that the Catholic Church action today is not based on those two documents any more. We have many texts of Vatican Council II that clearly state the line of action that the Church intends to follow in these matters.

As I explained to you, the schedule of the Holy Father is a very heavy one in this Jubilee Year and I am not sure that we will be able to arrange a special meeting with him for the group of leaders. Of course, I can forward the request without promising anything.

A meeting could more easily be arranged with Pontifical Council "Justice and Peace" (Cardinal Appiah Turkson). To this effect, I would need the complete list of people who would travel to Rome and the dates when they can do this.

I renew my deepest sympathy on the passing away of your cousin and in communion of prayers I am

Cordially yours in Christ

+G. Lazzarotto

Apostolic Nuncio

Bishop Riah, however, was not to be put off so easily. He had other contacts in Rome, and pursued matters right up until our arrival in Florence.

I didn't know he had his own problems, having been illegally expelled from the Diocese by his successor, Bishop Dawani, and dealing with the hostility of groups such as the Anglicans, friends of Israel. I liked him, and I liked talking to him.

Bishop Riah became for me the symbol of the Long March to Rome. I recall that, as the final weeks were approaching, two men — an Apostolic Delegate from Rome, and an Israeli Palestinian — were sitting in Nazareth, the birthplace of Jesus Christ, to discuss the impact of the Papal Bulls of Discovery. Interestingly, the Apostolic Delegate basically took the same position as the Diocese of Phoenix in 1984 — it was all ancient history. Except it wasn't for the simplest of all reasons. The Papal Bulls of Discovery were a sort of corporate playbook, and it continues to serve as the blueprint for people who are in the dubious enterprise of stealing what belongs to others — from Rio Tinto to Chinese state ventures to Pension funds investing in African mining ventures.

The Borgias were the world's first globalists. Genghis Khan had indeed covered a lot of territory, but the Borgias were the first to conceptualize the notion of creating a sub-caste of humanity to justify conquest. There was a sense among us that this was inevitable, and that even better, it was a win-win situation. It wasn't in the Church's interest to deny the confrontation of its own history. In fact, there was a parallel that would allow for an understanding of an event involving one of the other two Abrahamic religions.

The Catholic Church had in fact been hijacked in the fifteenth century by the Borgias. They were a Spanish house that used simony, bribery and murder to take control of the Holy See. And, although we're not really listening very much, in the heyday of ISIS, there was a similar pattern — intimidation, violence and the promise of gain to take control of Islamic mosques by Salafists hell-bent on world domination.

Bishop Riah was far from our only road to Rome, but our success was attracting long-time professionals in the game. In December of 2015, Bob Rae wrote to say that we needed to "engage the Canadian government in our process." I sent him a quick answer the same day:

> There are many developments at my end, and I was about to write you on this — I am engaged in ongoing discussions this week with an international indigenous caucus that is gaining in support at high levels — including Maori, other South Pacific leaders, possible participation of sub-Saharan nations, prestigious representatives of Caribbean and Central and South American indigenous and numerous US native leaders.

> I think there is a real opportunity here and am open to this development subject to a vital condition — the Long March to Rome has to be indigenous-led and it has to be publicly seen that the animus comes from the indigenous world. I don't want the Long March to Rome to become the equivalent of a Bob Geldof/Sean Penn show. But Justin Trudeau joining in with his heart as part of the Long March to Rome, perhaps alongside Perry Bellegarde, Justice Murray Sinclair, the new Justice Minister, and other leaders such as the Haida, with whom I am in contact, and other world indigenous leaders, would of course, be powerful.

But then, a day later, I had second thoughts, and sent a follow-up missive on December 18:

> I had two lengthy conversations with the Right Honourable Paul Martin last year, and another with his close friend, Archbishop Durocher of Gatineau, and can sense their hands behind this entire initiative. I anticipated that something of the sort of the Justin Trudeau announcement would be attempted. Mr. Martin asked me early on whether I knew Perry Bellegarde, so he was aware of the Special Chiefs' resolution endorsing the Long March to Rome. But the irony of the Canadian government purporting to lead this initiative will not be lost on indigenous peoples inside and outside Canada, if Trudeau insists on making it his own show.
>
> By the way, we are receiving several enquiries per day through our website from indigenous leaders, chiefs and elders, associations, NGOs, even renegade Catholic priests. The Long March to Rome has already begun. We just established a Northern Canada support

> group in NWT, including members of several first nations and a CBC media figure. I have been corresponding, just over the course of the last days, with Lakota, Haida, Ojibway, Metis, Cree, South American groups and Navajo/Dine and their participation isn't being steered by the backroom, but by their hearts. I can assure you that it is very powerful to witness first-hand. I am deeply impressed by the leaders and elders with whom I exchange in the days leading up to the Long March to Rome. New York's WNBC, APTN and other people are waiting to provide coverage.
>
> There is tremendous enthusiasm here in Europe as well.
>
> I will be in touch as soon as we are ready to go with the formal request.
>
> By the way, I deeply appreciate your support, and enjoy talking with you.

All of this was of course coming from every direction, and we were at the epicentre. It was making our lives in the Netherlands perfectly hellish. My business had come to a halt as I was spending hours throughout the day on Zoom speaking with leaders, legitimate, self-appointed, hereditary from around the world, NGOs, funders, and fielding an incredible array of offers to house the mission, which as far as the world via our website was concerned, was walking to Rome. But the core mission was moving along. It looked like the NAIA would be in our sights, and a national resolution from America to accompany the resolution of the First Nations would be powerful and impossible to ignore. But that was to ignore human nature, and the inability of some, when faced with certain success, to do everything in the power to make sure that everything implodes.

We were weeks away from the Gathering of Nations in Florence, and Hannah and I survived by going out for a daily walk in the forest nearby our home in the suburbs of Amsterdam. She had remarked that my posture was bad. We had found Enio, and Enio would make the Gathering of Nations a success.

"There's something I have to say."

"Go ahead."

"I know we're three weeks away, but I honestly don't think I can do this anymore."

"Trust me, I understand."

"It's too crazy. People are too unpredictable. They're coming at us from all directions."

"I'll just see what I can do. It's probably too dangerous for the kids."

"I'm sorry, David."

Of course, I concluded that she just was having a bad moment. She'd regret missing the trip. But now was no time to deal in hypotheticals. Not with disaster threatening on all fronts, and the near-certain prospect that there could be a crucifixion in Florence, and only one candidate for the cross.

A GREAT GIG IF YOU CAN GET INTO IT ...

I SUBMITTED "Chains of Title" to the *Canadian Journal of Native Studies*, a Brandon University review edited by a Métis poet named Lorraine Mayer. After I submitted the article, she contacted me to say that the two reviewers had vehemently opposed publication, without however providing any reasons in support. I pressed her—and she was sympathetic—for particulars, and she eventually sent me a review titled "I strongly recommend against publication," the thrust of which follows:

> "The authors also ignore the fact that the entire history of the medieval period is rife with conflict between the popes and the Kings/emperors as to supremacy. Sometimes popes had the upper hand, sometimes the secular leaders did—but neither side ever accepted the supremacy of the other's authority. The idea that any Protestant monarch is going to base his claims to land on the rejected authority of a pope simply beggars belief.

> "The authors also overlook that the late medieval period had long experience with non-Christians (Jews, Muslims, animists, pagans in Lithuania well

> into the 14thC) and persons of colour (Moors, Africans, Mongols, Indians from India as well as the fabulous peoples of the East that turn up in literature — the hairy Wild Man, the people with faces in their stomachs, one big foot ...). Encountering the other and the land they lived on did not begin in 1492."

There was no point in explaining among other things that Henry VII was not a "Protestant Monarch" but the very Catholic father of Henry VIII, married by Papal Bull, and very much deferring to both the spiritual and temporal authority of the Pope. Academia seethes with petty envy, but this reviewer didn't mind in the least showcasing his or her pig-ignorant dilettantism. So, to my eye, there was either a sizeable minority of blathering incompetents making things up as they went along, or some kind of a cronyistic clique selling a set of received ideas revolving around truth and reconciliation or it was a mix of both. In any event, "Chains of Title" stood up to criticism, and numerous readers in praised its straight-up legal examination of the US government's claim to radical title in present-day America. But it twigged my suspicions as to the nature and quality of experts in the field of aboriginal studies.

It is possible — although I have no evidence in support — that there is a fear among the Canadian establishment of just what the consequences would be to accepting our argument that the *Johnson v. M'Intosh* judgment was ill-founded under contemporary law, because it relied upon conquest and a Papal doctrine founded on the inferiority of heathen qua human beings. That fear, in my view, is well-founded, for the simple reason that *Johnson v. M'Intosh* was cited with approval by the Supreme Court of Canada in the Calder and Guerin cases, long bedrocks on the issue of aboriginal title.

So, if *Johnson v. M'Intosh* falls, so does the logic that the Canadian government holds radical title to Crown land. That's the elephant in the Canadian living room.

The fact is that, even with section 35 of the Constitution, nobody really understands what aboriginal title means. The most celebrated leading case in recent years is *Tsilhqot'in vs. The Queen*. The judgment in the case was followed by delirium throughout Tsilhqot'in territory and across the country. In the midst of celebrations, no-one seemed to care about the answer to the question: "What is aboriginal title?" And certainly, none of the honourable justices pointed out that, even where aboriginal law existed, it was subject to the rights of the beneficial holder — the Crown. And what is even less known is that the claim to radical title depends upon a notion "the assertion of sovereignty" that is rooted in *Johnson v. M'Intosh*.

Canada's fate — its very legitimacy as a nation — would appear to hinge upon an American doctrine: that of discovery born of a Faustian pact between a corrupt papacy run by the Borgias and Christian monarchs eager to divide up spoils. And the profits were derived primarily from the commerce of human beings themselves, a practice that would indicate that, if there was savagery afoot, the Christian monarchs and the papacy were more than the equal of the heathen they had relegated to inferiority.

On the European side, Willem van Genugten, Dean at Tilburg Law, chairman of the Hague Institute for International Justice and of the Committee on the Implementation of the Rights of Indigenous People of the International Law Association, had read "Chains of Title" with enthusiasm and vested it with gravitas by his approval. He wrote as follows:

> As you see it took me some time to have a look at your article. It is a very informative piece, not so much because of land title issues in general, but because of the role/views of The Vatican and the way these have been used in US case law, being the core of the article. It will definitely find a good readership!

Van Genugten had also provided six or seven suggestions for publication.

But it has to go on record that the most impressive analysis — and in the end, the most textured and the most corroborative — was that of Steven Newcomb, the senior journalist at *Indian Country Today*, the US indigenous outlet with 400,000 readers monthly. Newcomb is no ordinary man. If he were not indigenous, the world would know of him otherwise. He also enjoys a vice-grip over indigenous minds, who are reverential in their deference to him. Nothing survives in the indigenous world of the US or the UN without Steven Newcomb vetting it.

There's plenty about Steven's modus operandi I disagree with, but on the facts, his read of history is the most accurate, and the Vatican rightly fears him, not because he is a radical, but because they are sticking to a position that it knows is historically indefensible — that the Papal Bulls are "ancient history" and abrogated by the Papal Bull Sublimus Deus, a position they know is patently false.

As for Steven Newcomb, he would ultimately join the ranks of the Long March to Rome and leave his indelible mark. So, everything seemed to be happening at once. The world of Canadian academia — that was promoting either Truth & Reconciliation or other factitious inventions such as "Aboriginal Common Law" was censoring us. Himko

Kaps Kap, in the highest of implied tributes, had suggested I add his name as an author to the piece, a form of flattery I was forced to decline on cultural grounds.

Leaders and the non-indigenous activist world—from rock stars to daughters of ex-Presidents—were in contact, beating the digital door down to hitch their name to our wagon heading to Rome. It seemed for a time that the entire world was latching onto the cause, but the constant digital inflow increased our febrility and our sense of precarity. It was a matter of time before we cracked. The only question was when.

As Spring advanced, we seemed unable to see and enjoy our daily walks anymore in the Netherlands despite unprecedented good weather. I was spending my days with a passionate, humorous but fierce Maya named Quetzal Tzab, a former windsurfing champion of Mexico who had turned to activism, and evenings with Ariki, who was initiating me into the Maori thinking, or with the non-indigenous activists, heads of a series of think tanks and with major funders, none of whom appeared to be willing to front money without a commensurate surrender of control over the agenda.

And then, Phil Lane Jr., the ultimate hybrid of global warrior and self-designated hereditary chief, appeared on our horizon. Member of the Ihanktonwan Dakota and Chickasaw Nation, self-published author of the "Four Worlds International Institute," and a man who loved portraits of himself challenging the powers that be. When Lane Jr. parachuted in, he announced that "when I get involved, I do it in a big way," something we would learn within a couple of days of his arrival.

Repeatedly, Hannah and I reminded each other that our best guarantor of personal safety was to take no money, which of course ensured our financial ruin in the middle term, and to insist that we were answerable to an indigenous leadership whose contours fluctuated by the hour and covered countries on every continent. There was no other way, but our serenity was being stretched, feeling like an increasingly thin tarpaulin, sheltering us less and less from winds over which we had no control.

A lovely woman named Velma Whittington, Fort McMurray #468 First Nation Cree member, contacted us, as did an alliance of Navajo women known as the Indigenous sisters. Velma wished to bring a group of Cree survivors of the Residential School system — about twenty of them, with a traditional drum, and their inclusion was a formidable addition to those prepared to go. The Cree, Velma explained to me, particularly the northern Cree, were shy and only needed the opportunity to forgive, and had no interest in retribution.

Within days of the Long March to Rome delegation's scheduled arrival in Italy, the entire Cree delegation from Fort MacMurray disappeared, and my calls to Velma no longer returned.

Only hours later, on May 1st, during the Gathering of Nations, while we waited in Florence for word of our visit to Rome, disaster struck. On May 1, 2016, a wildfire began southwest of Fort McMurray, Alberta. On May 3, it swept through the community, forcing the largest wildfire evacuation in Alberta's history, with upwards of 88,000 people forced from their homes. It was Canada's greatest natural catastrophe ever.

I liken the timeline to the fire as coinciding identically with the timeline of the Long March to Rome and the peril that accompanied our every step. The fire broke out while we descended upon Rome, and spread across approximately 590,000 hectares (1,500,000 acres). It was declared to be under control on July 5, 2016, the date of the Assembly of First Nations annual meeting in Canada, where no mention was made of the meeting, despite the AFN being a principal backer of the mission.

It continued to smoulder, and was fully extinguished on August 2, 2017, on or about the date that Bob Rae parachuted into Rome to confer with Archbishop Tomasi and ensure that the Papal Bulls were deemed to be "ancient history," and everyone back in "turn-the-page" mode. The problem had been solved, and evil, like a cooling ember, was under control ready to flame again at another time and place yet to be determined.

ENIO

... **CAME OUT OF** nowhere, and the Creator sent him. Enio ran a free-love/indigenous-worshipping cult on the outskirts of Florence. Charles Manson minus the axe murdering. A place called Bagno a Ripoli, a Tuscan camp for runaway Italian girls who could engage in indigenous communion, Tuscan version, with Enio in exchange for free lodging in an RV he kept on the premises.

Enio appeared on Zoom one day. The other actors on the Zoom stage that day were Sacha, a former rock star — white — from Zimbabwe; Christina, a new age crony of Bono running a corporate makeover gig called Fountainhead after Ayn Rand; Al Gore's daughter; and a Sioux woman running a wellness centre with about a zillion followers down in California. Plus a Hispanic couple out of New York. Plus a recent and dangerous entry, the great, international shit-disturber supremo, Phil Lane Jr., and then, miraculously, Enio. I pretexted a bad connection, and signed off before Phil could do his protracted Choctaw/Cherokee screech of a prayer, and sent a private email to Enio, asking for his phone number.

"Enio, I've got a mission where you can put your name down on the history rolls."

"I'm listening, man."

"This is big, Enio."

"The Long March is big, a big thing."

"This could be even bigger. I'm talking a Gathering of Nations, Enio."

"Gathering of Nations. I like the sound of that man."

"I'm talking an invitation to every single delegate nation to show up at your place first."

"Like a fucking ambush."

"You got it. Descending from the seven hills of Rome. These guys have no idea how big or how small we are."

"So, how big are we?"

Enio, the man. We, he says.

"Somewhere between six and sixty thousand. Depending on whether the Maoris show up."

Enio paused.

"I saw all this in a dream. The indigenous leaders of the world descending from the skies on Bosco di Sacro. All of us holding hands."

"You're the man, Enio."

"I'll need money to do this. To receive them properly."

"We'll get you some money."

"How much?"

"Enough for some repairs to the site. We're not rich."

"Let's not talk about money today, my friend. Let's talk about the dream.

CLOSING THE DEAL

ON APRIL 28th, a Thursday, we arrived in Florence, with the other leaders scheduled to arrive over the coming days. Our plan was to hold some kind of ceremony, and I had done my best to warn everyone that the Vatican was not necessarily ready to meet with us. Ariki, the Maoris, the King of Hawaii, Charmaine Whiteface had withdrawn. Tiokasin Ghosthorse had stipulated he wanted nothing to do with drug addicts, without saying who the drug addicts were. Anyways, that was a secondary issue for me.

Quetzal Tzab and a retinue of African leaders were no-shows. Beatrice Long Visitor Holy Dance had given a moving show of support by video prior to passing on to the next world. Ariki Tohunga Te Wairemana, representing Aotearoa and certain South Pacific islands as Ariki, Tohunga in the spiritual realm of the Atua, had withdrawn his support along with a retinue of Maoris. Chief Phil Lane Jr, Ihanktonwan Dakota & Chickasaw nations, Chairman & Global Trustee-United Religions Initiative and the Four Worlds International Institute was busy persuading the Cree that Rome is too far for an aging delegation. Roberto "Mukaro Aguelbana" Borrero, Chief Damon Corrie, ISAU of the Bariria OROBAHADO LOKONO (Eagle Clan Arawaks) of Guyana Full-blooded descendant of Princess Marian

(b. 1879, d. 1928) the only surviving child of Hereditary Paramount Chief AMOROTAHE HAUBARIRIA—last full-blooded ruler of the ancient nobility (b. 1822, d. 1899) was incommunicado.

Judge Ted Strong, Chief Judge Emeritus, Yakama Nation, former Clinton appointee, Pablo Huaiquilao Huincaman Mapuche Werken (Traditional Tribal leader), from Pitrufquen, Chile. Loretta Afraid of Bear Cook and Barbara Dullknife of the Lakota Elders, were on their way. Theresa Two Bulls and Mila Yellow Hair were not. Shannon Rivers, Akimel O'otham Elder, Gila River Indian Community, was behind LMR, but couldn't make it.

The Indigenous Sisters, a Navajo-led international solidarity movement to advance the causes of indigenous women, would be represented by Belinda Ayze, on behalf of her sisters, Weyakpa Najin Win, Woman stands shining, Holy Earth Surface Walker, Life-Bringre, Life-Bearer and Big Mountain and Black Mesa resistant Louise Benally.

There were many others, from the Mapuche nations, the Sami, the Cayuse, the Haida, and particularly the Haudenosaunee, the Lenape, the Simpcw nation especially represented by ex-Chief Keith Matthew. Those people came to Florence on belief alone. They came with the prayers of their peoples. Some came because they said in our presence during those marvellous, volcanic days that they had already been to the Vatican, and had already met the Pope, but that this was just the playing out of what had already been.

As they arrived, my fears and certainty that I might die during these last days out of pure necessity subsided, and was replaced by a certainty that this would happen, that it had to happen.

The day prior to arrival, I received news that someone named Michael Hill was coming instead of Charmaine Whiteface. Hill was apparently an Apache, who had something to do with the UN Apache report. And Arthur Manuel, the indigenous Nelson Mandela, author of *Whose Land Is It Anyway? A Manual for Decolonization* had said he might "drop in" and then only six months later would suddenly die, like so many others. It was difficult to predict — the entire participation of people was like a shimmering veil, behind which the silhouettes of the indigenous were visible, without anything more than their contours discernible.

On Thursday, from our Tuscan hideaway, I phoned the Vatican, realizing that we had to get through and come up with something, at least a priest, or this was going to end badly. I decided to phone a nun I had come to establish a rapport with, Sister José de Maria de Jesus, one of the staff at the Pontifical Council for Justice and Peace, who usually responded to my calls by saying she would pass my message on to "her superiors." But now I had to have an answer. I still wasn't sure of anything, but dialled Palazzo San Pietro, and she picked up the line.

"Look, Sister, I need to talk to Archbishop Tomasi."

"Yes, something must be done."

"Oh, let's not worry about that. There's another problem ..."

"What?"

"Once these people get together, they're literally capable of anything. May I ask you a question?"

"Of course."

"When I landed in Florence, and I drove through the city, and up to the estate where we are staying, I looked up and saw the Tuscan sky, the turquoise and pastel sky. Do you know what I thought?"

"No," she replied softly.

"Flight. My first reaction was to flee. To leave these indigenous leaders to their own devices."

"Oh ..."

"I don't know whether I briefly lost my senses. But I couldn't help reflecting that it is really not my problem."

"..."

"... not my problem," I repeated.

"Momento."

After a moment, I heard a male voice.

"Good day, Mr MacKinnon. This is Archbishop Tomasi."

"Your excellency."

"How may I assist you?"

"I won't keep you long. There's been a rather fractious split in the delegation."

"A split."

"A breakaway faction. These things are not unusual with the indigenous. There are warrior nations and there are peacekeepers."

"I see."

"The breakaway portion wants to create a disturbance in St. Peter's Square."

The Archbishop remained silent for several moments.

"That will be difficult. Security is tight."

"The difficulty only encourages some of them. These are warriors, your excellency. There is a god of chaos in the indigenous world. The messier it gets, the happier they are. I can assure you, they are in their comfort zone. The Maoris, the Choctaws, the Maya. They want to march on Rome, with media in tow."

"What are they seeking?"

An opening. *They.*

"There's talk of melting down all the gold in the Sistine Chapel."

"I'm not sure. Logistically ..."

"They're very resourceful."

"Where are you?"

"Florence."

"Wait."

I heard a low discussion between Sister Jesus di Maria and his Excellency in Italian, then the return of the Archbishop on the phone.

"I have an hour next Wednesday."

"We need four."

"Two. Not a minute more."

THE SWEAT LODGE

ON SUNDAY MAY 2nd, everyone had arrived. One of the arrivals was Michael Hill. He had contacted me out of the blue, and said that he was being sent on behalf of Charmaine Whiteface of the Lakota Sioux. He was funny, and very engaging. JoDe Goudy, Chairman of the Yakama Nation, had also come. And Kenneth Deer, secretary of the Mohawk nation. We were placed in a circle around a burning fire, and each leader told personal stories of his or her suffering, preceded and followed by prayers and songs. It was quite extraordinary.

At the same time, tension was running very high. I had been a tuning fork for everything that could possibly go right or wrong, and now that we were on the verge of success, the atmosphere was electric. But within that tension, something was happening. We heard everything that day—about Ethiopia, about the uranium under the ground in the Black Hills, about children getting pins pushed through their tongue to "kill the Indian in the child."

Part way through the proceedings, a husky, tight-lipped pony-tailed man arrived and all eyes were upon him as he approached the circle where proceedings were underway. Dr. Kassahun Berhanu, the Ethiopian leader, was explaining the manner in which land grabs worked to the detriment of his people, but all eyes were riveted on the arrival. Steven

Newcomb had come fully equipped with a tripod, sophisticated camera equipment, and immediately began filming everyone, but remaining quiet. Whatever anybody else is in the indigenous world, Steven Newcomb stood apart, above, and as we would soon learn, viewed himself as both the guarantor of the purity of the indigenous message and a law unto himself. I still can only properly frame him in terms of the characters of the French revolution. There was much of Camille Desmoulins, the fiery editor of *Le Vieux Cordelier* in the pre-terror days. There was more than a resemblance to Robespierre in his uncompromising positions and I suspect that if it came down to it, there might be some Marat in the man. If Kenneth Deer was a Girondin, Newcomb was a Montagnard. His turn arrived to speak, and he talked about the Doctrine of Discovery, and how what had clearly been Christian discovery of America, conquest based on Vatican script, became airbrushed out of history. People had forgotten just how the world had been discovered and taken from the indigenous, and Steven Newcomb was there to remind them of the truth.

Since Friday, the meeting with the Pontifical Council for Justice and Peace had been confirmed for Monday in a hotel conference room. The leaders returned to their hotel, but Enio had been talking of a sweat lodge he had set up for them, and they enthusiastically accepted.

* * *

On Monday, May 3rd, we held the meeting at the hotel in Florence. The night before there had been a sweat lodge, and although we were privy to none of it, a look in the eyes of many of the delegates upon arrival in the morning at the hotel telegraphed that it didn't bode well for either Hannah or myself. At the beginning of the meeting, I spoke for a minute or two on organisational issues. Loretta Afraid of Bear Cook raised her hand to speak, and I yielded the floor.

"Barbara Dry Bones and I wish to say that Steven Newcomb speaks for us today."

Michael Hill concurred. On my right hand side were Kenneth Deer and Willie Littlechild. The American tribes — heavily weighted in favour of the Lakota Sioux, were about to make their play. Steven Newcomb was typing into a laptop and all eyes followed the editor of *Indian Country Today*. He finished his typing. I do not yield the floor to him because he has asked for it. I do so because it is a foregone conclusion.

"Steven?"

"What right do you have to come in and filibuster this entire process? You're not indigenous. This is our fight. You shouldn't even be here."

At this point, Kenneth Deer and Willie Littlechild have closed their eyes and appear to be sleeping.

"Uhh, that's an interesting point. Any thoughts? I'll be back in a moment, but I'm here to serve, and happy to hear what the consensus is on bringing this forward and preparing for the meeting."

I stepped outside into the corridor. Hannah was waiting there.

"Something's going on."

"I think Steven Newcomb, and I imagine a few others, want to take over the Long March to Rome."

"I'm not surprised. What are you going to do about it?"

"I'm going to give it to them."

"Totally agree."

I turned back and returned to the room, smiling and sat down. For the next half hour, I watched the other leaders buckle under. Herson Huinca Puitrin, the Mapuche delegate, spoke no English, and Dr. Berhanu, the Ethiopian had returned to Africa, further tilting the balance towards a dominant North American bias. The Lakota Sioux through Loretta Afraid of Bear Cook had already surrendered their vote to Steven. And the delegates from north of the 49th appeared to be in "wait and see" mode. I asked for the floor.

"This is remarkable. We have waited for this moment when we could pass off the reins of the Long March to Rome to the indigenous leadership. If I can be of any service in assisting you, please don't hesitate to ask. Congratulations. Maybe it's time for a break to absorb the significance of this extraordinary moment."

I stepped out in the hallway, where the hotel lounge served coffee and snacks. Steven Newcomb spotted me and approached.

"I guess that was a bit confrontational on my part."

"Oh, not to worry. You people have suffered enough indignities. But you do have a point. We really have no place in the discussion."

"Well, you do actually."

"Actually not. Look, I'll be honest. You can't really undertake this without becoming attached to the cause. But it probably is a good time for a reality check."

He didn't say anything, just watched. It was odd. He could say the most radical things, but you didn't see aggression when you looked in his eyes.

"From the outset our sole goal has been to get you — all of you — to a table with some Vatican officials on the other side. Nobody in between. Anyways, let's go back in. Just think of me from here on in as a protocol officer."

Newcomb didn't say anything. He was a curious combination of qualities. But I'd put him up against anyone in a fight. He was tough. Once inside, I felt there had been some discussion about things, and Keith Matthew was to confirm that.

"I'd like to ensure that David comes with us as a Corporate Secretary. I think we'll need him in that capacity. If he's willing to accept."

"Well, I'd be pleased to come," I said, "but not to speak on your behalf. That defeats the whole purpose of the mission. Steven was direct, but I want to be clear. He was right." I added, by way of an afterthought: "Something just occurred to me."

I didn't say anything for a moment. I was learning.

"You do realize how Archbishop Tomasi will be receiving you."

Silence.

"With a short prayer and a blessing."

No-one said anything.

"In other words, imposing upon you the Christian prayer without regard for you."

I let that sink in.

"It's pretty serious," said Keith.

"There is only one way to respond to this."

"Of course."

"With a prayer of your own. What about the Yakama hymn you were chanting in Bagno a Ripoli yesterday, Chairman JoDe?"

This was met with great enthusiasm. The chant of the Yakama, a bell-ringing cacophony of shouts, threats, grimaces and bell-ringing would be the delegation response to Tomasi's prayer. My work was done. I only had to return to our hilltop retreat and drink a couple of bottles of wine, lay in the pool and stare at the Tuscan sky. Or so I thought at the time. In twenty-four hours, we would be in Rome. The earth seemed to be moving beneath our feet, and it felt as if only the Creator could save us now.

THE BLUEPRINT FOR DISCOVERY

THE CANADIAN GOVERNMENT is haunted by two issues affecting indigenous north of the 49th, and that just will not go into that good night: the Indian Residential School issue and that of missing Aboriginal women. It is the former that cuts across the political, social and economic spheres like a swathe, because it is based upon a vile trope, that it is necessary to "kill the Indian in the child," implying that the existential and cultural essence of an aboriginal is something to be erased. It is a tragic issue, it resonates, but it is only one of a pleiade of indigenous tragedies around the world, each of which can be traced back to the Papal Bulls of Discovery. The UN estimates there are 370 million indigenous worldwide, representing over 5000 ethnic groups.

The goal of the Long March to Rome was both single-minded in its focus on the "blueprint for discovery" and broad in its implications, as the Papal Bulls were the enabling statute that legitimized the issuance of letters patent to the Cabots, who are credited with discovery of the Americas. To the extent possible, we also wanted to keep independent of politics or other considerations. It astounds me to this day that we didn't, or rather I didn't face up to the patent absurdity of considering that to be a reasonable expectation. It was exposing a flank without any hope of avoiding a debacle.

Canada also had its vulnerabilities, but they would only emerge in the 21st century as a result of processes that had begun in the 20th century and earlier. But there were unhealthy desires — the desire not to be good, but to be seen to be good. The desire not to be seen as American. The desire to deal with our past differently. But, because of our hubris, we failed to see some of the ironies staring us in the face. The first core reality of Canada is that it is a colony, but the fact that its faces were predominantly white until the 1990s cast a veil over the fact that we were no less a colony than African countries, particularly those who had been "decolonized" rather than opting for a revolution and a republic.

Somehow in the Canadian mind we still cultivate our complex that we are superior to the Americans — brave but without the racism. It is our greatest taboo, that we are instinctively not just good, but better than those south of the 49th. It is a taboo of recent vintage, our humble forefathers not having yet acquired the modern label of hubris. Yet, at the same time, we were burying the history of our soldiers, the very guarantors of our freedom. Something of our martial achievements, unrivalled in the world, was shunned by the ruling classes.

Other myths sprang up, that of a "natural governing party," that of multiculturalism and diversity. Of a Scandinavian sense of social justice. Hubris was the prevailing theme and would be embedded in the form of the 1982 Charter of Rights and Freedoms and section 35 that would grant supra-constitutional protection to aboriginal rights. That Pandora's Box would eventually become untenable, and now, the country is in a legal and political shamble, but one that no-one dares acknowledge.

All of this was done of course without much mention of Canada's historic role in dealing with its First Nations. It's odd, because in the beginning, they truly were treated as autonomous nations. That changed during a successive entrenchment of policies that more closely mirrored the American approach of "civilizing" indigenous peoples, and drawing them away from their collective notions of society:

> Thus, the old military partnership between British regular forces, Canadian militia, and Indian warriors was to be refashioned, and in its place, Imperial authorities, local officers of the British Indian department, and missionaries would work together to ensure the growth of Christian civilization among the "barbarous" and unsettled tribes of the Canadas[1].

This policy — and that of refusing rights of ownership to Canada's indigenous — was born directly of the Papal Bulls and the notion that non-Christians were barbarians. The Canadian government's approach — a truth and reconciliation commission à la South Africa, was what it was. Canada is not that different from Africa — the overriding issue is getting resources to market without being caught in a squeeze by multinationals or China or the US or all of the above. Reconciliation was about getting resources to market, and if truth had to be compromised along the way, well so be it.

While in Quebec, although always careful to not join the sovereignist cause, living side-by-side with nationalists

1. Leslie, John F., Commissions of Inquiry into Indian affairs in the Canadas, 1828–1858: Evolving a corporate memory for the Indian department, Indian and Northern Affairs Canada, February, 1985, p. 25.

left an enduring impression upon me. They had assumed I was a federalist, just "*pas comme les autres.*" Although I refused to state it, the fact was that I was more than sympathetic to the idea of Quebec sovereignty, and today believe they'd be better off to dictate their own terms of independence. And, I had seen the clear evidence through my research into 19th century history in Quebec and at the Sorbonne of the role of the Catholic Church in keeping the Québécois from political and social emancipation. The other was the tactic of the federal government to constantly reach accommodations rather than discuss root causes of discontent.

In the end, the Vatican held a position not that far from their original one—that the doctrine characterizing the indigenous as barbarians was "ancient history" and the indigenous had to work with the bishops if they wanted to get anywhere. End of story.

ANCIENT HISTORY

The Chiefs were extremely gracious. The Vatican, as always, remained silent. Bob Rae was convinced "there would be bumps" but remained hopeful. I felt like the hunchback of Notre Dame. I'd nearly brought ruination and even worse upon my own family for a cause that was not my own. "Sir," Niall said at the breakfast table the day following our return, breaking our silence. "Yes, sir." "Sir, no more big ideas." "Promise, Niall. No more big ideas."

Chief Littlechild wrote the kindest of letters, as did Chairman JoDe Goudy. An article appeared on the Aboriginal Peoples TV Network and in the *Khanawake News*. But it was Chief Littlechild's missive that touched our hearts and reassured us that it hadn't been entirely mad to bring this mission to Rome:

> Thanks to you and your family it was very historic and important. What you have done together for us will forever be etched in my memory. Words cannot truly express my gratitude for your persistence. It allowed me on behalf of the Truth and Reconciliation Commission of Canada to present our Calls to Action in particular those relating to the role of the Catholic Church, the Papal Bulls, the Doctrine of Discovery and Terra Nullius

and how important it is for Pope Francis to visit Canada in that regard. As you know these are directly related to the Indian Residential School history and legacy. There is apparent willingness for the need to continue working on these matters together to continue the good arguments presented today that could impact the actions of the Holy See because they are having ongoing impacts. That is a very positive signal for the "Long Road to Rome" as to the need to continue its work. For the TRC of Canada it gave me an opportunity to re-submit our Calls to Action directly to the Pontifical Council for which I am very thankful as it allowed us to direct focus on the role of the Catholic Church in this Residential Schools' history and legacy. So it was good in our objective of starting a process, inviting the Pope to Canada, and an added important issue of repatriation of sacred items of Indigenous Peoples. So, on my behalf and those I represent thank you, your wife and children and your colleagues for all your help. May the Great Spirit watch, bless and guide you!

Chief Willie Littlechild

That letter came on May 4th, the day of the visit. Bob Rae sent out his congratulations on the same day:

Willie,

As you may know, I did some background stickhandling to help set up the meeting in Rome. David sent me your e-mail and I was delighted to hear about the discussion, and for your very generous tribute to David.

Onward and upward!

Bob Rae

Not for the first time, I sat back and looked at this for what it was. Our mandate was not to settle a political problem for the Canadian government or to advance a reconciliation agenda. It was to put the Vatican four-square in front of a few people who for the ends of the mission, were representing 370 million people worldwide. There are 1.5 million indigenous in Canada, and they had some nasty things done to them by the government of Canada just as indigenous worldwide had been deprived of their fundamental rights by settler governments. I sympathized with them. My own grandfather was strapped daily for speaking Gaelic, and that within a few decades of the Highland clearances, an act of cultural genocide and spoliation equal to that suffered by the indigenous. But I never confused the fate of my clan with the indigenous, and never assumed either that the Canadian problems were the sum total of the wrongs done by Christian monarchs and the explorers acting under the seal of the Pope. And, I learned through the Long March to Rome an overriding truth that prevents a resolution of this issue—the fact that the world, as far as the indigenous are concerned, has been governed by a sort of invisible Balfour declaration—their very boundaries imposed by men in far off places who had never even seen their lands. And to this day, Canadian politicians equate indigenous politics with solely those indigenous north of the 49th, when major nations such as the Haudenosaunee see things in a broader, transnational light.

Rae had informed me only a month earlier that there was no way he could guarantee a meeting with Cardinal Turkson, the President of the Pontifical Council for Justice and Peace. Clearly, the conspiracy between Church and government wasn't quite as tight as the activists believed. From my standpoint, if the government was so cozy with Rome, they wouldn't have stooped to asking to become part of the Long March to Rome. So, the success of the Rome trip presented a problem. It was a problem with a simple solution, but alas, when one party has to get resources to market in an extraction economy and has shot itself in the foot by creating a Pandora's box of ill-defined, fluid aboriginal rights and the second "co-conspirator" is still hanging onto the idea that the Pope is infallible, more stickhandling was inevitable.

On June 28, I received the next missive addressed to myself, Chiefs Ed John and Grand Chief Willie Littlechild. The letter spoke of reaching out to a priest who was a member of the Pontifical Council's secretariat, and of a meeting he'd had with Archbishop Tomasi. Among other things, there was some discussion of a possible Papal visit, and I'm taking the liberty to quote a small portion of this letter since the proposed 2017 visit never took place, if only to evidence the extent to which the main parties in the drama were looking in the same direction at the same time for the briefest of moments during Summer 2016.

> Friends,
>
> The Archbishop says that letters are being prepared for Cardinal Turkson's signature in response to the letters and documents they received during and after the visit in late April/May.
>
> There is a chance that Pope Francis will visit Canada in 2017, he has received an invite from Mr. Trudeau, and the Mayor of Montreal, Denis Coderre. In preparation for the visit, the Archbishop signalled that discussions needed to begin on the Pope's response to the process of reconciliation proposed in the Truth and Reconciliation Commission report.
>
> If the Pope comes, there would then be an

> opportunity for an official response, which will require some preparatory work and dialogue.
>
> If the Pope cannot come, there is a suggestion of a conference in Rome in 2017, to be followed by an official response from the Pope. This would also involve some dialogue.
>
> I personally see these developments as very positive. The Archbishop emphasized that the Vatican has wholly endorsed the UN Declaration on the Rights of Indigenous People, and that the Papal Bulls and the Doctrine of Discovery are "ancient history" and of no 'current effect.'
>
> He hoped that with a focus on the Sinclair Commission and its recommendations it would be possible to find a "good path."
>
> He also emphasized that the Canadian Council of Bishops would need to be involved in any dialogue, as well as the Secretariat in Rome and the Papal Nuncio in Ottawa.
>
> Warm regards to all. We are making progress.

About a week later, the annual Assembly of First Nations meeting was held in Canada. I contacted Keith Matthew in its aftermath to see how they had received news of the successful mission, as former chief Matthew represented their interests in Rome by special mandate and under the Special Chiefs resolution.

"It's stale news, David."

"Stale news? You waited 523 years, and six weeks after the meeting, it's stale news?"

"Yup."

I ran the news past Hannah.

"I'm not surprised."

"Well, neither am I. Still, it's disappointing."

"David, Bob Rae is a politician and he works for a law firm specializing in aboriginal law. Honestly, what did you expect? Mother Teresa?"

"I didn't expect Talleyrand."

"You give the man too much credit. Actually, from a political standpoint, you could do a lot worse than Bob Rae. Read his letter."

"I've read it."

"No, you haven't. You've broken the lawyer's first rule of survival — getting emotionally involved with your client. Say what you like about Bob Rae, he doesn't make that mistake. Read the letter."

"You're actually saying he's right."

"Well, to coin the cliché, he's reaching out, isn't he? He reached out to the Vatican; he reached out to the Truth & Reconciliation Commission and to individual leaders. He even reached out to you. Sorry, Mr. President, but on the political level, it's pretty irreproachable."

"Private gig."

"David, I love you, but you and I both know that's quasi-delusional rubbish."

Every single thing that has ever been said about the Dutch is true. They're reasonable, logical and literal. It may be the one thing I still know.

"David, please. For our sake, take a step back."

"Well, maybe they can use an adviser. Consultancy."

"I think that's a poor idea."

"Why?"

"Do I have to elaborate?"

"Yes."

"Well, you'll be transforming yourself into a beggar at your own banquet."

"It's too late."

I showed an email I'd sent to Bob earlier in the day.

> On the basis of the May 4th letter, it seems to me that a logical first step would be a response formulated by the AFN and/or the TRC, signed by Murray Sinclair, Willie Littlechild, Ed John at the very least, welcoming the overture in the August 1st letter in general terms, and inviting Archbishop Tomasi and His Holiness Pope Francis to come and hear stories and testimony first-hand about the effects of the Papal Bulls in Canada, details to be worked out by the respective delegations.
>
> Given that the Long March to Rome has been the platform for communication to date, and that your support has been crucial in vesting the mission with gravitas and dignity, I suggest that you and I jointly could write the cover letter to accompany their response.

"Jesus, David, you're kowtowing to the man. Show me his reply."

"Just look beneath; it's in the same thread."

> I think the Canadian "leadership" has to take charge. That includes the people you've named. And the next, immediate step of engagement is with the Canadian Council of Bishops.

She whistled.

"He's a politician all right."

"It's actually simple. Drop him a thank you note. Say you couldn't agree more. That you're looking forward to hearing from the Canadian 'leadership'. And David..."

"Yea, I know. Don't respond to his email."

I typed out the email in front of her.

Thank you very much for your note, Bob. I'm looking forward to hearing from the Canadian "leadership".

Best regards,

David

"Ready?"

"Ready."

As I clicked *Send*, I thought back to the remark of the Vancouver solicitor at the outset of this adventure — that Aboriginal politics was a great gig if you could get into it. Even better if you can get out of it. And this was our chance. It was no secret in my own home. I needed something like this to happen or I'd never loosen my shackles, but that email saved me. And things did calm down eventually. There were a couple of good articles in *Indian Country Today* and in the *Kahnawake News* but people had gone back to their lives. Harvard University was eager. Under the direction of Pierre Bélanger, Associate Professor of Landscape Architecture, a group of students at the Harvard Graduate School of Design were researching resource extraction as it relates to territory and urbanization. Their primary focus was on Canada's extraction industry, which, as they had rightly observed, has a long history of Indigenous subjugation and, not coincidentally, is the most productive mining country in the world. That had been our hope from the outset — that people would see that the issuance of the Papal Bulls as a corporate strategy, using a device — a manufactured inequality — to steal land and resources. And then we returned to our day-to-day lives. And there was another benefit, one that was painful, and which I observed during our daily debriefings on the Long March to Rome.

"We're lucky to see firsthand that both the Vatican and the Canadian government were willing to fudge the truth on the existence of the Papal Bulls. When push came to shove, they reverted to denial."

"They didn't fudge the truth, David. They shaped it. So, give it back straight. But then let it go. It's not your domain. You're a writer."

"I admit it's an addiction and I'm no more immune than the other fanatics. It's a recurrent desire to see the thing through. Not terribly rational.

"David, do I have to repeat myself?" she replied, yet somehow, after everything that had occurred, still reining in her exasperation, "there's nothing whatsoever to see through except for *him*. I can guess, but tell me, how did he react?"

"He said 'For my part, I'd always presumed *all of this* was pro bono.'"

Hannah laughed. *Men*, that laugh seemed to say. All of us.

"He would say that, wouldn't he?"

"Nothing more to say?"

"Well, what is there to add? Something witty on Greeks bearing gifts?"

In Autumn 2017, a retired Catholic priest, Father John Tritschler, contacted me by email from Maple Ridge, British Columbia:

> I am a retired priest of the Archdiocese of Vancouver and presently residing at St. Pat's, Maple Ridge. As I have done on four previous occasions, so last winter I spent serving the people of the Sahtu, NWT. While I was there Bishop Mark Hagemoen, whose mother

incidentally died a few days ago, emailed me the attached email.

I am writing an extensive article on the attempts to harmonize the Catholic Church and the Native people of Canada. I would like to use in my article extracts of the attached emails relating to the Doctrine of Discovery and Terra Nullius and your organizing of the walk to Rome, Would you give me permission to use extracts from the Letter of Archbishop Tomasi to yourself and your letter to Bishop Crosby relating to the Long March to Rome?

Peace,
Fr. John Tritschler

Father John didn't need to know about the fistfight that broke out between two of the chiefs following the meeting with the Pontifical Council, and he didn't need to know about the prolonged war prayer of the Yakama ringing out in the hallowed halls of the Pontifical Council, while ringing bells and performing a Yakama war dance, or that Loretta Afraid of Bear Cook called Tomasi out and said she didn't like him, or that Michael Hill had chosen to speak extempore on clandestine Vatican operations tracking aliens he had discovered on Apache lands. Although I think he would have agreed with me, they weren't antics, but the damaged expression of the unspeakable wrongs committed against the indigenous.

"I've learned a lot through the Long March to Rome," he said during a phone conversation after he'd finished his last draft of the article.

"So have I."

"Do feel any responsibility yourself?"

"Only a priest could ask such a question. No, wait a minute, let me try to answer that. I actually do feel responsible for a lot of the things I've done in life and even some I haven't done. But not this. It's in a league of its own."

"I was just curious."

"Sure, I know. But I think we're a long way from this harmony you talk about in your paper. Harmony is just not on the indigenous agenda. It's a top-down, federally-imposed agenda."

"And I'm not so sure it's reconciliation the indigenous are after. I never thought it was a workable concept in the first place. I would never reconcile with the Christian Brothers after what they did to my friends. Why would any truly free indigenous person want to reconcile with the Church or the Canadian government? They haven't changed at all, really. And don't think I've gone native either. These Ottawa people and Vatican people will stoop to virtually anything to keep their game going. That's my final conclusion."

"You sound disappointed."

"I never thought I'd say this, but you're right. I am disappointed. All Tomasi had to do was say yes, we admit it."

"You know all this talk about apologies?"

"Sure. Trudeau keeps bringing it up."

"Well, the bishops don't feel much like apologizing anymore."

"I don't think anybody should apologize. The notion is obscene. You know I met some of the real leaders, not the propped-up strawmen of the AFN. The ones that show their wounds openly. They talk about a lot of things but reconciliation isn't one of them."

"Well, what do they want then?"

"Funny, you're the first priest I've ever heard ask that

question. Isn't it odd that in over five hundred years, nobody has ever asked the indigenous what they want? Why do you suppose that is?"

"Well, what do they want?"

"They want restoration."

"Of what?"

"Everything. Plus interest and interest on interest. They actually do want to melt down the gold of the Vatican."

"Well, that's not going to wash."

"Oh, we're back to cleanliness, are we?"

"I'm going back to my pastoral work. Let's just render unto Caesar what is Caesar's, shall we?"

"I'm with you on that, Father."

"Peace, my friend."

It was only after I hung up the phone that I recalled that I had a recording of the two-hour session between the indigenous and Tomasi that I had never properly listened to. Now, how did I forget about that?

We corresponded for about a year after that, and he didn't run for cover on the issue of the Church's responsibility. But one of his letters clarified a point I think gets to the nub of the matter for Canada:

> The mistake of forbidding native language to be spoken in residential schools, and the removal of native children from their homes was federal government policy and Church members who staffed the schools, clergy and laity, followed that policy in the administration of the schools.

SUBLIMUS DEUS

RECENTLY, I SPOKE with the executive assistant to the Archbishop of the Vatican who met with the indigenous delegation in Rome in 2016. Alessio is a nice fellow, lawyer in his own right, and clearly someone, like me, who is structuring all the policy while the Archbishop presides over meetings although Alessio would be the first to deny this, and is meticulous in his observation of protocol and deference to his "superiors." Alessio informs me that the Pontifical Council for Justice and Peace has been dissolved, as have several other "organs" of the Vatican, and are now reborn, as it were, as the Dicastery for the Promotion of Integral Human Development. Alessio assures me both that he is not jesting about the reorganisation and that he and his superiors still care very much about the indigenous, but that they have been very busy with nuclear disarmament and the migrant issue. They are also quite busy in the Curia with another issue which they fear far more than a few aboriginals decrying some ancient practices of individual priests — the charges of sexual abuse, seemingly multiplying in number, a virus hitting them from every corner, and being exposed by the diabolical medium of social media. Their office has the same phone number and even emails, but apparently, they no longer exist.

Because Alessio and I have an implied understanding, he does not reprimand me when I say that the Archbishop was displaying less fear from the prospect of a nuclear holocaust than from the prospect of having to sit at the same table again with some of the Apaches he'd had the privilege to encounter through the Long March to Rome. Alessio and I don't discuss; we engage in commiseration by proxy, and we both sympathize with the Archbishop, despite the millennial sins of the church and its seeming inability to admit them and *tarnish the ensign* of Papal infallibility.

Sometimes I gently remind Alessio that it might be useful for the former Papal Nuncio to recall that the indigenous confederacy is the world's oldest democracy, two-row Wampum treaty *oblige* ... "and no Alessio, the Papal Bulls were not revoked by *Sublimus Deus*, haven't you read the enforcement bull, *Pastorale Officium*, and please, as a courtesy, remember to exempt the delegation from the presentation of letters of credence," etc., etc.

Another delegation has since travelled to Rome in 2018 — a youth delegation from the Minneapolis area, in addition to the Haudenosaunee who are keeping the contact alive. From what I heard, it went well. It must be a bit strange, everybody in their historical costumes — priests, nuns and aboriginals.

As for us, we are left with our own small lives, and now that we have placed ourselves somewhat outside the perimeter of risk, my reflections and readings remind me that maybe the Creator has his own way of dealing with things. The whole African slave trade took wing in 1455 with the issuance of *Romanus Pontifex* by Pope Nicholas V, that authorized the Portuguese monarchy — Henry the Navigator — to engage in the lucrative African slave trade. 400,000

African slaves arrived in Lisbon between 1444 and 1761. The only Portuguese who didn't have slaves in the 16th century were the beggars. Then you have the estimated 5.8 million Africans shipped to Brazil between 1501 and 1857[1]. A seemingly limitless treasure chest of riches, all diverted towards the greater glory of the Portugese monarchy.

But then, at the height of this, on the 300th anniversary of *Romanus Pontifex*, on All Saints Day, 1755, the gods visited a carnage upon Lisbon described by Goethe as "diabolic terror." "In seven minutes one of the most powerful earthquakes to hit Europe obliterated one tenth of Lisbon's population, two thirds of its houses, 36 churches, the world's most sumptuous opera house, and a royal palace containing priceless archives from Portugal's golden Age of Discovery. All that was left after the tsunami, the fires and 250 aftershocks was 'a vast heap of ruins.' Lisbon never altogether recovered."[2]

The fate of Lisbon turned my mind back to that of another man set to conquer the world—Emperor Zhu Di, he of the Forbidden City. On 8 March 1421, the largest fleet ever seen in the world, some of the 26,000 boats up to more than 150 metres long, all of them under the command of Zheng He and the emperor's other eunuch admirals, set sail "to proceed all the way to the end of the earth" and to subject all peoples to kowtow and pay tribute to the heavenly-mandated Emperor.

On the night of 9 May, two months later, lightning struck the newly constructed palace of the Emperor. The fire that ensued could not be contained and the inferno raged across the city:

---

1. Hatton, Barry, *Queen of the Sea: A History of Lisbon*, C. Hurst & Co.

2. *The Spectator*, 14 July 2018, Nicholas Shakespeare reviewing "Queen of the Sea."

> Balls of fire appeared to travel down the Imperial Way itself, long the very axis of the Forbidden City, destroying what now is called the Hall of Great Harmony and the Hall of Preserving Harmony—the magnificent palaces where Zhu Di had received leaders of the world three months earlier. The emperor's throne was burned to cinders ... the shock killed the emperor's favourite concubine.[1]

And his concubines, even upon pain of death, mocked him as having lost his "yang power." The razing of his empire in a single stroke had also excised his manhood. It was more than a tragedy. It was a divine rape. A violation of the vain aspirations of man. And a warning. A halt was placed on voyages of future treasure fleets and foreign travel was prohibited. China turned in upon itself, and truly only re-emerged in the years following the cultural revolution, 550 years later. As Chinese emperors believed they ruled with the mandate of heaven, the destruction of the Forbidden City had unequivocally signalled their displeasure and the end of the Emperor's reign, and even his lineage.

It's passing strange that as I wrote the previous passage, I noticed a *Times of London* leader, titled: "Vatican bows to Beijing over Bishops." The Chinese government has just announced a historic agreement with the Catholic Church, whereby future bishops will be approved by Beijing and mandated by the Pope. The deal calls for two bishops nominated by the Pope to step aside in the dioceses of Shantou and Mindong and certain excommunication, but Beijing-sponsored bishops to be reinstated. So, five hundred years

1. Menzies, Gavin, *1421: The Year China discovered the World*, Bantom, 2003.

after both the Catholic Church and the Forbidden City were last involved in an attempt to go to the ends of the earth, the Holy See is cutting a deal with Xi Jinping, bartering for the souls of the world's most populous country.

Even as this deal is being closed, in the far western region of Xinjiang, up to one million Uighurs and other Muslims are thought to be held for political indoctrination, in the biggest re-education programme since the Cultural Revolution. Business has never been better. The Muslims are suppressed. The Church is in a partnership with a rising global power. It's back to the good old days. Mandarinus Pontifex.

I shared this with Hannah, who didn't react, as if I were weaning myself off opiates.

"Well, looking back at the Long March, I would have enjoyed being a fly-on-the-wall when Bob Rae was talking to Tomasi."

"Why? I think his letter is pretty clear."

"Is it?"

"Of course it is. Men secretly drawing immaculately straight lines across maps of places from a far-off capital. Spheres of influence. It's basically the way the French and Brits chopped up Arab regions in 1916 after the collapse of the Ottoman Empire. With a ruler. Drawing straight lines across the region, with no account taken of ethnic or sectarian groupings."

"Like the Papal Bulls of Discovery. Queen Isabella and Pope Alexander VI carving up the world with the cleanest stroke of a pen in history. Dividing the world into believers and non-believers."

"Now, where have I heard that one before?"

"Actually, here's one for you. The Spanish conquistadores used to read out a document called the *Requerimiento* to indigenous populations, ordering submission and adherence to the Catholic faith upon pain of excommunication, enslavement and death."

"Goes to show, evil doesn't have to be banal."

"They borrowed the idea from an 8th century Daesh practice."

"It's interesting, but none of this has anything to do with us anymore, really. It's time for others to shout it from the rooftops."

"So, there's one thing I don't get. Why wouldn't either the Vatican or the Canadian government just opt for the simple, straightforward truth? An admission of the wrong would do so much to turn the page. Call me naïve again, but the truth will set you free."

"In Madagascar, in the end, the truth is only of secondary importance. You have to presume certain things true to understand the Malagasy."

"...so long as people believe them to be true. A modus vivendi."

"Oh," she laughed, "some things they believe true, others not. The important thing is to get people to say it's true, and then to act on the premise that it is true. That is what *fomba gasy* is. Tradition. Customs."

"Didn't Sister Maria once say 'tradition kills'?"

"Of course."

"So, it's irrelevant whether anyone has any core beliefs? It's all realpolitiek?"

"It's not about core beliefs. It's a tactic each of them learned somewhere. The tactic works in the short term."

She paused, considering her remark."

"You said he was a Rhodes Scholar?"

"Yes."

"It comes down to entitlement, David. Men drawing

straight lines over maps with rulers, and men carving up the globe when they don't even know whether lands exist or not. It keeps us anthropologists in business."

"So, where does that leave us?"

"Us? We just get on with it, mister ex-Director."

"Just like that."

"Correct. Just like that. We, actually you, David, get on with it. None of these people want to change. The saviours don't want to save and the victims don't want to be saved. So, let's just get on with it, all right? Let's save ourselves, for once."

THE HECTOR

THE HECTOR WAS a full-rigged Fluyt built in the Netherlands and is the most famous of the ships transporting Gaelic families from the Hebrides to Nova Scotia after the *Fuadaich nan Gaidheal* or Scottish Highland Clearances. In 1773, it landed in Pictou with 189 settlers. The ship departed during the second week of July. The settlers — 23 families, 25 single men, were "obscure, illiterate crofters and artisans from Northern Scotland who spoke Gaelic.[1] The trip took 11 weeks, including a two-week delay, blowing them off course nearby Newfoundland. It eventually arrived on September 15, but dysentery and smallpox had taken the lives of 18 passengers[2].

I'd heard from family oral histories that we had come over on a ship called the Hector in 1791, so we drove up to Pictou from River John as we'd learned there was a replica of the Hector moored in Pictou harbour. The agent at the dock where the Hector was moored was a stocky red-head. He showed us the ship's berths and briefly described the trip, where eighteen children had died, marking the end of

1. MacKay, Donald, *Scotland Farewell: The People of the Hector* (Toronto: Natural Heritage/Natural History Inc. 2001), vii.

2. Ron Wallis, "The Hector Story," Town of Pictou Nova Scotia, cited in *Wikipedia*.

a tough life and the beginning of another life with little promise of better as the winter approached.

"You couldn't exactly call them refugees, but it wasn't easy."

"Why wouldn't you call them refugees?" I asked.

"It's a misleading term. They were actually crofters who had been offered acreage in the area."

"Well, you say they were four to a berth."

"That's right."

"And that eighteen children perished on the trip over."

"Yup."

"Well, these people, as you call them had been cleared out of their lands, lost their language, mode of dress and culture. What's it take to be called a refugee?"

"Well, you have to understand, many of them came voluntarily."

"Voluntarily, you call that? What's your name by the way?"

"Campbell."

"The MacKinnons did not come to these parts of their own volition. They were shoved onto the Hector under horrendous conditions."

"I'm sorry to disappoint you, but there were no MacKinnons on the Hector."

"No MacKinnons."

"Check for yourself. There's a copy of the passenger list on the second floor."

The museum itself was built like a ship. We climbed up the stairs, past a video room, playing a re-enactment of the trip. There it was on the wall. The Hector passenger list. No MacKinnons.

"Well, that can be explained. This passenger list is for 1775. The MacKinnons arrived in 1791."

"I'm sorry, sir, but the Hector only sailed to Nova Scotia once."

Agent Campbell was standing behind me with a book.

"There was a ship in the year 1791, though. Could be the one you're looking for."

He opened the volume, titled *Ships from Scotland to America, 1628-1828, Volume 1.*

"Here's the entry."

Ship	Dunkfield	Sept 1791	From the Hebrides, arrived at Pictou 9.1791 with passengers; Most Removed to Cape Breton or Antigonish

"The 400-ton vessel was also called the Dunkenfield or the Dunkeld. Simon Fraser was the emigration agent. Mainly Roman Catholics from the Western Isles. Dispersed to P.E.I., Antigonish and Cape Breton."

It made sense. The family had stayed entirely in the Maryvale area until the departure of Grandpa for Saskatchewan.

"Well, funny after all this time that a Campbell would help a MacKinnon find his way to his family."

Pictou's a small town. Our car was parked on its main street, a block away from the Hector. I thanked Campbell, and we found ourselves back on Main street. I noticed we were parked close by the town library.

"We might as well do a bit of research, long as we're here."

The library was up on the second floor, over the post office. While I spoke with a research librarian, Hannah looked through the shelves herself. I rejoined her at a table in the reference area, sitting in front of a book titled *A History of the County of Antigonish, Nova Scotia.* By the Rev. D.J. Rankin. At page 305, I discovered the following:

> John, son of Ronald, son of John, son of Donald, pioneer, married Annie MacDougall with issue: Dougald, died as an ecclesiastic student. He contracted illness in Rome and came home hoping to recover; he is buried at Marydale. William married to Miss MacGillivrary; John married to Miss MacDonald; Dan J. married away; Mary Ann not married; Sarah died young. Angus, son of Ronald, son of John, married Mary MacGillivray, with issue: Andrew G. married to Miss MacMaster, lawyer in Regina ...

"Andrew G. is my grandfather. Miss MacMaster is Grandma. Angus, son of Ronald, son of John, son of Donald pioneer was my great-grandfather. He was the homesteader who built our family home in Maryvale, close to Antigonish."

Antigonish is another small town in Pictou country, and the place where I had heard the MacKinnons had primarily settled. St. Francis Xavier was the alma mater of Grandpa, where he'd played rugby, edited the student newspaper. We decided to start at the Antigonish Public Library on Main street. As I began our inquiry at the front desk, a man walking by interrupted.

"Sorry to jump in to the conversation, but if you want to know anything about your ancestors, go see Jocelyn Gillis down at the Heritage Centre."

The heritage centre was located in a small railway station at the end of Main Street, on the outskirts. Inside, the exhibits, photos and documents were focussed on the emigration of the Scots to Pictou county.

"Jocelyn Gillis? That would be me," she responded, as

we entered, and when I mentioned that we were seeking information on the MacKinnons.

"A Dr. MacKinnon was a long time mayor of the city, another had been Rector of the university. I'm not sure what there is on your grandfather, so a little bit of digging is in order."

She retrieved a folder from a grey filing cabinet by her desk.

"Here's something. It's a census of the small Isles 1764-1765 for the Isles of Eigg, Muck, Rum, and Cama. In the left column, a sub-head: 'Here following a list of the papists in Eigg. And under that, the names of John MacKinnon, aged 21 and his brother Donald, aged 16, sons of Donald MacKinnon and Mary MacKay.' Those appear to be your ancestors, the pioneers who are mentioned in the *History of Antigonish*."

She turned her back and spent a few minutes more digging through microfiches.

"I've found something."

I examined the photo more closely. The house was vernacular, one and a half storey with a central chimney, a shed dormer and a 3-bay façade flanked with an open verandah, with a one-storey extension. The cladding was shingles and the foundation stone.

There was a notation taken from the microfiche from the land registry:

Town: Maryvale
County: Antigonish Co, N.S.
Year Built: c. 1880
Historical Comment: This house is long known as a MacKinnon homestead. It was built c. 1880 as the family home of Angus and Margaret MacKinnon. Currently the owner is Angus MacKinnon.
Contextual comment: The house appears to have remained unchanged since construction over 100 years ago.

"I'd like to visit the location."

"Just go back to Hawthorne, which is Route 245, and take it until you're five minutes outside of town; you'll see Maryvale Church on your right. Then a sign for MacGillivray farms. Three driveways further on, you'll come across a large property, largely overgrown. If you see the Fire Hall on your left, you've gone too far."

"Who owns the house now?"

"Well, that's just it, isn't it? The house no longer exists. And there's just tall grass and weeds. All that remains of the MacKinnon homestead is grass."

"Unchanged, that is," I said as we left the converted railway station, "until Angus MacKinnon tore it down."

"Do you want to see it?"

"No. It's what happened to all our land in British Columbia. We were too busy saving people to hang onto our properties."

"Would you have it any other way?"

"Of course not. It's in our DNA. It's actually beyond our control. Other people are Lotharios; we are Samaritans."

"Could you see yourself here?"

"Well, it's a bit like Victoria a half century ago, I suppose. That has its attractions. But I'd probably be down fist-fighting at the local pub before long and then there'd be no end of it. Nothing bad has happened yet. Let's let sleeping MacKinnons lie, shall we?"

We drove out of town. After twenty minutes, we were passing by the fake-Hector replica.

"Look, there it is in the harbour."

I caught Hannah's glance for a moment. The kids would know when it was time to return. Not because we wanted to or didn't want to. Because we would have no choice in the matter. We also would have to replicate the emigration of our forefathers, and land in the same province Nova Scotia. And then the children would just have to *get on with it.*

ABOUT THE AUTHOR

A Voluntary Crucifixion traces the story of 20th century Canada through the MacKinnon clan and David J MacKinnon's life. Disillusioned with the slow death of the soul promised by life at a major Montreal law firm, MacKinnon ripped himself untimely from the profession, making a personal vow to discover society "from the bottom up." *A Voluntary Crucifixion* recounts the tale of MacKinnon's adventures and misadventures from post-Tiananmen Hong Kong to various ports of call in the Indian Ocean, offering MacKinnon's views on everything from censorship to indigenous issues, all of which reflect his ethos that the key to life is to refuse to adapt, and to fight tooth-and-nail for every square inch of your freedom before others wrench it from you.

The author is a Sorbonne graduate in history cum laude, a member of two law societies, and has translated for the international criminal tribunals of Rwanda, the Hague and Yugoslavia. He currently serves on the Board of Directors of the Canadian Association of Legal Translators. David J. MacKinnon is co-founder and Director of the Long March to Rome, an indigenous-led mission seeking repeal of the Papal Bulls of Discovery. In earlier days, he worked as oil field roughneck, toilet factory worker, longshoreman and morgue attendant. MacKinnon has walked the ancient Santiago de

Compostela pilgrim's trail and to Chartres several times. He has published two earlier novels with Guernica, *Leper Tango* and *The Eel*, and a critically-acclaimed translation of radio interviews of the French vagabond poet Blaise Cendrars in *Blaise Cendrars Speaks*.